P9-DFG-306

# Responsive Curriculum Development

## THEORY AND ACTION

# Glenys G. Unruh

*Assistant Superintendent, Curriculum and Instruction*
*School District of University City, Missouri*

McCutchan Publishing Corporation
2526 Grove Street
Berkeley, California 94704

Library of Congress Catalog Card Number 74-24476
ISBN 0-8211-2002-6

Printed in the United States of America

# Contents

PREFACE                                                                    V

## Part I
### ABOUT CURRICULUM DEVELOPMENT
### THEORY AND ACTION

ONE        Problems and Progress in Curriculum Development     3

TWO        Values and Alternative Futures                     35

THREE      Theory and the Practitioner                        59

FOUR       Curriculum Development in a Responsive Context      75

FIVE       Roles and Responsibilities of Participants          97

## Part II
### PROPOSITIONS FOR A THEORY OF RESPONSIVE
### CURRICULUM DEVELOPMENT AND ACTION

SIX        Freedom and Moral Values                           123

SEVEN      Culture and Curriculum Development                 143

EIGHT      Democratic Goals and Means                         161

NINE       Future Awareness and Planned Change                181

TEN        Need as a Factor in Curriculum Development         201

ELEVEN     Strengthening Links among Participants             223

TWELVE     Systems Concepts in Curriculum Development         247

THIRTEEN   Toward a Theory of Responsive Development          277

# Preface

This book is addressed to the problem of responsive, responsible renewal in curriculum development—to the necessity for theoretical frameworks for curriculum development that will aid in continual analysis, revision, and growth, that will respond to new knowledge, that will relate complex decisions to one another and to forces acting on the school, that will be applicable in diverse situations, and that will look to the future. A review of curriculum development activities in the past provides some insights into the need for constructing an adequate theory of curriculum development. We have experienced successive waves of polarized viewpoints, limited approaches to curriculum development, and dissatisfaction with school offerings. Numerous sources, woven into this text, point to widespread emphasis on a single-principle basis for curriculum development, such as subject matter content, the needs of society, or the needs of the learner. A seeming lack of rigorous, systematic thinking about curriculum development has, over past decades, produced unfortunate patterns of either/or thinking that are reflected in such "opposing" views as interest versus subject matter, life-centeredness versus subject-centeredness, process versus content, emotional development versus intellectual growth, and basic skills versus experiential learning.

Building a theory of curriculum development to meet the needs of schools in a complex and changing society requires a forward vision, not a past orientation. To be responsive to the needs of individuals and society in a dynamic changing world, a theory must be based on humanistic values and the democratic ideals of American origin. A theoretical framework is presented in this book for responsive, responsible curriculum development, focused on elementary and secondary public school education, although applications can be drawn for other types and levels of education.

Chapter one points out contemporary dissatisfactions with curriculum development and views several crises and reforms in the past, including the effects of immigration and industrialization on the curriculum, the mental discipline point of view, John Dewey's influence on democracy in education, and the gains and losses of the progressive education movement. The "Eight Year Study," life adjustment, Sputnik, the curriculum projects of the 1960s, the student revolts at the turn of the 1970s, the calls for relevance and accountability, and proposals for alternatives in public schools are also discussed.

Chapter two speaks to the influence of futures research on the world around the schools and its inevitable impact in such areas as population expansion, economic growth, and dwindling resources; communications technology; global interdependence and other environmental factors; and biochemical futures. A comparison is made of four value bases—materialistic, humanistic, behavioristic, and democratic—and evidence of a reconception of values in the face of a crisis society is examined.

Chapter three discusses the theory problem in general and misunderstandings by both practitioners and professors about the need for theory. It distinguishes what theory is from what it is not and offers definitions that are essential in clarifying this approach to theory building. Elements of theory, criteria for judging the quality of a theory, steps in constructing a theory, and the functions of a theory are described in this chapter.

Chapter four defines curriculum, instruction, and curriculum development for the purposes of clarification. Various models for, processes of, and factors affecting curriculum development are noted. Responsive curriculum development is contrasted with unresponsive curriculum development.

Chapter five discusses the problems of cooperative decision-making and defines the roles and responsibilities, as well as irresponsible behavior, of the various participants and referent groups in the curriculum development process.

Part II presents seven propositions for a theory of responsive curriculum development and then brings them together in a matrix. At points of intersection, propositions, general constructs, and hypotheses for testing are analyzed.

Chapter six supports a proposition on freedom and moral values with a discussion of observations and data related to freedom in the schools; choice as an element of freedom; social, ethical, and moral values; stages of moral development; and present-day shifts in society's value bases.

Chapter seven proposes that the total culture be acknowledged and drawn on for curriculum development. It describes distortions in present views of culture and the contributions to culture of the subject matter disciplines, interdisciplinary methods, and multidisciplinary approaches. This chapter speaks to the human quest, the realities of the classroom, and national and world events that influence curriculum development, and it suggests a unifying principle.

Chapter eight discusses democratic ideals that have not been met, the dilemmas of democracy, the status of democracy in the schools, and gaps in education, and it proposes some democratic means to reach educational goals.

Chapter nine advocates a commitment to planned change so that curriculum development can become responsive to dynamic and futuristic technological and social developments. Present barriers to change, the problem of bringing knowledge and action together, and resistance to mechanistic systems approaches are shown to affect attitudes toward planned change. The necessity for planning, if we are to live in a free society, is noted, and its potential for producing creativity, leadership, freedom, and examination of values is explored. Planning aids, strategies for change, and the dynamics of change are also discussed.

Chapter ten notes the recent discovery of need in curriculum planning and emphasizes both educational and psychological needs.

Needs assessment procedures and their uses are described. They range from personal interviews between teacher and student to the involvement of widespread multiple groups in identifying needs through open-ended surveys, discussion sessions, and professionally designed instruments.

Chapter eleven stresses the necessity for links among the participants. It speaks to democratic ideals, distinguishing participants and nonparticipants, involvement problems, human relations studies, organizational theories, research and development in education, school-university collaborations, student involvement, and community involvement.

Chapter twelve defines systems concepts, both open and closed, traces the historical roots of systems approaches, identifies the elements of these approaches, provides models, discusses objections to systems approaches, and gives illustrations of curricular and teaching situations in both open and closed systems.

Each proposition has an underlying concept that contributes, as a determinant or cause, to a responsive effect, result, or consequence in curriculum development. Chapter thirteen recognizes the complexity of these interrelationships. It arranges the theoretical propositions in a matrix, with determinants on the horizontal axis and results on the vertical axis. An expanded effect is produced at each point of interaction. The matrix provides an inventory of propositions and a means for studying their relationships at each intersection and at combinations of intersections. Each proposition contributes to the power of each other, but in varying ways. The types of relationships are described in the chapter. Constructs are formed at each point of intersection, and each construct is analyzed in terms of its type or types of relationships, so that causal relations can be identified. Each construct provides possibilities for generating new knowledge, hypotheses for testing, and means for strengthening the quality of curriculum development with suggestions for action in the schools.

Before closing this preface, and getting on with the text, I wish to express my appreciation and gratitude to my family, particularly my husband, Adolph Unruh, who not only tolerated the concentrated and prolonged periods of reflection and action (writing) required by this work but also encouraged me to carry through and covered other bases for me while I was working on the book. To my professional colleagues in education, in addition to Adolph, I wish to acknowledge a debt of gratitude for books, ideas, research studies, journals, discussions, conferences, and the many opportunities I have had to glean knowledge about curriculum development and the need for theory. Several professional organizations have been helpful in providing source material, and the Association for Supervision and Curriculum Development deserves particular mention.

It is my hope that this volume will open further discussion on the need for a theoretical framework for responsive and responsible curriculum development.

## PART I

# About
# Curriculum Development
# Theory and Action

CHAPTER ONE

# Problems and Progress in Curriculum Development

Critics of school curriculum have frequently made best-seller lists with passionate accounts of crises in education and calls for reform. Today, as in the past, critics focus on an element or elements they perceive to be missing in the curriculum and instructional processes, or they call attention to flagrant abuses within the schools. Most frequently they dwell on the oughts or ought nots, without providing much assistance to curriculum developers on the whys (comprehensive theoretical concepts), the whats (matters to be included), or the hows (ways to achieve desired results in curriculum development).

Historical accounts of public education reaching back into the nineteenth century reveal successive waves of polarization of viewpoints, limited approaches to curriculum development, and recurring upsurges of dissatisfaction with school offerings. Curriculum development activities in the past show a seeming lack of rigorous, systematic thinking about curriculum development and give insight into the need for an adequate theory of curriculum development. Without a comprehensive theory of curriculum development, child-centered, society-centered, subject-centered, and other approaches of limited dimensions will continue to compete with each other as exclusive routes to curriculum planning.

## CONTEMPORARY DISSATISFACTIONS

Currently, a major source of dissatisfaction is the failure of schools to provide effective education for all. Some critics charge elitism, which implies that some students are predestined to fail. Others charge that overworship of the subject matter aspects of schooling has depersonalized and dehumanized schools to such an extent that many students are turned off, apathetic, and seeking ways to escape from school. From another quarter, the free school movement has provoked new accusations of antiintellectualism in schools.

Active critics and reformers on the contemporary scene can be classified roughly into three categories. One includes those who focus on individual freedom in learning. They are sometimes termed the "romantics" or "radicals," and they advocate free schools or the elimination of schools as they now exist. The free school movement can be traced to the publication of A. S. Neill's *Summerhill* in 1960 and became manifested in various types of "free schools," emphasizing experiential learning that places the highest priority on the "self" of the individual. Advocates of deschooling see hope in a network of opportunities for incidental education through which each child can discover himself or herself and pursue his or her particular interests in special ways.

Another point of view is expressed by the reorganizers—those who would solve educational problems through various reorganizational approaches. Examples are the exit-reentry plans in which a student may choose his or her own time spans for attending school; multiage classrooms, usually associated with "pods" or open-space schools; and voucher plans, which give parents financial support to buy whatever kind of education they want for their children either at a nearby school or elsewhere.

A third and powerful group may be designated the social reformers, who are interested in using education to improve society. Growing out of the civil rights movement, the urgency of urban school problems, an increasing awareness of global interdependence, and the concern about dwindling resources and increasing population, this approach places considerable emphasis on a curriculum that confronts social issues. Social reformers would bring teachers and students together to identify the societal problems they consider important and to collaborate with community resources beyond the classroom in working for social change.

Each of these approaches emphasizes a single principle, such as the needs of the learner, the organizational setting, or the needs of society, and all are weak at the point of theory: they are not asking questions of sufficient scope, depth, and intensity and, as in the past, are producing unfortunate patterns of either/or thinking.

## CURRICULUM DEVELOPMENT IN THE PAST

### Early American Background

Evidence of a long succession of limited approaches to curriculum development may be found in historical literature. In the colonial era, free public schooling had not yet been conceived. The prevailing concept at that time, borrowed from European schools, was that education was for the elite—a view that haunted public education in one way or another for generations.

The American Revolution added new power to the emerging spirit of democracy and focused new attention on schools and education. The colonial view that formal schooling was only for the upper classes came into question, and public schooling was introduced in this country. Its expressed purposes in the postrevolutionary period were to inculcate moral standards by transmitting the traditional culture—a job previously assigned to the home and the church—and to create a uniform national American culture out of the diverse cultures brought here by immigrants from many countries. Jefferson and his followers did not view public education as a means for doing away with social classes, but rather as a means to provide lower-class citizens with basic skills and practical learning while offering the children of the elite a more classical education. It was recognized, however, that geniuses could rise from the lower classes when sufficiently motivated. The first large wave of European immigrants arrived in the 1830s and seemed to accept the prevailing rationale for curriculum planning, which was the welfare of the American public at large, not the individual.

Next came the common school movement, headed by such renowned reformers as Horace Mann and Henry Barnard. Their work characterized the period from the 1830s to the Civil War. The common school crusaders were concerned for the individual child. They respected cultural diversity and were anxious to improve the educational welfare of the masses crowding into urban centers. They extolled free public education as the remedy for ignorance and vice and the means to assimilate immigrants into a national point of view.

The postbellum period saw a phenomenal expansion of industrialization, which has exercised a pervasive influence on various aspects of public schooling since that time. In the 1880s and 1890s a second and huge wave of immigrants arrived and settled in both rural and urban locations. The two influences of immigration and industrialization brought new demands on the curriculum and on instruction in the schools.

## Immigration and Industrialization

Industrialism and the "closing of the frontier" in the late nineteenth century brought a population movement to the cities. Urban life and American life in general became more complex. Higher levels of skills were needed to find employment in factories, to cope with public transportation, to negotiate credit, and to participate in political life. Immigrants from southern and eastern Europe arrived in large numbers and settled in ghettos in the eastern cities, unlike the western Europeans who had scattered into the West and Midwest. Paralleling the intellectual interests of the upper social classes were industrial and agricultural interests of businessmen and farmers.

Lawrence Cremin (1962) tells us that ideas for industrial training were introduced to the United States when the Moscow Imperial Technical School brought them to the Philadelphia Centennial Exposition of 1876. Almost immediately schools of mechanic arts, led by the Massachusetts Institute of Technology, began to appear in major cities. A new vision of the secondary school was born that was intended to marry the intellectual or mental discipline approach and the manual education approach to prepare people for life in an industrial society.

In St. Louis, Calvin M. Woodward instituted the Manual Training School of Washington University in 1879. It provided a three-year secondary program divided equally between mental and manual labor. Woodward's goals at the outset were not vocational; he set out to increase the students' mental competence in mathematics by teaching them to build mathematical models that required carpentry and tool work. Business interests, while giving lip service to Woodward's concept of manual skills as a support system to mental development, saw the manual training curriculum of the secondary schools as a way to provide practical trade training to relieve industrial management from the growing labor union regulation of apprenticeships. Ultimately, labor interests combined with management to support the industrial and trade schools, and their intellectual aspects were emphasized less and less. Public high schools expanded, and 2,500 were in existence by 1890.

The vocational education movement was not exclusively urban in orientation; it also received strong support from agrarian interests. Agricultural colleges founded under the Morrill Act of 1862, agricultural experiment stations provided under the Hatch Act of 1882, and People's Parties appearing in the Midwest by 1890 gave impetus for establishing agricultural curricula in the schools. Pressure grew to emphasize elementary botany, agricultural chemistry, domestic science, and dairy husbandry and to relate the various branches of English, mathematics, and science to agriculture.

By 1914 the appointment of a Commission on National Aid to Vocational Education had secured federal money to support the salaries of teachers and supervisors of trade, industrial, and agricultural subjects and to assist in training teachers in agricultural, trade, industrial, and home economics subjects. Aid was directed toward (1) secondary schools that devoted about half of their time to actual training for a vocation, (2) part-time schools designed to extend the vocational skills of young workers over fourteen years of age, and (3) evening schools to extend the vocational knowledge of older workers over sixteen years of age.

## Mental Discipline

While the vocational training movement grew, professional educators tried to ignore the political and economic interests around them and continued to view high school as a college preparatory institution for the elite, although emphasis on use of the classics for mental discipline diminished somewhat.

A landmark in its effect on curriculum planning was the 1893 report of the Committee of Ten, appointed by the National Education Association, which summarized the "mental discipline" thinking of the preceding generation: high school was designed for the intellectually elite as a college preparatory institution, and the best way to improve intellectual ability was to discipline the mind on the materials of languages, the humanities, and the sciences. The same report proposed four types of curricula for high schools, reflecting some concern for the diversity of the American population; however, the elitist emphasis was uppermost.

The National Education Association then appointed a Committee of Fifteen (Committee on College Entrance Requirements), which, in 1895, defined a six-year sequence, for grades seven to twelve, and specified course requirements more clearly. The Carnegie unit for measuring high school credits was established in 1906 and still exists. Although the Committee of Fifteen had observed that the child, not the subject of study, was the guide to the teacher's efforts, its report concentrating on subject matter continued for some time to influence educators' perceptions of the mission of high school as a college preparatory institution.

## Changing Views of Public Education

Outside the fortress of elitism in secondary education, political, social, and educational leaders began to awaken to the broader responsibilities of the schools and to look to the public schools for constructive approaches to the public's needs and problems. Horace Mann's dynamic pre-Civil War philosophy began to demonstrate the power of a principle that has since characterized much of the "ideal" vision of American public education. Mann and other leaders of his time stressed the need for lay control over a system of universal education that could be the "great equalizer" of human conditions, the "balance wheel of the social machinery," and the "creator of wealth undreamed of." Poverty would most assuredly disappear, and with it the rancorous discord between the "haves" and the "have-nots" that had marked all of human history. Crime would diminish; sickness would abate; and life for the common man would be longer, better, and happier. Here was a total faith in the power of education to shape the destiny of the country—a philosophy that fired the optimism of the American public.

Stronger educational leadership was emerging, and as early as 1896 Nicholas Murray Butler argued that intelligent citizenship as well as scientific knowledge and literary culture should be among the aims of the schools. Butler's conception of citizenship was of the broadest scope, embracing social as well as political responsibilities. Growing demands from industry and labor pressed for trade, commercial, and agricultural instruction in the schools. Public schools began to be more aware of immigrant education problems and political, economic, and social changes foreshadowed new demands on the schools.

Among the efforts to "Americanize" immigrants was the settlement house idea, an attempt to bring about social improvement through family and community education, which was increasingly foisted on the schools. This meant that schools would be ultimately concerned with the total lives of individuals, rather than restrictively or even primarily with things intellectual. This notion was expressed later in the "whole child" concept.

## Democracy and Education

In the early 1900s political reformers also looked to the schools. Problems of exploitation of resources and labor for personal gain, unequal distribution of wealth, personal misery brought about by industrialization, and corruption in politics all came in for sharp criticism by crusading humanitarians, resulting in reform legislation. The exhortations of Jane Addams, Jacob Riis, William Jennings Bryan, and Theodore Roosevelt spurred the concept of progressivism in social and political life, and progressivism in education as well emerged.

Francis W. Parker in 1891 had proclaimed the theme of democracy in education: that every school should be an embryonic democracy protecting children's rights, preserving their freedoms, and building on their natural gifts. John Dewey's classic, *Democracy and Education,* appeared in 1916. Dewey carefully analyzed the fundamental conditions of democracy and sought educational arrangements to nurture and support these conditions.

Harry Broudy's review of the status of democratic processes in education (1971) notes that Dewey cast the problem of democracy in education in fundamental terms and provided an internally consistent set of conceptual tools for dealing with it. The Dewey concept emphasized shareability—that the sense of community is constantly deepened by the sharing of pooled resources and communication that applies methods of intelligence to new problems. Dewey elevated the scientific method to humanistic levels and spelled out steps in thinking and problem-solving. He viewed group inquiry as suited to a range of abilities and as the answer to elitism in education.

Although educators viewed the Dewey concept as desirable, they disagreed on how to carry it out in practice. To some it meant a school without structure or predetermined objectives and content. Harold Rugg viewed such superficial interpretations with alarm in 1926 and urged educators to realize that curriculum-making is a complex, highly specialized task that must be the cooperative endeavor of many minds. Despite its varied interpretations, the Dewey concept brought an upsurge of curriculum development in the 1920s and 1930s that moved away from traditional classicism and toward emphasis on the needs of the individual and of society.

New currents of educational thought were reflected in the report *Cardinal Principles of Secondary Education*, released in 1918 by the Commission on the Reorganization of Secondary Education, which had been appointed by the National Education Association five years earlier. The report manifested a shift in the conception of the high school from an institution for the few to an institution for all. It favored the comprehensive high school, embracing both vocational and academic curricula in one unified organization. Seven primary educational objectives were recommended as central aims of education at the elementary, secondary, and higher education levels. These were: health, command of fundamental processes, worthy home membership, vocation, citizenship, worthy use of leisure, and ethical character. The specific task of the secondary school was to realize these objectives in the lives of *all* children from about twelve to eighteen years of age. For the next forty years or so the cardinal principles provided the orientation and terminology for the development of secondary education.

### Progressive Education

The Progressive Education Association, formed in 1919, was another significant influence on curriculum development. What had been a loosely formed movement against the mental discipline approach and formalism in education became an organized movement. Through the decade of the 1920s the association emphasized progressivism in *elementary* education; in the 1930s it shifted to secondary education with its sponsorship of an eight-year study by the Commission on the Relation of School and College.

Conflicting schools of thought within the Progressive Education Association led to internal strife. Lawrence Cremin (1962) identified these as scientism, sentimentalism, and radicalism. The trend of scientism is illustrated by those who took the testing and measurement boom stimulated by Edward L. Thorndike's mental testing during the military recruitment drives of World War I and applied it to the labeling of children. In many schools this led to prejudgment of children and assignment to curriculum tracks for their supposed levels in life. Sentimentalism encompassed the rhetoric of child-centered curricula, which led to some bizarre applications in a few schools, such as planless classes engaged in chaotic self-expression. Radicalism included the social reform movement led by George Counts (1952), who charged the schools with responsibility for changing the social order. Counts called for recognition of a world society and for bringing progressive education to all social classes, not just the upper middle class.

William Van Til (1974) in an essay originally published in 1962, reminds us that basic questions raised by the leaders of the progressive education movement of the 1920s and 1930s—John Dewey, William Heard Kilpatrick, George Counts, and Boyd H. Bode—have not yet been answered: What are the aims of education? On what foundations should the curriculum be built? Given such aims and foundations, what should the schools teach?

Kilpatrick's mark on curriculum development was his faith in the potential of the learner when that potential is cultivated by skillful and sensitive teachers. Bode saw the method of intelligence in human affairs to be the road out of the value confusion between democratic and authoritarian influences. Each of these—Bode, Counts, and Kilpatrick—touched on a part of the whole. Dewey visualized reconciliation of the individual, society, and philosophical foundations, but he did not achieve translation of his ideas into a new curriculum.

Hilda Taba (1962), too, recognized the conflicts within the progressive education movement and the opposition from without, but she emphasized that the underlying concepts and the experimentation and research of the day contained the essential elements of a renaissance in a theory of curriculum building. Unfortunately this did not come about; however, several important principles began to emerge.

In a review of progress in curriculum development Robert Schaefer (1971) identifies elements of curricular and pedagogical theory on which there was relative consensus by the 1920s. These are:

1. Education must take account of the developmental needs of children.
2. Learning cannot be externally imposed but rather must involve activity of the mind of the learner.
3. Knowledge is gained through participation in social life.
4. Curricular decisions may be improved by application of the scientific method.
5. Curriculum and instruction must take account of individual differences in learners.
6. Curriculum and instruction must take account of the needs of society.
7. Schools in a democracy should maximize development of the individual.

The shortcomings of the progressive education movement are also identified by Schaefer (1971). He sees the ultimate failure of the work of the Progressive Education Association (which terminated in 1955) as its failure to comprehend the fundamental forces that move American education and to involve appropriate groups in decision-making and curriculum-planning. Lay power to sustain the movement was missing. The movement centered in the upper middle class and seemed to ignore the great transformation of society that was taking place because of the rise of industrialism. Fewer and fewer persons like Jacob Riis, Jane Addams, Woodrow Wilson, and Theodore Roosevelt concerned themselves with educational reform as educators isolated themselves from community and culture.

The field of education also became isolated from the university as a whole. Teachers' colleges and schools of education came into control of curriculum planning, and the split between "scholars" and "educationists" began. The experimental schools of the 1920s and 1930s were not conceived as laboratories in inquiry but as prescriptive exemplars. Teachers did not become students of society, of the child, or of curriculum. There was little or no attempt to develop or evaluate theories of curriculum. The exhilaration of the revolt from formalism brought a reaction of zeal and enthusiasm on the part of teachers rather than disciplined inquiry and testing of hypotheses. At the same time, the entire responsibility to learn how to cope with all conditions seemed to be placed on the teacher in the classroom. No supportive technology was offered by the universities for the teacher's use in the workaday world.

Nevertheless, concepts from the progressive education movement can be found in practice in the 1970s. And the movement produced a study that continues to provoke questions and stimulate thinking about curriculum and evaluation.

## The Eight Year Study

Significant to the field of curriculum development is the Eight Year Study, a longitudinal study covering the period from 1932 to 1940 (Aiken 1942). Sponsored by the Commission on the Relation of School and College of the Progressive Education Association, the Study was designed to explore possibilities for allowing secondary schools freedom to attempt fundamental reconstruction. Thirty public and private high schools were invited to participate, and more than three hundred colleges and universities agreed to allow these schools to ignore the usual college entrance requirements. Each school planned its own program within general frameworks that were variously designated "broad fields," "problem approach," "experience curriculum," and similar terms. General purposes of the study were to achieve greater mastery and continuity of learning, clearer understanding of the problems of civilization, increased social responsibility, release of creative energies, greater freedom for students and teachers, and greater emphasis on guidance and counseling. Wilford M. Aiken, chairman of the commission, wrote in 1942, "We are trying to develop students who regard education as an enduring quest for meanings rather than credit accumulation."

Evaluation of the Eight Year Study was done under the direction of Ralph W. Tyler of the University of Chicago. The evaluation procedure was to match each of 1,475 graduates of the experimental schools who entered college with graduates of other secondary schools who were also in college. The pairs were matched for similarities in socioeconomic background, aptitude, interests, age, race, sex, and other variables. Uncontrolled variables included teacher competence and financial expenditures of the schools. Results of the study showed that graduates of the experimental schools attained higher levels of performance in several important areas, including problem-solving, intellectual curiosity and drive, and resourcefulness in meeting new situations. Only a slightly higher total grade average was achieved by the experimental group, but it had higher grade averages in all subject fields except foreign languages. Aiken's general conclusion was that success in college was not predicated on completion of traditional units of college preparatory subjects.

Tyler has identified some conclusions of the Eight Year Study that are related to curriculum development (1971, pp. 42-43):

1. Although a number of state and regional studies drew upon the experience of the Eight Year Study and developed curriculum materials, units, and ideas, teachers and students made little use of the products of commissions unless they were deeply involved themselves in developing, modifying, and trying out curriculum plans.

2. Summer workshops, in which teachers and consultants worked together in drawing upon materials developed by distant commissions, enabled teachers to adapt and use units built by others.

3. Pupil-teacher planning in the summer workshops was found to be a useful means of developing and selecting learning activities consonant with the purposes and interests of the students and at the same time devising learning experiences appropriate for the larger educational objectives.

4. The importance of evaluation as an essential part of curriculum making was established. As new courses were formed and resource units developed, the evaluation staff of the Eight Year Study was helping teachers and specialists clarify their objectives, define them in terms of behavior, and identify situations in which students' behavior could be appraised.

Unfortunately, the impact of the Eight Year Study on curriculum development was minimal in its day. The five volumes of the report were released in 1942, at a time when our nation's interests were absorbed in World War II.

## Arrested Progress in Curriculum Development

After the war ended, curriculum development suffered from arrested progress, according to Taba (1962), and entered a lengthy bypass. The vacuum in curriculum development is attributed by L. Craig Wilson (1971) to several factors: postwar relaxation; general acceptance of the idea that intelligence is inborn and unlikely to be changed much, if at all, by environmental remedies; unquestioned acceptance of the traditional orientation of academic subjects; little attention to minority group needs; and fragmentation of school improvement theories. Despite repeated warnings about single-minded solutions to curriculum problems, these continued to be offered through the 1950s and early 1960s. Many educators hoped to influence the next generation through child-centered schools; some aimed at the parents and advocated community schools. Not until the 1960s did the question of comprehensive strategies for curriculum change begin to receive attention.

As the 1950s began, construction rather than curriculum was uppermost in the minds of most school administrators. The tasks of accommodating a 33-percent increase in students, recruiting staff, and managing a building program diverted the attention of educators from curriculum. Some sporadic efforts were made to improve education for the gifted, to increase international understanding, to expand the use of audiovisual materials, to use group dynamics in teacher education, to improve school guidance programs, and to expand community involvement in school affairs.

The Joe McCarthy "witch-hunt" influence was particularly destructive of the nation's heritage of academic freedom. Senator McCarthy and other right-wing and reactionary individuals charged subversion in governmental, military, and intellectual circles. Carrying the attack over to education, they repeatedly assailed the public school curriculum as socialistic, communistic, atheistic, and unpatriotic.

From still other sources, distant rumblings of dissatisfaction with the quality of education in the public schools began to be heard in the early 1950s and erupted into a storm before the end of the decade. This criticism came from the academicians— who were not associated with the right-wing reactionaries—and focused on the apparent superficialities of "life adjustment" education.

## Life Adjustment

From its conception in 1945 to its demise, through withdrawal of federal funds, in 1954, the life adjustment movement achieved notoriety from vociferous critics. It originated in the activities of the Vocational Education Division of the United States Office of Education and was described in a paper prepared for a conference sponsored by that division in the summer of 1945 (U.S. Office of Education 1945, p. 15). The position taken was that vocational schools of a community can prepare 20 percent of the youth of secondary school age to enter desired skill occupations, high schools should continue to prepare another 20 percent for college entrance, and the remaining 60 percent should receive "life adjustment training."

The emphasis on adjustment *to* existing conditions and the implication that the main job of the school should be to keep students happy, make them well behaved, and guide them toward assuming necessary job responsibilities in the community triggered a torrent of criticism. A number of writers attracted the attention of readers of the popular press. David Hulburd's *This Happened in Pasadena* (1951) proved of absorbing interest to a wide audience. Arthur Bestor's *Educational Wastelands* (1953) and Mortimer Smith's *The Diminished Mind* (1954) were among the works that gave the death blow to life adjustment education and, by association, to the progressive education movement. Bestor's writings were particularly influential.

Accusations were that elementary schools had failed to transmit the traditional wisdom of the culture, that the high schools were merely coddling young minds rather than developing them, and that the colleges, by surrendering to utilitarian goals, had deprived the nation of an educated leadership. The great subversion of American education, Bestor emphasized, had been the separation of the schools and colleges of teacher education from the academic arts and sciences. He stressed the need to train all students in the ability to think, so that intellectual power would be distributed widely among the people. Curriculum reform again became a national issue.

### The Influence of Sputnik

Although the orbiting of the earth by Sputnik in 1957 is generally credited with triggering the curriculum reform movement of the 1950s and 1960s, reform was already on the way. That the Sputnik influence was great, however, is unquestionable. Joining the "academic" professors in a crusade for curriculum reform, was an influential figure from outside educational circles, Admiral Hyman G. Rickover, whose theme was that education could not safely be left to the "professional" educators, that progressive educators and life-adjustment curricula had fooled the American people into thinking that all was well with the schools. American social hysteria increased, and zeal mounted for increasing the academic rigor of the separate subject fields.

Inspired by fears for national defense, the federal government and private foundations poured funds into "curriculum reform" projects. From initial efforts in mathematics and science, the reform movement spread into other subject fields. Curricular redesign in the 1950s was essentially directed at the elite students—college-bound youngsters whose ambitious parents and teachers were most likely to be found in the resource-rich suburban communities.

Again, a single principle was the basis for curriculum development. The work of Jerome Bruner (1960) and others emphasized the "structure of the disciplines" as a basis for curriculum design. Bruner called attention to the general usefulness of structure within a discipline as an organizing principle, but he did not set forth a comprehensive curriculum development theory. Hilda Taba (1962) noted that the either/or practice still prevailed and that, while in the 1930s the cry was for attention to the child, in the 1950s the battle was to reintroduce disciplined content, with the problem of balance still unresolved.

James Macdonald (1971) observed that the "curriculum reform movement" of the 1950s and 1960s was in no real sense a *movement,* because its separate parts were never really related or coordinated.   Rather, it was a historical accident— a combination of Sputnik, McCarthyism, interested professors, federal money, and the ambitions of commercial publishers.

## Curriculum Projects

In the late 1950s and into the 1960s large sums of money were granted by the federal government and private foundations for curriculum development projects. In 1959 the Woods Hole Conference was called, and psychologists ranging from Freudian to behaviorist in approach engaged with representatives of the various curriculum projects in an examination of the learning process, motivation, and the nature of intelligence as these related to problems of curriculum content. Bruner's 1960 report of the Woods Hole Conference, *The Process of Education,* seemed to fuse nineteenth-century subject matter emphases with elements of progressive education.

In the early 1960s a pattern of characteristics began to emerge in curriculum projects:

1. The emphasis was on discrete academic disciplines such as

biology, chemistry, physics, economics, geography, literature, and grammar.

2. Curriculum content was built around concepts, key ideas, and principles, even though in some cases these were devised after the selection of new content and not as prior direction to the selection process.

3. Modes of inquiry, inductive thinking, and ways to lead the student to discover for himself were built into the curriculum plans.

4. The projects employed a wide variety of materials, such as books, films, and laboratory equipment.

Although schools were slow to adopt the new curriculum programs in the early 1960s, there was a movement toward clarification and redefinition of the goals of education, a movement away from such limited objectives as "covering" a body of factual information, and a movement toward educating students in modes of inquiry.

### Contributions of the 1960s

An important contribution of the decade to curriculum development was the wider collaboration of scholars and a few selected teachers in the creation of curriculum guides and materials that offered new patterns to replace mediocre approaches to curriculum development. Although curriculum committees in local school systems had been writing numerous curriculum guides, these were for the most part outlines of content and activities lifted from several textbooks. The textbook publishers in turn had customarily collected curriculum guides and published more textbooks, setting up a cycle of limited content and ideas. Collaborative efforts in the 1960s led to wider involvement by many groups in curriculum-making in the 1970s.

The stress on "inquiry" in the curriculum developments of the 1960s continues to affect curriculum and instruction. Teachers feel uncomfortable if they find themselves merely "covering" a body of factual information in their instructional approaches without engaging the students in problem-formulation and introducing higher thought processes.

The curriculum projects, although widely diverse in subject matter, methods, and materials, shared a common commitment to teaching students how to learn, encouraged them to acquire skills and insights as well as information, and led them to discover ideas and arrive at general principles and concepts. Students were not expected to rediscover all knowledge but to learn how to use knowledge and facts to find connections between ideas and to develop solutions to problems.

Another major contribution of the curriculum development decade was its emphasis on variety and alternatives in materials and procedures. A rich array of materials and media began to be available to curriculum developers. Pamphlets, source books, readings, and original documents began to compete with traditional textbooks. Multimedia kits, audiovisual resources, simulations, models, and non-verbal games became widely known. In the science laboratories, students approached unknowns through original experimentation rather than being confined to repetitive laboratory exercises, although both had a rightful place in maintaining the balance between the known and the unknown. Technical equipment invaded the libraries and caused a welcome upheaval in the role of the librarian.

In all, the combined effects of wider involvement in curriculum-making, emphasis on inquiry and thought processes, fresh content, and growing variety in curriculum materials and resources have produced lasting gains. However, shortcomings must also be noted.

## Shortcomings of the Curriculum Projects

As the new curriculum developments came, subject by subject, into the schools, there was a tendency toward separation of and competition among subject field interests and little attention was paid to design of the curriculum as a whole.

The new curriculum developments emerged from the separate disciplines; therefore, the division of knowledge and skills into various subjects was maintained, and reading, mathematics, social studies, science, music, and art each emphasized the known fundamentals. Little attention was given to the more integrative qualities of knowledge—appreciations, understandings, and insights that are frequently, although not exclusively, triggered by interrelated and interdisciplinary approaches to learning.

Students, during the curriculum development decade, seemed to be the participants who were least consulted in curriculum planning, and they reacted in many cases with either extreme apathy or extreme activism. In the inner cities, a barren environment and human indifference had reduced schools to barely endurable custodial institutions. In the suburbs, more affluent students began to resent the adult pressures for college acceptance and social conformity that seemed to be blighting their growing-up years.

Preoccupation of the curriculum developers with curriculum structure and new teaching styles left them somewhat unprepared for the shock of the "crisis" that gained national attention in the late 1960s. American education seemed to have failed to respond to changing social needs.

### New Crises and Reforms

Belatedly, the special needs of large segments of the population attracted the attention of courts and legislators. The 1954 Supreme Court decision in *Brown v. Board of Education* outlawing segregated education initiated the civil rights movement, which forced public attention on the problems of blacks and other minority groups. The mass media of the nation now turned from demanding curriculum reform in the teaching of mathematics, science, and other subjects, to a new focus on the plight of urban and rural disadvantaged children. Schools were forced to heed the urgent cry of minority citizens.

At the same time from another quarter came further charges of school inadequacies. From education's New Left came forth a flow of exciting and also disquieting publications about the nature of schooling. Kozol's *Death at an Early Age* (1967), Holt's *How Children Fail* (1964), Dennison's *Lives of Children* (1967), and others of a similar tone captured wide audiences, both lay and professional. Their concern was for relevance, individuality, freedom, autonomy, responsive environments, cultural pride, honesty, value clarification, meaningful communication, and ethical growth. Disenchanted students from affluent suburban schools joined militant blacks in challenging the curricular and instructional offerings of the schools.

Congress entered more heavily into the education arena in the 1960s and from 1963 to 1968 enacted twenty-four major pieces of educational legislation. The new laws touched every aspect of education from preschool to postdoctoral. Funds were poured into early childhood, compensatory, and other programs designed to reach the handicapped and disadvantaged.

Bruner (1971) looked back over the curriculum reform movement of the early 1960s and concluded that the revisions of curriculum made then were insufficient to meet society's problems. Vietnam, urban ghettos, poverty, and racism had brought disillusionment with the idealistic vision of the American way of life. In a revolt against the establishment, Ivan Illich (1971) and others called for new forms of schooling. Bruner found that American education had entered a state of crisis. He concluded that the educational system was, in effect, a way of maintaining a class system—a group at the bottom.

## Calls for Relevance

That the curriculum lacked relevance for many students became a new watchword. Unresponsiveness of the schools to the changing culture, social issues, and the needs of youth was dramatized in the late 1960s and early 1970s by student disruptions in numerous high schools. A 1968-69 survey of American high schools by the House Subcommittee on General Education ("Disruption in the Nation's High Schools" 1970) revealed that 2,710 high schools had reported riots as a form of protest activity occurring during that academic year. Protests and demonstrations were widespread for several succeeding years.

Implications of the student uprisings for curriculum development were clear. *Toward a More Relevant Curriculum*, a report of a national seminar held in 1970, emphasized that the most important single change needed in the schools was development of responsiveness in curriculum. Diagnosing group needs as well as individual needs was seen as an important function of those responsible for improving curriculum and instruction.

Mark Chesler, a frequent observer and consultant in disrupted schools, gained some insights into procedures that seem to hold promise for constructive change. In "School Crisis and Change" (1970), he asserts that when school officials sought only superficial techniques for reestablishing the status quo, stress and turmoil were more likely to continue. When collaborative decision-making procedures were instituted among students, community people, school executives, and faculty, meaningful and positive curriculum improvements began to take place. Chesler does not advocate "replacing the principal with six youngsters," which would mean wresting power from the hands of one group and establishing new autocrats. He recommends preparing students, faculty, and administrators for shared decision-making and corresponding responsibilities to work together in revising the curriculum, instructional styles, and teaching procedures.

Concerns about the magnitude of student unrest have been matched recently by concerns about the magnitude of student discouragement and apathy. Charles Silberman's field study *Crisis in the Classroom* reported that, in many of the classes observed by the study staff, students remained uninvolved in their own education. Schools seemed to "educate for docility," and teachers seemed to assume that the students should be passive—that the teacher should dominate the classroom.

Thus, students who have no experience in making decisions or assuming responsibility for their learning may become apathetic or react through disruptive behavior.

### Alternatives

One answer to the problem of irrelevance in the school curriculum has been the rise of the alternative school movement, which entered the public school scene minimally in 1964 and grew steadily through the following decade, as reported in *Changing Schools* (no. 008, 1973), a newsletter on alternative public schools. A survey identified more than six hundred alternative public schools in 1973. Secondary alternatives outnumbered elementary alternative schools by four to one, and there was a handful of K-12 alternative organizations.

Various types and combinations of types were manifested, which may be roughly classified as follows:

*Open schools* are inspired by the British integrated-day concept of open education, in which learning activities are individualized and organized around interest centers within the classroom or building. This form of alternative school is most common at the elementary level.

*Schools-without-walls* provide learning activities throughout the community and are usually centered in nonschool facilities such as store fronts, business establishments, museum facilities, and other locations outside the traditional school building.

*Learning centers* concentrate learning resources in one location available to all students in the community and include magnet schools, centers for the arts, career education programs, and other interest facilities.

*Continuation schools* provide education for students whose conventional schooling has been interrupted or has been unsatisfactory for various reasons and include dropout centers, reentry programs, and inner-city street academies.

*Multicultural schools* emphasize cultural pluralism and ethnic and racial awareness. They usually serve a multicultural student body and may provide bilingual education.

*Free schools* emphasize greater freedom for students and teachers and are usually nonpublic alternative schools, although they are sometimes available by choice within public school systems.

*Schools-within-schools* include minischools and satellite schools, which may be within the traditional school building or at a separate location. They maintain fairly strong administrative ties to their parent schools, while emphasizing a different kind of learning program, usually much more informal than the traditional school offering.

Advocates of alternatives in public education are characterized by their zeal and enthusiasm for educational reform. A position statement in *Changing Schools* (no. 001, 1972) expresses the concept of alternatives as a means of educational reform.

Something is happening in our schools, and it holds deep significance to all American youth. For just as the education profession was beginning to settle into a sense of troubling despair over the failure of an apocalyptic decade of intensive curriculum reform to render significant changes in our nation's schools, indications have begun to appear that signal a new era for public education in America. Not since the Eight Year Study has such bold creativity and experimentation been attempted, and once again the profession is being vitalized with an exciting new hope for educational reform. What is particularly surprising about this reform movement, is that it is not the one the pros in the field have been predicting for so long and have worked so hard to make happen. Almost unnoticed by national educational leaders, this wave of experimentation has occurred as a widely diverse and uncoordinated grass-roots movement that is attempting to provide school youth with meaningful educational experiences. And while the experimentation is characterized by its diversity, there is one common factor that is ever-present—the desire to provide students with alternative learning options within the public schools.

Leaders of the alternative school movement emphasize the consistency of the concept with our democratic heritage and political philosophy—with the pluralistic nature of American culture, the need for institutional self-renewal of public education, the need for financial austerity, and the need for community involvement in public education.

Possibly the fact that the pressure for alternatives has come from students, parents, and teachers at the local level is of most significance. The spirit of the alternative schools may be much closer to the challenge posed by George S. Counts in his 1932 pamphlet *Dare the School Build a New Social Order?* than to the progressive education movement as noted by *Changing Schools*. Counts said, "Schools could never be the prime movers of an industrial civilization, but they could, by remaining close to society, become the cultural instruments for humanizing it. Here is an educational opportunity unparalleled in history; dare teachers take up the challenge?"

Cremin, writing perceptively about progressive education twelve years after the Progressive Education Association disbanded, contrasts the alternative school movement with that movement (1973, p. 3):

> What is most striking, perhaps, in any comparison of the two movements is the notoriously a-theoretical, a-historical character of the free school movement in our time. The present movement has been far less profound in the questions it has raised about the nature and character of education and in the debate it has pursued around those questions. . . . It has been far less willing to look to history for ideas. . . . Further, the movement has had immense difficulty going from protest to reform, to the kinds of detailed alternative strategies that will give us better educational programs than we now have. . . . Where they have failed, it seems to me, is at the point of theory: they have not asked the right questions insistently enough, and as a result they have tended to come up with superficial and shop-worn answers.

Cremin also points out that when children come to school they have already been educated and miseducated and that youngsters in the schools have been taught and are being taught by many sources outside the school, such as radio and television, peer groups, advertising agencies, libraries and museums, and the many provincial viewpoints of family and geographic location. For these reasons it is increasingly important to encourage collaborative participation in curriculum development.

## NEED FOR COLLABORATIVE PARTICIPATION

That a change process can be effective when parents, teachers, and students collaborate with school authorities in decisions about curriculum development has been illustrated by conventional schools as well as alternative schools.

Analogous to the situation in which the needs of the student-recipient are defined and determined exclusively by the teacher-sender are situations in which the teacher becomes the recipient and the administrator the sender, or the administrator the recipient of programs devised by others without his participation. Eliot Spack (1971) studied the use of knowledge about curriculum change within the ES '70 (Educational Systems for the Seventies) consortium of seventeen school systems in various parts of the country. Spack concluded that a major weakness of curriculum development was a serious lack of collaborative participation in curriculum decisions by all persons affected. Schools seemed to behave passively in using innovative curriculum plans and processes when these were determined largely by curriculum projects, state departments of education, or school executives, without the involvement of the potential recipients or users—that is, the teachers, the students, and the community. However, he found that, when the users were involved in recognizing and diagnosing key problems and issues, their orientation changed from a passive to an active role, and they became engaged in seeking changes and using resources more effectively to suit particular local problems.

Possibly because the curriculum developers were preoccupied with concepts, key ideas, and lofty goals, they omitted specification of goals based on local needs and improvement of the appraisal process to provide feedback for modification. It was not until after the curriculum revision era had reached its peak that attention was directed toward the potential power of combining goals, needs, alternative procedures, and materials, with evaluation processes to achieve responsiveness in curriculum development.

## ACCOUNTABILITY: ABUSES AND PROMISES

Even the process of setting goals and relevant evaluation procedures can be subverted into a narrow approach to curriculum development, however, as is illustrated by abuses of the concept of accountability that entered the scene in the 1970s with assistance from federal and state educational funding agencies.

Accountability as a broad societal concept is highly acceptable. Watergate inquiries, Ralph Nader's investigations on behalf of consumer interests, the work of environmentalists, attention to population growth in relation to poverty and starvation, cost accounting in the schools—all of these reflect concern for the responsibility of individuals and institutions for the consequences of their decisions and actions. In the realm of education, however, "accountability" is in danger of developing into an operational definition that focuses at the state level on the urgency of student acquisition of basic skills in reading and arithmetic as measured by standardized tests. Carried to extremes, accountability may include the factoring of per student allocations of state funds into some kind of equation with student achievement scores. The question of accountability related to money has been raised by taxpayers who want to know what they are getting for their education tax dollar. Although billions of dollars were poured into the schools during the 1960s, current school critics claim they cannot detect a much better product than they had a decade earlier.

By 1973, thirty-three states had passed legislation or joint resolutions featuring some aspect of accountability, with another dozen states considering action of some kind at that time. Over four thousand books and articles on accountability were published from 1969 to 1972. The Michigan accountability plan is typical of those enacted in many states, although it has gone further into implementation than most. Stated features of the Michigan plan include needs assessment and goal-setting through citizen participation, translation of goals into specific behavioral objectives, testing alternative delivery systems, improving local evaluation capability, using evaluation as feedback for guiding state and local educational policy, and using norm-referenced tests and objective-referenced tests to rank schools that are to be rewarded financially if poor achievers attain minimal standards in reading and mathematics.

These statements barely conceal the hidden implication that the classroom teacher is to be held accountable for student achievement measured by standardized test scores of basic skills. This implication was identified publicly by Congressman John Brademas in a speech delivered at a symposium on accountability held at Memphis State University and later published in the *Congressional Record* of December 10, 1973. He stated, "It is the weapon we have long been seeking that will let us punish the teachers who can't make our children learn" (Elam 1974, p. 657).

Terry Herndon (1974), speaking as executive secretary of the

National Education Association, responded by taking a strong stand on behalf of teachers. He said that they willingly accept their appropriate share of responsibility for the effectiveness of the nation's educational programs, but they do not accept the simplistic, bureaucratic approach to teacher accountability that is prevalent in the United States today. The current "Big Brother" idea has the government looking over the teacher's shoulder and applying a business-industrial concept of accountability, in which teachers are held to task for their results or "products," based on batteries of tests of student achievement. Herndon pointed out that a corollary to statewide testing is the development of a statewide curriculum, and this carries the danger of invidious thought control, hardly conducive to the kind of open democracy that the United States at its best represents.

Educators stress that there are too many factors affecting what students do in school, and how well they do it, to make the present simplistic measures of accountability acceptable. Education is a social process in which human beings are continually interacting with other human beings in ways that are imperfectly measurable or predictable. Values, attitudes, and aesthetics may be more important than the few things that can be readily measured. So educators must help young people develop their individual potential, teach them how to make the democratic system work, foster their creativity and aid them in getting along with their fellow men. These basic goals of education must never be bartered away (1974, p. 26).

Herndon also quoted a statement adopted by the NEA's Representative Assembly:

The Association believes that educators can be accountable only to the degree that they share responsibility in educational decision making and to the degree that other parties who share this responsibility—legislators, other governmental officials, school board, parents, students, and taxpayers—are also held accountable (1974, p. 26).

A statewide assessment of the Michigan plan, conducted by Ernest House, Wendell Rivers, and Daniel Stufflebeam (1974), reflected general support of the accountability process in principle but was highly critical of the implementation of the plan in Michigan. The evaluators pointed out that attention had been limited mainly to reading and arithmetic at two grade levels, that no constructive purpose had been gained by ranking schools on norm-referenced tests, and that the promise of providing needs assessment in relation to the full scope of goals had not been pursued. Other criticisms included (1) failure to provide for a continuous updating of goals, (2) limitation of the objectives to cognitive areas to the neglect of affective areas, (3) participation of too few people in choosing objectives, (4) high cost and excessive time spent in testing every pupil, and (5) misinterpretation of published test scores by the public. The evaluation panel also expressed its view that tying money to test scores was potentially harmful.

Thus the accountability crusade of the 1970s, admirable though its purposes may have been at the outset, is in danger of becoming one more in a long series of narrowly interpreted approaches to curriculum development. Arthur Combs (1972), taking a strong position, outlines the hazards of accountability programs that focus almost exclusively on test scores of detailed behavioral objectives. A truly comprehensive approach to accountability, he says, must consider at least five major problems related to curriculum and instruction:

1. *Basic skills.* Specific, atomistic behavioral objectives can be applied successfully only to simple skills and problems for which they are appropriate and must be constantly updated. The information explosion and rapidity of change make "right" behaviors rapidly obsolete.

2. *Intelligence and holistic behavior.* Accountability must contribute maximally to intelligent behavior and problem-solving action directed toward fulfillment of the individual's and society's needs.

3. *The nature of learning and the causes of behavior.* Attention should be concentrated on the causes of behavior rather than on behavior itself. Personal meanings are the causes of behavior, and these are formed through two aspects of learning: the provision of new information or experience, and the discovery by the learner of its personal meaning for him.

4. *Humanistic goals of education.* Developing humane qualities, self-actualization of the individual, good citizenship, learning to care for others, and working together are all aspects of humanism for which schools must be accountable. "We can live with a bad reader," says Combs, "but a bigot is a danger to everyone."

5. *Professional accountability.* Teachers can and should be held accountable for professional behavior: being informed in subject

matter, being concerned about the welfare of students, being knowledgeable about their behavior, and understanding human behavior in general. Professional educators may be held professionally responsible for the purposes they seek to carry out and the methods they use.

Accountability, in a comprehensive view, has important implications for curriculum development; a limited view will again reveal the need for a broad theory base for curriculum development.

## NEED FOR THEORY

Taking a long view of curriculum development over decades of time makes it evident that investigators have constantly discovered and deplored piecemeal approaches to curriculum development, lack of a comprehensive theory of curriculum development, and lack of a philosophical value base for the theory that can unite and use the viewpoints of the nation's diverse people.

Investigative studies are numerous, and the following are representative. Ole Sand and Donald A. Myers (1967) note that, given the complex nature of curriculum development, which poses the need to construct conceptual frameworks, few conceptual models or theories can be found in the field that have attempted to include a logical place for all components. Robert Emans (1966) observes that American education has been characterized by polarized approaches, and "what seems to be needed is a framework which is so designed as to aid in continual examination, revision and growth" (p. 327). Harry Broudy (1966) argues that the only defensible basis for curriculum decisions is a theory that rationally weaves together the objectives of the culture, life outcomes, and school outcomes. James Macdonald (1967) suggests that applications of systems theory can stimulate curriculum development processes in which both technological and aesthetic rationality can take place, and integrity of content, persons, and groups can be maintained. The challenge thus becomes one of taking curriculum development out of the "accidental" category and introducing some form of general rational input into planning, while maintaining the participation and integrity of the persons and groups involved.

The scope of the challenge to curriculum developers is defined by

Warren Bryan Martin (1974, p. 33), in discussing the need for an underlying philosophy, ethic, and theory on which to base curricular decisions and actions:

The sought-after social philosophy must unite and utilize the experiences of a lot of different people. It must take into account the evolving experience of race in America. It will need to deal with current skepticism about government, and with the widespread ambivalence about human nature, and with the insights of Eastern thought. In this movement and struggle from confusion to clarity, we may very well be groping toward a new human pantheism. . . . Theory is unquestionably important, for without it training programs will be devoid of purpose. But action is required if theory is to be tested. . . . An educational institution will allow for the importance of objective analysis and may even advocate intellectual rigor. It does not necessarily scorn the academic tradition and its accomplishments. But in an educational institution the perspective is broader, more contextual, emphatically relational. The education of the total person becomes more than a cliché. Emphasis is placed on affecting mind, body, and spirit, so as to enlist all of the human being in teaching and learning. Thus, intellectual training is matched by experiential enrichment—field experience, work-study, personal involvement. And by what Theodore Roszak calls "transcendent vision," the utilization of human sensibilities to achieve perceptions that transcend the human. The key words are: action, vitality, practice, contact, imagination, the metaphoric, sacramental, poetic, the symbolic, and spiritual.

The succeeding chapters of this book discuss the development of value bases for theory building, considerations in theory construction, and building a theory of responsive curriculum development for a complex, changing society. The review of problems in curriculum development presented in this chapter concludes with a statement of my own assumptions.

The problems of society and of individual self-actualization are the problems of the schools, and we must direct our curriculum development resources into a concerted and intensive effort to find ways to reach all individuals—not just the eager motivated learners, but all—with relevant processes and content. Curriculum development is needed that can help individuals learn to draw effectively on growing realms of knowledge and act constructively when faced with subtle and unresolved problems for which there are no clear-cut answers. Serious attention to needs can increase the improvement in educational programs. Ways can be found to expand the capability of education to teach individuals how to continue learning and developing new skills in a rapidly changing world, how to develop new insights and new approaches to solving problems. Both young and mature citizens need to interact and work with others across cultures and classes, to have empathy with other people of diverse viewpoints, and to understand, aid, and cooperate with people of all socio-economic levels and all beliefs.

## REFERENCES

Aiken, Wilford M. *The Story of the Eight Year Study.* New York: Harper and Row, 1942.

Bestor, Arthur. *Educational Wastelands.* Urbana: University of Illinois Press, 1953.

Broudy, Harry S. "Democratic Values and Educational Goals." In *The Curriculum: Retrospect and Prospect,* part I, pp. 113-52. Seventieth Yearbook of the National Society for the Study of Education. Chicago: University of Chicago Press, 1971.

——. "Needed: A Unifying Theory of Education." In *Curriculum Change: Direction and Process,* edited by Robert R. Leeper, pp. 15-26. Washington, D.C.: Association for Supervision and Curriculum Development, 1966.

Bruner, Jerome S. "The Process of Education Reconsidered." In *Dare to Care, Dare to Act,* edited by Robert R. Leeper, pp. 19-32. Washington, D.C.: Association for Supervision and Curriculum Development, 1971.

——. *Toward a Theory of Instruction.* New York: W. W. Norton, 1966.

——. *The Process of Education.* Cambridge: Harvard University Press, 1960.

*Changing Schools,* nos. 001, 008 (1972, 1973). Newsletter published by the Educational Alternatives Project of Indiana University.

Chesler, Mark A. "School Crisis and Change." In *Student Unrest: Threat or Promise?* edited by Richard L. Hart and J. Galen Saylor, pp. 100-21. Washington, D.C.: Association for Supervision and Curriculum Development, 1970.

Combs, Arthur W. *Educational Accountability.* Washington, D.C.: Association for Supervision and Curriculum Development, 1972.

Commission on the Reorganization of Secondary Education. *Cardinal Principles of Secondary Education.* Washington, D.C.: National Education Association, 1918.

Counts, George S. *Education and American Civilization.* New York: Bureau of Publications, Teachers College, Columbia University, 1952.

——. *Dare the School Build a New Social Order?* New York: John Day, 1932.

Cremin, Lawrence A. "The Free School Movement: A Perspective." *Notes on Education,* October 1973, p. 3. Newsletter published by Teachers College, Columbia University.

——. *The Transformation of the School.* New York: Alfred A. Knopf, 1962.

——. "The Problem of Curriculum Making: An Historical Perspective." In *What Shall the High Schools Teach?* pp. 6-26. Yearbook of the Association for Supervision and Curriculum Development. Washington, D.C.: ASCD, 1956.

Dennison, George. *The Lives of Children.* New York: Random House, 1967.

Dewey, John. *Democracy and Education.* New York: Macmillan, 1916.

"Disruption in the Nation's High Schools: House Subcommittee's Survey of Unrest." */I/D/E/A/ Reporter,* special issue, 1970, p. 3. Published by the Institute for the Development of Educational Activities, Melbourne, Fla.

Elam, Stanley M. "Holding the Accountability Movement Accountable." *Phi Delta Kappan* 55 (June 1974): 657, 674.

Emans, Robert. "A Proposed Conceptual Framework for Curriculum Development." *Journal of Educational Research* 59 (1966): 327-32.

Herndon, Terry E. "Why Teachers Get Mad About 'Accountability.' " *Compact,* January-February 1974, pp. 24-26.

Holt, John. *How Children Fail.* New York: Pitman, 1964.

House, Ernest R.; Rivers, Wendell; and Stufflebeam, Daniel L. "An Assessment of the Michigan Accountability System." *Phi Delta Kappan* 55 (June 1974): 663-69.

Hulburd, David. *This Happened in Pasadena.* New York: Macmillan, 1951.

Illich, Ivan. *Deschooling Society.* New York: Harper and Row, 1971.

Kozol, Jonathan. *Death at an Early Age.* Boston: Houghton Mifflin, 1967.

Macdonald, James B. "Curriculum Development in Relation to Social and Intellectual Systems." In *The Curriculum: Retrospect and Prospect,* part I, pp. 97-112. Seventieth Yearbook of the National Society for the Study of Education. Chicago: University of Chicago Press, 1971.

———. "An Example of Disciplined Curriculum Thinking." *Theory into Practice* 6 (October 1967): 166-71.

Martin, Warren Bryan. "The Ethical Crisis in Education." *Change* 6 (June 1974): 28-33.

Neill, A. S. *Summerhill.* New York: Hart, 1960.

Rickover, Hyman G. *Education and Freedom.* New York: E. P. Dutton, 1959.

Rugg, Harold, ed. "Curriculum-making: Points of Emphasis." In *The Foundations and Technique of Curriculum-making,* part I. Twenty-sixth Yearbook of the National Society for the Study of Education. Bloomington, Ill.: Public School Publishing, 1926.

Sand, Ole, and Myers, Donald A. "Creating a Productive Dialogue, Research, Discussion and Rationale." In *Rational Planning in Curriculum and in Instruction,* pp. 53-60. Washington, D.C.: National Education Association, 1967.

Schaefer, Robert J. "Retrospect and Prospect." In *The Curriculum: Retrospect and Prospect,* part I, pp. 3-25. Seventieth Yearbook of the National Society for the Study of Education. Chicago: University of Chicago Press, 1971.

Silberman, Charles E. *Crisis in the Classroom.* New York: Random House, 1970.

Smith, Mortimer. *The Diminished Mind.* Westport, Conn.: Greenwood Press, 1954.

Spack, Eliot G. "ES '70: A Model of Knowledge Utilization by the Public Schools." Paper presented at the American Educational Research Association Convention, February 6, 1971.

Taba, Hilda. *Curriculum Development: Theory and Practice.* New York: Harcourt, Brace and World, 1962.

"Toward a More Relevant Curriculum." Report of a national seminar. Published by the Institute for Development of Educational Activities, Melbourne, Fla., 1970.

Tyler, Ralph W. "Curriculum Development in the Twenties and Thirties." In *The Curriculum: Retrospect and Prospect*, part I, pp. 26-44. Seventieth Yearbook of the National Society for the Study of Education. Chicago: University of Chicago Press, 1971.

U.S. Office of Education. *Life Adjustment for Every Youth*. Washington, D.C.: USOE, 1945.

Vallance, Elizabeth. "Hiding the Hidden Curriculum." *Curriculum Theory Network* 4, no. 1 (1973-74): 5-22.

Van Til, William. "Prologue: Is Progressive Education Obsolete?" In *Curriculum: Quest for Relevance*, edited by William Van Til, pp. 9-17. 2d ed. Boston: Houghton Mifflin, 1974.

Wilson, L. Craig. *The Open Access Curriculum*. Boston: Allyn and Bacon, 1971.

## ADDITIONAL READINGS

Argyris, Chris. "Alternative Schools: A Behavioral Analysis." *Teachers College Record* 75 (May 1974): 429-52.

Berkson, I. B. *The Ideal and the Community*. Westport, Conn.: Greenwood Press, 1958.

Callahan, Raymond. *Education and the Cult of Efficiency*. Chicago: University of Chicago Press, 1962.

DeNovellis, Richard L., and Lewis, Arthur J. *Schools Become Accountable*. Washington, D.C.: Association for Supervision and Curriculum Development, 1974.

Dropkin, Stan; Full, Harold; and Schwartz, Ernest, eds. *Contemporary American Education: An Anthology of Issues, Problems, Challenges*. New York: Macmillan, 1965.

Eisner, Elliot W., and Vallance, Elizabeth, eds. *Conflicting Conceptions of Curriculum*. Berkeley: McCutchan, 1974.

Frazier, Alexander. *Open Schools for Children*. Washington, D.C.: Association for Supervision and Curriculum Development, 1972.

Friedenberg, Edgar Z. "New Value Conflicts in American Education." *School Review* 74 (spring 1966): 66-94.

Goodman, Paul. *Growing Up Absurd*. New York: Random House, 1966.

Gorton, Richard A. *Conflict, Controversy, and Crisis in School Administration: Issues, Cases, and Concepts for the '70s*. Dubuque, Iowa: William C. Brown, 1972.

Katz, Michael B., ed. *School Reform: Past and Present*. Boston: Little, Brown, 1971.

Kimball, Solon, and McClellan, James. *Education and the New America*. New York: Random House, 1962.

Kohl, Herbert. *Half the House*. New York: E. P. Dutton, 1974.

Krug, Edward A. *The Shaping of the American High School*. New York: Harper and Row, 1964.

Olson, Arthur V., and Richardson, Joe A., eds. *Accountability: Curricular Applications*. Scranton, Pa.: Intext Educational Publishers, 1972.

Overly, Norman, ed. *The Unstudied Curriculum*. Washington, D.C.: Association for Supervision and Curriculum Development, 1970.

Saxe, Richard W., ed. *Opening the Schools: Alternative Ways of Learning*. Berkeley: McCutchan, 1972.

Schrag, Peter. *Village School Downtown: Politics and Education*. Boston: Beacon Press, 1967.

Squire, James R. *A New Look at Progressive Education*. Yearbook of the Association for Supervision and Curriculum Development. Washington, D.C.: ASCD, 1972.

Tyack, David. *Turning Points in American Educational History*. Waltham, Mass.: Blaisdell, 1967.

Unruh, Glenys G., and Alexander, William M. *Innovations in Secondary Education*. 2d ed. New York: Holt, Rinehart and Winston, 1974.

Walberg, Herbert J., and Rasher, Sue Pinzer. "Public School Effectiveness and Equality: New Evidence and Its Implications." *Phi Delta Kappan* 56 (September 1974): 3-9.

Welch, I. David; Richards, Fred; and Richards, Anne Cohen, eds. *Educational Accountability: A Humanistic Perspective*. Fort Collins, Colo.: Shields, 1973.

*What Shall the High Schools Teach?* Yearbook of the Association for Supervision and Curriculum Development. Washington, D.C.: ASCD, 1956.

CHAPTER TWO

# Values and
# Alternative Futures

Building a theory of curriculum development to meet the needs of schools in a complex and changing society requires a forward vision, not a past orientation. This means that it behooves curriculum developers to examine the work of futures researchers in relation to curriculum development, to examine value systems presently operating in our society, to consider alternative futures, and then to develop value bases on which to build theory.

Forecasts and trends based on information presently available indicate that the United States, which changed from an agricultural economy to an industrial economy a century ago, is now changing to a service economy. This process is likely to be replicated in many other industrial nations. Accompanying this transition and based on probable future trends are signs of a major conceptual shift from materialistic to humanistic values. The service economy is described by Daniel Bell (1973) as a postindustrial society. Others refer to a postmarket society, a technological society, a technetronic era, a communications era, and a superindustrial society.

In essence an industrial society is a goods-producing society, engaged in expansion of manufacturing, transportation, and invention. A postindustrial society, as described by various analysts, is a society that has attained industrialization, has the built-in capacity to produce or obtain everything it needs, and is prepared to move forward to the next stage of human societal development. Ideally, the chief focus of that stage will be humanistic or person-centered activities, creating the conditions that provide genuine opportunity for each member of society to develop his or her full human potential. Emphasis will be on professional and human services. Theoretical knowledge will gain new importance, because, in an age of growing complexity, the process of asking questions and generating hypotheses will become more and more necessary to the formation of public policy. Choices made by the present generation will determine which of several alternative futures described by analysts of futures research our grandchildren and great-grandchildren will inhabit.

## INFLUENCE OF FUTURES RESEARCH

For curriculum developers, the implications of futures studies are significant. Harold Shane (1973, p. 1) defines futures research as "a new discipline concerned with sharpening the data and improving the processes on the basis of which policy decisions are made in various fields of human endeavor such as business, government, or education." Terms such as "policies research" or "futures studies" are frequently used interchangeably with "futures research." Shane conducted an extensive survey through visits to centers in which futurists are at work—RAND, the Hudson Institute, the Institute for the Future, and various others—and contacts with specialists not connected with centers. He sought answers to questions bearing on the implication of futures research for education. Some of the trends, signs, and portents he identified are briefly reviewed here to clarify the basic value concepts from which planning for the future stems and that must underlie curriculum development.

### Population

Currently the world's population is increasing at about 2 percent annually, doubling every thirty-five years. In 1830, one billion people inhabited the earth, and it had taken two million years to reach this figure. Only a hundred years later the second billion had populated the earth, by 1960 there were three billion, and in 1975 four billion. By 1995, six billion people are expected, according to figures prepared by Lester Brown (1972b). Population is growing rapidly because man has succeeded to an unprecedented degree in controlling disease and feeding the world's people. While more babies are surviving to become adults and the death rate has been reduced, nations have been slow to reduce their high birth rates and thus keep the population level stable. Rapid population increases in recent years have widened the rich-poor gap, increased hunger and starvation, caused unemployment levels to rise in poor countries, and contributed to the deterioration of the physical environment. Continuing population growth is steadily reducing the per capita global supply of living space, fresh water, forest products, industrial raw materials, energy fuels, and arable land.

## Gap between Rich and Poor

Of the four billion persons populating the world in 1975, one billion will populate the technology-rich nations and be ready for the postindustrial era of humanism. Three billion will occupy the poor or underdeveloped countries. The rich nations consist of English-speaking North America, Europe, the Soviet Union, Japan, and portions of the Mideast. The poor include large areas of Latin America, Africa, and Asia. The rich countries are generally literate, industrial, urban, overfed, overweight, and consumption-oriented. The poor countries are generally illiterate, agrarian, rural, hungry, malnourished, and survival-oriented.

Brown (1972a) notes that the rich-poor gap among nations emerged rather recently in history. Before the industrial revolution, there was little difference between living standards in Western Europe and those in China; all were poor, illiterate, malnourished, and suffering from disease. On the average, people did not live more than about thirty years. But with the rapid rise of industrializing societies, the gap between incomes in the rich countries and those in the poor increased swiftly. The income disparity may reach a ratio of 30 to 1 by the end of the present century. This increasing gap between incomes is stimulated by recent technology that enables man to harness new sources of power and energy. In the industrial countries, one technological advance leads to another, while elsewhere productivity increases little if at all. In fact, the industrialized countries tend to discriminate against the products of poor countries and to inhibit their industrialization. The rich countries depend extensively on the raw materials of the underdeveloped countries, however.

The *United Nations Statistical Yearbook of 1970* reports that in the preceding year, North America, with 6 percent of the world's population, consumed 37 percent of the world's liquid fuel and 37 percent of its total energy. The United States in that year consumed 24 percent of the world's steel, 41 percent of its rubber, and 32 percent of its tin. The quantities of materials used in the last few decades vastly exceed the total consumption in all previous time.

## Urbanization

Related to population growth, particularly in the underdeveloped countries, is runaway urbanization, which is producing congested living conditions. If the present rate of growth in squatter settlements surrounding large urban centers in the poorer countries of the world continues, much of mankind will be living in slums and shantytowns by the end of the century. Because of improved agricultural methods, rural employment has declined drastically, and rural people began several years ago to migrate to the cities, although they were unprepared for urban employment and had difficulty being absorbed into the economy. Among the rich countries, a comparable situation occurred in the United States, beginning about 1940, when blacks from the rural South migrated to the urban North. In the following two decades, employment on farms in the Mississippi Delta declined nearly 90 percent, as mechanical cotton pickers and chemical weed killers replaced hand labor. Hundreds of thousands of blacks settled in Cleveland, Detroit, Newark, Chicago, and other large cities. Many were unable to find work and were confined to ghettos. Their bitter and alienated feelings erupted into the riots of the late 1960s.

## Economic Growth

Galbraith (1973) emphasizes that the most basic tendency of modern economic society has been for constituent firms to become vast and to keep on growing. In the United States, one thousand manufacturing, merchandising, transportation, power, and financial corporations produce approximately half of all the goods and services not provided by the state. In manufacturing the concentration is even greater. In fact, says Galbraith, "there exists an extremely asymmetrical industrial structure, with the bulk of economic (i.e., industrial) activity controlled by an elite of a few hundred enormous corporations and the remainder divided among four hundred thousand small and medium-sized manufacturing businesses" (1973, p. 43).

Growth then becomes a major purpose of the economic system and, consequently, of the society it serves. Growth of a corporation brings both monetary and career rewards to its members. In a firm that does not grow, an individual's advancement to a higher position must await creation of a vacancy through death, disability, or retirement of those above him. If he shows ambitions to displace a person on a higher level, he may face the same ambitions by those who aspire to his position.

In a growing corporation, however, new jobs are created by expansion. Many more opportunities are presented for advancement, for success, and for cooperative working relationships. Galbraith finds it not surprising that so many influential people, on finding the growth of the firm and the associated growth of the economy to their advantage, conclude that economic growth is a good thing. Consequently, economic growth has become a social goal, and competition has been considered the remedy for all industrial ills.

## Consumption and Depletion of Resources

Closely allied to the "growth is good" concept is consumer management. Americans are flooded with ingenious advertisements by television, radio, billboards, magazines, and newspapers—all stressing that the consumption of goods is the foundation of human happiness, the greatest source of pleasure, and the mark of status. From cake mixes, detergents, hair dressings, and intoxicants to automobiles, advertising on a united front contributes to the concept that the possession and use of goods enhances life. Newness, quite apart from any other characteristic, is used as a persuasive argument for acquisition. Advertising has stimulated a popular view that a newly invented product is better than one invented a year or ten years ago. Promotion along this line developed the principle of built-in obsolescence, which continues to encourage the discarding of old automobiles and the purchase of new, throwaway products, new clothing styles, and so forth.

Unhappily, however, unrestricted growth and consumerism require vast amounts of raw materials and natural resources, many of which cannot be replenished or replaced with another. A practical illustration of increasing consumption and diminishing resources was the energy crisis of 1973-74. Futures researchers, before that time, had consistently warned that the per capita consumption of energy in the United States was growing at an alarming rate, that our major sources of energy—petroleum, gas, and oil—were nonrenewable, and that once used they would be gone forever. Lawrence Rocks and Richard Runyon (1972) predicted that massive energy shortages were inevitable unless energy conservation and new sources of energy were developed. Warnings of brownouts and blackouts were given, as the electrical utility industry became unable to keep pace with the growth of the electrical products industry. It was predicted that gasoline and oil products would sharply increase in price, restrictions would be placed on the use of luxuries, air conditioners would be prohibited or severely limited in use, and oil for heat in the home would be cut back. Rationing of gasoline and fuel oil might be mandated, Rocks and Runyon said, and people encouraged or required to use mass transportation or to form car pools to get to and from work. Pleasure driving would be a thing of the past. Decreased use of the automobile would necessitate drastic cutbacks in automobile manufacturing, with massive layoffs in the industry. Industries dependent on automobile manufacturing would suffer corresponding layoffs. Although food production would be a first priority, transportation systems would suffer fuel shortages, and difficulties in transporting necessities to and from the farm would make us comprehend the extent to which our incredible agricultural productivity is dependent on oil. These predictions were not yet fully realized in 1973 and 1974.

Although negotiations between the Mideast and the United States in 1974 alleviated the energy crisis temporarily, the energy dilemma remains. Needless to say, the crisis spurred new and intensive efforts in energy research directed toward generating power from sources other than oil. It would be an oversimplification to say that we must learn to adjust to a constant level of material benefits rather than a constantly rising level. The social implications of such an adjustment are highly complex. Do we increase electrical production until everyone has an air conditioner, for example, or do we declare that no one may have an air conditioner? Only a comprehensive planning system can discipline growth without excluding it, align it with public purposes, and use economic power in the public interest.

## Environmental Damage

Increasing concern about the deterioration of the world's natural environment has been publicized by environmentalists in recent years. Alarms have been raised over the increasingly polluted air and water, polluted beaches, and destruction of fish. Wild animals are disappearing, and more and more species of animal life are becoming endangered. Intolerable levels of nonbiodegradable pesticides threaten extinction of the bald eagle and other animal life. Emphysema, a disease associated with air pollution, is rising rapidly in the United States. Environmental damage is not done only by industries. Tourists, farmers, food vendors, and service station operators all contribute to pollution. When the belief prevails that nothing should interfere with economic growth, its diverse effects on air, water, tranquillity of urban life, or the beauty of the countryside are ignored.

Various remedies have been suggested for environmental damage. One is that public money be used to employ a sufficient work force and provide a sufficient amount of equipment to keep the streets clean. Public money might also be used to provide adequate sewers and treatment plants for sewage. However, the modern economy systematically discriminates against these expenditures for public services. Galbraith (1973) notes that public services that are important for the economic system or that purchase its products are more handsomely financed than those that have no industrial base, such as relief of privation, provision of nontechnical education, and administration of justice. This was exemplified a few years ago when the national administration cut back education funds in an economy drive and because of the low "cost-effectiveness" of educational programs. At the same time, defense expenditures were being increased, despite peace and the avowed need to economize, and with no claims being made for their cost-effectiveness.

Other proposed solutions to environmental problems include requiring industries to assume the costs of prevention or reparation of environmental damage. This is generally an inadequate solution and becomes impractical when applied to noise pollution from airplanes, visual pollution from ugly man-made structures, or smoking in public places.

One suggestion is to continue economic growth but to specify its parameters by legislation. In several ways this alternative is already being forced on the various levels of government. A more radical proposal is to limit growth. A provocative volume by Meadows et al. (1972) on this approach has stimulated international concern over the shape of tomorrow and has had an effect on planning. Through the catalytic initiative of a few people, the consciousness of many is being raised, and there are signs in urban centers of more thoughtful planning for the future. The concluding statement of the Meadows book (p. 205) points up the resources available to mankind and the "missing ingredients":

If there is cause for deep concern, there is also cause for hope. Deliberately limiting growth would be difficult, but not impossible. The way to proceed is clear, and the necessary steps, although they are new ones for human society, are well within human capabilities. Man possesses, for a small moment in his history, the most powerful combination of knowledge, tools, and resources the world has ever known. He has all that is physically necessary to create a totally new form of human society—one that would be built to last for generations. The two missing ingredients are a realistic, long-term goal that can guide mankind to the equilibrium society and the human will to achieve that goal. Without such a goal and a commitment to it, short-term concerns will generate the exponential growth that drives the world system toward the limits of the earth and ultimate collapse. With that goal and that commitment, mankind would be ready now to begin a controlled, orderly transition from growth to global equilibrium.

## Global Interdependence

Environmental pollution, depletion of energy resources, and other potential problems cited by futures researchers are not confined by national boundaries. The unity of the biosphere does not recognize political boundaries, and nonbiodegradable insecticides circulate everywhere. Lester Brown (1972b) notes that DDT has been found in the tissues of penguins in Antarctica, in the bodies of children in villages in Thailand, and in mothers' milk in India, as well as in the United States. Controlling the level of DDT in the biosphere is only one of the problems that will require international cooperation. Weapons control, the fishing industry, and exchange of necessary goods are other examples. Energy interdependence is materially different from other forms of interdependence, because interruptions in the flow of petroleum affect so many products that a national economy deprived of oil could scarcely function at all.

No part of the earth is self-sufficient in all its critical needs. The net effect of international cooperation in economic activities would be more jobs and higher living levels in the poorer countries and more equitable global distribution of wealth and income. The energy crisis, population growth, and environmental problems have posed basic challenges for man's institutions and values:

> Not only are many of man's institutions incapable of resolving the problems he now faces, but his values, inherited largely from the past, are inconsistent with his survival. Values which are widely held, many of them built into the economic system, such as "growth is good," "planned obsolescence," "reverence for motherhood," and the nationalistic feelings which many of us hold are becoming threats to our future well-being. Man must evolve a new social ethic, one which emphasizes economic and demographic stability and the recycling of raw materials. Such an ethic replaces international competition with global cooperation and sees man in harmony with nature rather than having dominion over nature (Brown 1972, p. 39).

Hopeful signs are appearing in various parts of the world. The battle against illiteracy in the underdeveloped nations is progressing, although it is far from won. Birth rates are dropping in several countries, with some approaching zero population growth. The world's transportation systems are rapidly improving, and international tourism is skyrocketing. As people cross national borders more and more frequently, they tend to adopt less of an attitude of "we" versus "they" and more of an attitude that supports the need for interrelated, interdependent cooperation.

## Communications Technology

Advances presently available in communications technology give promise of a coming communications revolution that will offer ways to solve some of man's literacy, food production, urban density, and job-related problems.

Communications satellites have become much more powerful since the first commercial satellite was launched in 1965. While the original satellite had a capacity equivalent to 240 telephone circuits, the most recent one has 20,000 circuits. Among other capabilities, satellites provide a means for broadcasting to rural areas that are uneconomical to reach by conventional transmissions. For example, by means of satellite broadcasts and cheap transistor radios, uneducated populations in Asia and Africa can learn about family planning, modern agricultural techniques, and new job opportunities.

In the summer of 1974, the Applications Technology Satellite

(ATS-6) was launched from Cape Kennedy to provide an experimental technology tool for school systems in rural areas of Appalachia, the Rocky Mountains, and Alaska. In the Appalachian region, teachers received in-service education in career education and techniques for dealing with reading problems of individual students. The Rocky Mountain experiment included career education for junior high students and evening programs for adults on subjects of local concern. Alaska's portion of the experiment focused on early childhood education, oral language, and health education, plus public television programs for adults on such subjects as land claims, the arts, and oil pipeline implications.

The National Aeronautics and Space Administration launched the same satellite over India in 1975, with sufficient power to be picked up by domestic television for a year-long experiment in mass education. Education, literacy, improved hygiene, and agricultural techniques can be brought to every human being on this planet for about a dollar per person per year, says Arthur Clarke (1972), who in 1945 conceived the idea of space communications via satellites stationed above the earth. Presently, eighty-three nations have joined the International Telecommunications Satellite Consortium (INTELSAT) and operate internationally owned satellites, which are launched by NASA on a cost-reimbursement basis.

Another major area for problem-solving that can be aided by communications technology is urban density. One of the factors that makes population growth a problem is the concentration of populations in cities and suburbs. About 90 percent of the United States population lives on less than 10 percent of the land, while migrations of people to urban areas have depressed rural areas economically and left many without essential services.

Applying communications technology to establish new living patterns based on fuller use of the nation's land resources is a project of the National Academy of Engineering, chaired by Peter Goldmark, and with supportive sponsorship by several governmental agencies. From the work of this group, plans are developing that could create a new rural society (Goldmark 1972).

Through telecommunications developments, choices will be increased: the employee will be able to select from urban and rural environments, and a company or agency will have a wider choice of areas in which to locate. Internal communications networks in new rural communities will include two-way random-access networks able to accommodate voices, data, and videophones; AM-FM radio and television channels for network affiliations and educational programs; broadband cable television systems carrying numerous channels into individual homes with call-back capabilities (especially useful for participating in town board meetings, public opinion polls, etc.); and emergency service channels such as those now available with the "911" system.

External communications will keep the new rural city or urban center in touch with the world. Businesses and other agencies will be connected to related operations by broadband cable or microwave circuits. Long-distance broadband circuits will interconnect telephone and videophone services with those of other cities. Printed material, graphic displays, computer access, and data access will all be transmitted between towns. Conferences will be held via television or videophone.

Thus, communications technology can offer assistance in solving some of mankind's problems. The capabilities described already exist; but the magnitude of the task will require the combined efforts of business, government, education systems, health care interests, and cultural agencies to succeed.

## Biochemical Futures

Futures research is justified by the desire to make the future a matter of rational choice rather than helpless victimization. Rational choice for the future is in no area more critical than in the field of biochemical technology. Robert Sinsheimer (1974), in one of a series of essays that appeared in metropolitan newspapers throughout the United States, noted that biochemical, physiological, and genetic understanding have already led to the discovery of many substances to improve man's health: antibiotics for combatting microbial disease, hormones for correcting metabolic defects, special diets for solving some genetic "errors of metabolism," and palliative drugs for relieving psychic trauma. Capsules are available to alter our states of mind: to stimulate, to calm, to sleep, to dull pain, to enhance color and tone, and to distort perception. Delicate instruments created in the electronic space science laboratories and adapted to the body's needs may in the future devise new organs for seeing and hearing and artificial hearts. New organisms have been spawned in science laboratories: an animal virus with genes acquired from a bacterium, a plant cell with the chloroplasts of another species, dozens of identical twin salamanders with no natural parents, and mice whose cells bear the genes from four parents.

Biochemical technology brings new powers and new responsibilities whenever man intervenes to change the natural order. The most probable rational choice is for man to continue to intervene in order to relieve infection, genetic and metabolic disease, hormonal imbalance or deficit, cancer, and psychic disorders. As we learn to reduce disease, we may also learn to slow aging and extend the human life span markedly. As we learn to correct genetic handicaps, we may also learn to modify the genetic character of man in other directions. By studying the biochemistry underlying mental illness, we may learn how to vary the dimensions of thought.

A simple means for preselecting the sex of a child or developing exact genetic reproduction or making sure that all humans have high intelligence can have social consequences that strain our powers of imagination. The possibilities now envisioned are new in the history of the human species—so new that their ethical, social, and philosophical implications have scarcely been explored. Answers to questions raised from developments in biochemical technology are not to be found in our present values, for these are unprecedented and surprising problems. The answers found and the choices made will demand reflection on the very deepest principles underlying our perception of human purpose, the relationships of humans to one another, and their relationship to the universe about them. A democratic society should provide for extensive discussion of these and other basic issues, as the future of democracy will depend on the choices made. Education and communication are the tools available for studying these fundamental questions.

Interestingly, in a poll prepared by the Institute for the Future, members of the World Future Society rated biochemical developments generally lower in desirability than possible technological developments in other fields. See figure 1.

These possible technological developments may seem improbable to us today, yet we know that science and industry can produce fabulous accomplishments. Man can travel through space, can communicate instantaneously with any other place in the world, and has the capacity to destroy the planet with his weapons. The industrial state has brought greater affluence to more people than at any other time in history. Nevertheless, we are facing a future in which the cumulative effects of population growth, urbanization, environmental problems, accelerating technology, international tension, and disparity between rich and poor can lead to ultimate disaster unless we undertake a searching examination of values and a basic change in approach. There is evidence that we are living in a period of transformation of our values, a period that John D. Rockefeller 3rd has

FIGURE 1

Technological Developments Ranked According to
Desirability by Readers of The Futurist

| Technological Development | Percentage of Maximum Possible Score (100%) |
|---|---|
| 1. Cheap and clean electrical power from thermonuclear (fusion) plants | 52.4% |
| 2. Increased (by a factor of 2) world agricultural production | 46.1% |
| 3. Mass economic fertility control agents in water and food | 38.7% |
| 4. Corporate employment at home via improved communications | 21.6% |
| 5. Drugs to raise intelligence levels | 17.4% |
| 6. Chemical control over hereditary defects by gene modification | 14.7% |
| 7. Chemical control of aging to extend life and vigor by 50 years | 14.7% |
| 8. Effective regional weather control at acceptable costs | 12.4% |
| 9. Drug control and change of personality characteristics such as anxiety and aggressiveness | 10.7% |
| 10. Comprehending computers with IQs of 150 | 9.1% |
| 11. Major world cities linked by high-speed ground, rail, and air vehicles | 7.9% |
| 12. Construction of cities under ground or under water | 4.3% |

From Gerald R. Salancik, "Choosing Technology for a Better World," *Futurist* 6 (October 1972): 209, published by the World Future Society, P.O. Box 30369 (Bethesda), Washington, D.C. 20014. Reprinted by permission.

styled "the second American revolution." Other observers have
pointed to evidence of a major conceptual shift in societal values.
Before examining whether there is evidence of such a shift, it may be
useful to describe differing belief-and-value positions.

### COMPARISON OF VALUE BASES

Four general value classifications, adapted from Willis Harman
(1970) and others, are identified here by the terms *materialistic,
humanistic, behavioristic,* and *democratic.* These value premises are
presently interacting in society, and the emergence of some above
others may well determine which of several alternative futures will be
ours.

### Materialistic

The traditional middle-class values are in the materialistic category.
Material progress is seen as the meaning of social progress, and, while
humanitarianism and a moral orientation are important, they are
sometimes subordinated to the goals of scientific, technological, and
economic progress. An underlying belief is that man can better himself through his own efforts. Thus, competitiveness and other characteristics of an industrial society govern this set of values. The traditional middle-class values generally include concern for equality,
justice, pursuit of happiness, freedom, property rights, and essential
respect for human beings. However, there is a tendency to value
profit and property higher than human considerations.

Value is placed on an orderly society, in which social roles and
rules are well defined and domestic and civic virtues are commonly
held. Pleasantness of environment and the esteem of others are
prized. Meaning in life centers around success and achievement in
terms of money, property, power, and status. Personal materialistic
characteristics include self-discipline, hard work, efficiency, industri-
ousness, integrity, dependability, self-sufficiency, control of inner
feelings, moderation, conformity, cleanliness, rationality, patriotism,
and productivity.

### Humanistic

The humanistic value base emphasizes self-awareness or individuality plus social consciousness. It is a composite of the "new

values," an expression stemming from the works of Fromm (1968), Maslow (1961), Rogers (1974), and others; the goal of a "person-centered" society, advocated by Platt (1973-74), Boulding (1964), Theobald (1968), and others; and a true concern for social problems and for serving others.

The emerging values of humanism have matured and deepened since the 1960s, when a "humanist" appeared to be someone mainly preoccupied with himself or herself and not necessarily deeply concerned with the welfare of others. The humanist movement was a refreshing and creative development that appeared as a reaction to the dehumanization of an advanced industrial society. Unfortunately, some of the specific techniques and procedures used to probe the self (e.g., those commonly associated with sensitivity training or encounter groups) appeared superficial if not bizarre to many Americans, and the potential of group dynamics has not been adequately developed in educational circles. Carl Rogers (1974) notes that, paradoxically, American industry more than any other institution has used techniques to improve interpersonal relationships, to open communication, and to develop regard for the importance of persons. He foresees more sophisticated future development of group processes, in which groups will wrestle with the ethical, moral, and philosophical questions posed by a rapidly changing world, thus providing a means for individuals to forge value stances and to change these stances as data continually come in.

The sharpened social awareness of the 1970s has brought true meaning to the concept of humanism. It encompasses the qualities of autonomy, responsibility, self-actualization, problem-solving, tolerance, and concern for others. A high value is placed on the individual's right to pursue self-fulfillment and essential respect as a human being. Not only self-discovery experiences are sought but also awareness of the need to change environments that do not presently support human dignity.

Personal humanistic characteristics include openness, authenticity, integrity, aliveness, spontaneity, honesty, a sense of community, willingness to engage in problem-solving action, and a view that work is not merely the price one pays to obtain the material things of life, but rather man's opportunity to reflect, create, and serve.

## Behavioristic

In the behavioristic frame of reference, change in behavior comes
about as the response of the organism to the application of stimuli.
Underlying premises are found in the work of B. F. Skinner (1973,
1971) and other psychologists interested in behavior modification
through conditioning accomplished by the manipulation of stimuli.
A basic belief is that socially acceptable behavior is shaped and controlled by means of rewards and punishments and that altruistic
behavior has to be instilled by the culture, as it is basically at vari-
ance with man's instinctual nature. Social order, justice, social consciousness, democracy, humanitarianism, public service, morality,
and achievement are perpetuated because of their usefulness; they
have no deeper roots. Free will is an illusion. Skinner (1973) illustrates these points by calling for "cultural designers" to shape a
better world for man before it is too late; he points out that, although a government can arrange positive contrived reinforcers to
induce individuals to shape a better world for man, our institutional
reinforcers are particularly weak and will not work. Without institutional reinforcers, people tend to turn to the surviving immediate
gratifiers, such as food, drugs, and sex.

Behaviorists hold the view that scientific objectivity, intelligence,
and impassivity are all culturally imposed, not choices, and that the
future of our society depends on the extent to which its leaders
make use of principles of punishment, reward, and reinforcement in
designing a desirable future.

## Democratic

Democratic values are the values implicit in the founding documents of our nation, elaborated in the Declaration of Independence
and a few years later in the Constitution. They are concerned with
equality and justice; they assert that "all men are created equal,"
that they are endowed "with certain inalienable rights," including
"life, liberty, and the pursuit of happiness." The founding documents established a governmental system to secure those rights. The
values of American origin rest on faith in the goodness, dignity, and
rationality of people generally, and hold that governments derive
their "just powers from the consent of the governed." They place the
person at the center, transcending material values.

However, increasingly over the years, the nation's citizens have come to regard the founding values as the ideal world and the material values as the real world. The founding fathers viewed the nation's mission to be that of bringing a new order, a democratically established order, into the world. Values in this concept of democracy are a binding, just, and adaptive system of law; harmonious human relations; individual responsibility; and equality and mutual obligation among individuals.

Personal democratic characteristics include integrity, responsibility, rationality, industry, self-sufficiency, fairness, spirituality, patriotism, humanitarianism, and idealism.

## A CRISIS SOCIETY?

The values declared by our founding fathers and the materialistic values that have predominated throughout the history of the nation have often been in conflict. Other contradictions among the value positions just described have also arisen.

Crisis seems to follow crisis in contemporary times: campus unrest, Vietnam, assassinations of prominent leaders, Wounded Knee, and Watergate are examples that come readily to mind. Some writers have described the contemporary era as a crisis of crises, and futurists warn us to prepare to be surprised in the future. We can expect discontinuities, turning points, and "system breaks." Alvin Toffler (1974, 1970) and John Platt (1973-74, 1966) warn us that a decade of disasters may be just ahead of us, possibly entailing famines, nuclear war, oil scarcities, and quarrels over ocean resources; they note the recent hijackings, kidnapings, and streakings as bizarre phenomena that are part of a crisis society. We need responsible planners for the future who recognize traps in time to prevent them or find ways to get out of them.

Harold Shane (1973) looks at the crises of our nation and the world and extracts several components or problems to be faced by responsible planners:

*The value crisis.* It is said that many people today cannot distinguish right from wrong—that permissiveness has undermined moral character.

*Disagreement about the good life.* Diverse opinions on desirable life-styles have raised conflicts between generations and between ethnic groups on ecological, industrial, religious, and business-labor problems.

*The credibility gap.* The loss of credibility by persons and groups in authority and positions of responsibility is creating a national dilemma that is eroding public confidence in social and governmental institutions.

*Institutional overload.* Critical difficulties arising in a complex, rapidly changing society have contributed to the incapacity of institutions such as schools, courts of law, and religious organizations to adjust and adapt to the new tasks that face them.

*Equity as opposed to equality.* Some people are questioning whether equal treatment is just or whether justice depends rather on equitable treatment, which implies special provision for the disadvantaged, the culturally different, the gifted, the handicapped, the very young, the elderly, and other special groups.

*Naive use of technology.* The phenomenal growth of technology in the recent past has clearly created crises: energy problems, depletion of arable lands, environmental pollution, an increase in emphysema, and many others.

*The haves and the have-nots.* Dilemmas are posed by the gap between rich and poor and by various forms of discrimination against segments of the population.

Despite this formidable list of crises, reordered values are emerging and are being applied to the problems we face today. Futurists are hopeful that minor disasters or crises will provide us with the learning and coping skills to avoid ultimate disaster. Rockefeller (1973, p. 42), a thoughtful observer of the scene, says:

> We are groping toward a post-industrial humanistic society, and this implies a long-term and complex process of diffusion, not a single dramatic event or series of events. It is a process in which values will emerge and re-emerge, to be tested and retested with clashes, confusion, doubt, rejection, acceptance, culminating eventually in a synthesis—a new value-system as the basis for action and change. This is the most complex form of social change, conditioned by the pace of events, by reform efforts, by pressure, leadership, but in the last analysis conditioned most of all by millions of personal decisions made by millions of individual Americans.

## EVIDENCE OF RECONCEIVED VALUES

Several writers and analysts other than Rockefeller have noted evidence of a shift in basic value concepts. John Platt (1973-74), an analyst of trends, has no doubt that mankind is now passing through the greatest transformation in history. He cites as evidence several events and movements since 1970 that are altering the social directions we have held for decades or centuries: the moon landings, the new peace moves between the major nuclear nations, the emergence of powerful new movements concerned with ecology, zero population growth, and consumerism, and the new emphasis on religion. Platt continues (p. 82):

In the U.S., there are new demands for rights and a new recognition of pluralism in life styles, from black power and women's lib to the communes and the eighteen-year-old vote. For the first time, there is an experimental approach to housing, education, and guaranteed income. International trade and development becomes a major business, and future forecasting becomes a major study. And there is suddenly an immense ferment of change in psychology, psychiatry, education, health, economics, and law.

Platt also notes that there are setbacks and that not all new solutions have been good. He recommends that we find ways to move rationally, deliberately—not just accidentally—into designing safer and more humane and responsive structures for this new age. He emphasizes that, while encouraging diversity of different groups and cultures to allow people to reach their full human potential, we must also design patterns that will provide the global security and abundance that the great new technologies have made possible.

Political scientists have noted an increasingly humanistic quality of life and give much credit to the courts, which, over the past twenty years, have functioned increasingly as designers of improved models of human relationships. Judicial rulings in educational policymaking have grown in importance and had far-reaching significance. Open board meetings, parent and student access to student records, examination of questions about equity in school finance, and numerous increases in student rights are examples of the results.

Courts have become more and more responsive to the analyses and advice of social scientists in grappling with such intractable modes of moral behavior as segregation, discrimination, and racism. Interestingly, the impetus for humanitarian movements such as the civil rights movement has come from the courts rather than from religious organizations, which seem unable to respond quickly enough to meet immediate needs or to give sufficiently structured assistance to the nation in removing an injustice or an unwarranted limitation on an individual's freedom.

The Watergate affair, which might be considered a predictor of national moral decline, may well prove to be the turning point for the nation toward squarely facing moral decisions and examining values in relation to substantive issues and interests. Surveys and polls of public opinion have consistently registered condemnation of the Watergate behavior and its associated motives.

Clare Graves (1974), a psychologist whose twenty-year research studies on human values indicate that something is indeed happening to these values, has developed a psychological theory that, as man's existential problems change, lower order behaviors are replaced by newer, higher order behavior systems. Western man has moved from the earliest subsistence level, based on physiological needs, to a tribalistic existence focused on survival, to the egocentric level (Machiavellian individualism), to a saintly level (suffer in this life to be worthy of a later life), to a materialistic level (devotion to material goals as a means of achieving status), then to a personalistic or self-realization level, centrally concerned with peace of the inner self and the relation of self to others. Going on, man begins to see the problems of the external world and moves to the cognitive or symbolic level, attains a future orientation, and realizes the necessity for giving, contributing, and constructing as opposed to getting, taking, and destroying. In man's next step, his values are based on accumulating knowledge rather than remaining fixed on a single set of values that may have been good for him at an earlier stage of development. Constantly accumulating knowledge will create new problems and compel man to continue developing, as his existential conditions change.

Graves notes that the recent problem identified as the "generation gap" was in reality a values gap, when examined in reference to his theory. At the present moment, he finds our society attempting to negotiate the most difficult transition the human race has faced thus far. We are moving from the personalistic to the cognitive level of behavior while facing three possible alternative futures: (1) through successive catastrophes regressing to the subsistence level, (2)

becoming fixated in a societal complex of saintly/materialistic/per-
sonalistic behaviors, or (3) emerging and advancing to the cognitive
level and proceeding toward stabilization of our world so that all life
can continue.

## THEORY AND VALUES

What, then, is the import of this discussion of the influence of
futures research on basic value concepts, or descriptions of contrasting value systems, and what is the significance of value bases in
building a theory of curriculum development? The adequacy of our
concepts for curriculum choice and planning will be tested by the
adequacy of the value system from which we are developing theory.

If curriculum development is to be responsive to the needs of
individuals and society in a dynamic changing world, based on
present knowledge and predictable alternative futures, an adequate
theory must be based on humanistic values and American democratic
ideals, while using materialism as the support system for human service. To paraphrase Galbraith (1973), a theory should lead to plau-
sible conclusions. A proposition related to values, futures studies, and
curriculum development is developed in chapter six.

## REFERENCES

Bell, Daniel. *The Coming of Post-industrial Society: A Venture in Social
Forecasting.* New York: Basic Books, 1973.
Boulding, Kenneth E. *The Meaning of the 20th Century: The Great Transition.*
New York: Harper and Row, 1964.
Brown, Lester R. "An Overview of World Trends." *Futurist* 6 (December 1972a):
225-32.
———. *World without Borders.* New York: Random House, 1972b.
Clarke, Arthur C. "Satellites and the 'United States of Earth.' " *Futurist*
6 (April 1972): 61.
Fantini, Mario. "Humanizing the Humanism Movement." *Phi Delta Kappan* 55
(February 1974): 400-402.
Fromm, Erich. *The Revolution of Hope: Toward a Humanized Technology.*
New York: Bantam Books, 1968.
Galbraith, John K. *Economics and the Public Purpose.* Boston: Houghton
Mifflin, 1973.
Goldmark, Peter C. "Tomorrow We Will Communicate to Our Jobs." *Futurist*
6 (April 1972): 55-58.

Graves, Clare W. "Human Nature Prepares for a Momentous Leap." *Futurist* 8 (April 1974): 72-82.

Harman, Willis W. "Nature of Our Changing Society: Implications for Schools." In *Social and Technological Change*, edited by Philip K. Piele, Terry L. Eidell, and Stuart C. Smith, pp. 1-70. Eugene: Center for the Advanced Study of Educational Administration, University of Oregon, 1970.

Maslow, Abraham H. "Eupsychia—the Good Society." *Journal of Humanistic Psychology* 1 (1961): 1-11.

Meadows, Donnella H.; Meadows, Dennis L.; Randers, Jorgen; and Behrens, William W., III. *The Limits to Growth*. A report for the Club of Rome's Project on the Predicament of Mankind. New York: Universe Books, 1972.

Platt, John R. "The Future Is in Our Hands." *Fields within Fields*, winter 1973-74, pp. 81-82.

———. *The Step to Man*. New York: John Wiley, 1966.

Rockefeller, John D., 3rd. *The Second American Revolution*. New York: Harper and Row, 1973.

Rocks, Lawrence, and Runyon, Richard P. *The Energy Crisis*. New York: Crown Publishers, 1972.

Rogers, Carl R. "Interpersonal Relationships: U.S.A. 2000." In *Curriculum: Quest for Relevance*, edited by William Van Til. 2d ed. Boston: Houghton Mifflin, 1974.

Salancik, Gerald R. "Choosing Technology for a Better World." *Futurist* 6 (October 1972): 209.

Shalala, Donna E., and Kelly, James A. "Politics, the Courts, and Educational Policy." *Teachers College Record* 75 (December 1973): 223-37.

Shane, Harold G. *The Educational Significance of the Future*. Bloomington, Ind.: Phi Delta Kappa, 1973.

Sinsheimer, Robert. "A New Perspective of Human Purpose." Essay #18 in the adult education course by newspaper *America and the Future of Man*. Berkeley: University of California, 1973. Distributed to newspapers across the country by Copley News Service. Appeared in *St. Louis Globe-Democrat*, 16-17 March 1974, p. 5E.

Skinner, B. F. "Shaping a Better World." *Intellect* 102 (October 1973): 7-8.

———. *Beyond Freedom and Dignity*. New York: Alfred A. Knopf, 1971.

Theobald, Robert. *An Alternative Future for America*. Chicago: Swallow Press, 1968.

Toffler, Alvin. *Future Shock*. New York: Bantam Books, 1970.

———, ed. *Learning for Tomorrow*. New York: Random House, 1974.

## ADDITIONAL READINGS

Anderson, Robert H; Almy, Millie; Shane, Harold G.; and Tyler, Ralph. *Education in Anticipation of Tomorrow*. Worthington, Ohio: Charles A. Jones, 1973.

Bassett, T. Robert. "It's the Side Effects of Education That Count." *Phi Delta Kappan* 54 (September 1972): 16-17.

Becker, James. *Education for a Global Society*. Bloomington, Ind.: Phi Delta Kappa, 1973.

Boulding, Kenneth E. *Meaning of the 20th Century: The Great Transition*. New York: Harper and Row, 1964.

Chase, Allen. *Biological Imperatives*. New York: Holt, Rinehart and Winston, 1972.

Clarke, Arthur C. *Profile of the Future*. New York: Harper and Row, 1973.

Combs, Arthur W., ed. *Perceiving, Behaving, Becoming*. Yearbook of the Association for Supervision and Curriculum Development. Washington, D.C.: ASCD, 1962.

Commoner, Barry. *The Closing Circle*. New York: Alfred A. Knopf, 1971.

de Brigard, Raul, and Helmer, Olaf. *Some Potential Developments: 1970-2000*. Middletown, Conn.: Institute for the Future, 1970.

de Chardin, Teilhard. *The Phenomenon of Man*. Evanston: Harper and Row, 1955.

Della-Dora, Delmo, and House, James E., eds. *Education for an Open Society*. Yearbook of the Association for Supervision and Curriculum Development. Washington, D.C.: ASCD, 1974.

Drucker, Peter F. *The Age of Discontinuity*. New York: Harper and Row, 1969.

Frazier, Alexander, ed. *New Insights and the Curriculum*. Yearbook of the Association for Supervision and Curriculum Development. Washington, D.C.: ASCD, 1963.

Gabor, Dennis. *The Mature Society*. New York: Praeger Publishers, 1972.

Gardner, John. *Self-renewal: The Individual and the Innovative Society*. New York: Harper and Row, 1963.

Hardin, Garrett. *Exploring New Ethics for Survival*. New York: Viking Press, 1972.

Harrington, Michael. *The Accidental Century*. New York: Macmillan, 1965.

Heilbronner, Robert L. *An Inquiry into the Human Prospect*. New York: W. W. Norton, 1974.

Kohn, Herman, and Wiener, Anthony J. *The Year 2000, A Framework for Speculation*. New York: Macmillan, 1967.

McHale, John. *The Future of the Future*. New York: George Braziller, 1969.

Marien, Michael. *Essential Reading for the Future of Education*. Rev. ed. Syracuse: Educational Policies Research Center, 1971.

Purpel, David E., and Belanger, Maurice. "Toward a Humanistic Curriculum Theory." In *Curriculum and the Cultural Revolution*, edited by David E. Purpel and Maurice Belanger, pp. 64-74. Berkeley: McCutchan, 1972.

Rogers, Carl R. *Freedom to Learn*. Columbus: Charles E. Merrill, 1969.

Sutherland, John W. "Beyond Behaviorism and Determinism." *Fields within Fields*, winter 1973-74, pp. 32-46.

Theobald, Robert, ed. *Futures Conditional*. Indianapolis: Bobbs-Merrill, 1972.

Thompson, William Irwin. *At the Edge of History*. New York: Harper and Row, 1971.

# CHAPTER THREE

# Theory and
# the Practitioner

## THE PRACTITIONER AND THE PROFESSOR

Theory is based on a value position and interrelated concepts, a belief system that provides criteria to guide the practitioner—in making rational choices among alternative courses of action and sources of knowledge, in making value decisions, and in predicting the consequences of various solutions to dilemmas. Theory provides a frame of reference against which the practitioner can raise questions and test hypotheses. Since the curriculum developer does not work in isolation, curriculum-related questions such as the following will be raised, calling for decisions that affect others:

1. What role does advanced technology in communications media play in curriculum development and instruction? How shall the curriculum cope with the power of the mass media to shape opinions and attitudes?

2. In view of the world's dwindling natural resources, its increasing population, the threat of irrevocable damage to the biosphere, and

the apparent need to reverse the "growth is good" concept, what should be taught in economics, science, sociology, aesthetics, and other fields?

3. If new values are needed by the human race, what issues and dilemmas are to be faced, and what processes and content shall be used to face them? What experiences shall be made available to students? What disciplines shall be drawn upon for knowledge? How shall the planner assist students in developing the valuing and decision-making skills they need for making reasoned choices?

4. Is a new work ethic arising that can give direction to curriculum development—an ethic in which job satisfaction, the feeling of contribution, cooperation, or creation, takes precedence over the income earned? If so, how can individual self-realization and mutual responsibility for social problems be developed in relation to this ethic?

5. What types of learning environments and physical facilities will be needed as a support system for the curriculum? Should the curriculum developer look to the home, the school, the community, or all as the setting for the curriculum? What relationship should the curriculum developer advocate between open, action, and experiential learning on the one hand and didactics, directives, and rote on the other? Alvin Toffler (1970) reminds us that the industrial age ushered in a form of mass education that was a perfect introduction to industrial society: its regimentation, lack of individualization, rigid systems of seating, grouping, grading, and marking, and authoritarian role of the teacher were precisely those that would make education an effective instrument for adapting the population to industrialism. The student was not expected to make decisions; they were made for him. At the other extreme, in our day, imitations of the Summerhill model are criticized for their total permissiveness and lack of apparent direction. What theories underlie the many important and varied curriculum decisions needed today?

These are some types of questions illustrating the practitioner's need for theory. But a theory cannot be delivered to the practitioner ready-made for adoption; practitioners must take part in its construction if it is to be meaningful.

George Beauchamp (1968, pp. 33-34) has synthesized other commentators on theory, and he points out that

the operational vistas opened up and explained by theories increase the possible choices of behaving for the practitioner; the theories, however, do not tell him how to act. A theory may clarify relationships among any given set of events. . . . Theory is not what is practiced. A person cannot practice a set of logically related statements; he performs an activity. Theories of instruction, for example, might account for classroom discipline, grouping practices, lesson planning, and instructional materials as components of instruction, but the theories cannot tell teachers how to behave with respect to those functions. . . . Nevertheless, it is the job of educational theory to guide educational practices. In turn, theory is modified by practice and research that emanate from it.

Clear though the need for theory may be, however, practitioners have persistent difficulties understanding what theory is and how it is developed, as the history of and problems associated with theory development in education reveal. This chapter recaps that history and then identifies the elements of theory, including definitions, concepts, steps in constructing theory, and functions of theory. Although some confusion exists about how theory-making applies to education and thus to curriculum development, a substantial degree of consensus is emerging.

## THE THEORY PROBLEM

Early leaders in the effort to call the attention of educators to the significance of theory in education were amazed and disappointed to find unexpected ignorance, indifference, and even hostility to learning more about the meaning of theory. The "breakthrough" in the development of theory in education came in educational administration in the 1950s, and, after a slow start, the development gained ground and spread to other areas of education, such as instruction and curriculum. Daniel Griffiths in 1959 reviewed the "theory problem," and the following historical comments are largely drawn from his observations and those of other contributors to his volume. Griffiths's review pertains to educational administration, but parallel situations regarding understandings about theory also exist in curriculum development and other fields of education, and analogies can be drawn.

Griffiths traced the stimulus for theory development to the Kellogg Foundation, which provided grants to several universities between 1946 and 1959 for the study and improvement of educational administration. In 1947, several professors of educational administration and a few interested practitioners formed an organization known as the National Conference of Professors of Educational

Administration (NCPEA), and from this group a significant movement emerged. Before 1950, the content of educational administration seemed to be comprised of folklore, testimonials of administrators from wealthy or innovative districts, speculations of college professors, and opinions of administrators and professors who had written or lectured widely. The content of courses in educational administration generally consisted of a description of practices, cautious
recommendations of promising techniques, personal success stories,
and lively anecdotes, all surrounded with the halo of common sense
conferred by a professor or reportedly successful administrator.
There was no well-defined and organized body of subject matter and
no theoretical structure.

An important turning point occurred in 1954. At the summer
conference of the NCPEA, a number of theorists of human behavior
from social science fields met with professors of educational administration, and together they challenged the type of thinking that had
been prevalent in educational administration. They offered suggestions for new approaches to thinking in the field and inspired a
critical analysis reported by Arthur Coladarci and Jacob Getzels
(1955).

One year later, the University Council for Educational Administration (UCEA) was organized. With financial assistance from the
Kellogg Foundation, it worked actively toward the development of
theory by stimulating seminars and research studies. Progress was
slow, however, as revealed by Hollis Moore's 1957 review of research
activities. A critique by Andrew Halpin (1958) of the reported
research noted that a prolific effort had been made to collect information, but it was exhortations, how-to-do-it prescriptions, catalogs
of opinion, or status investigations that did not permit generalization
beyond the immediate data.

By the time of Griffiths's 1959 publication, it had become evident
to the leaders in theory development that they had gone far beyond
the general comprehension of the meaning of theory. Disappoint-
ingly they found not only lack of acquaintance with theory, but also
resistance to it. A prevalent view among both practitioners and professors of education was that theory was useless.

A typical scoffer's comment was made by a professor who pointed
out proudly that his course titled "Principles of School Administration" was a "practical course, none of that theory stuff." An

observer knowledgeable in theory commented that the syllabus failed to reveal any "principles" and agreed that there was certainly no theory in the course!

Why were educators adverse to theory? Coladarci and Getzels identified several factors explaining the antitheory bias in the mid-1950s:

1. *Factualism*. "Get the facts" seemed to be almost a national slogan, but with no regard paid to interrelationships among facts, as though education could be merely an encyclopedia of facts.

2. *Authority*. There appeared to be an unwarranted and even alarming amount of respect for prominent speakers and writers, whose chief claim to fame might be merely that they came from a well-known school district or university.

3. *Lack of definitions*. There was little consistency at that time in the use of terms to describe events, and the same words were frequently used with a wide variety of meanings in discussions of theory.

4. *Personal opinion*. A major drawback to progress in the development of theory was jealousy about ideas held by various individuals. Ideas were personalized, and it seemed that to criticize an idea was to criticize an individual.

5. *Impracticality*. A common complaint was that it was better to be practical than theoretical. For example, if an individual or group advocated the use of lay committees in a school system, it was more often because a neighboring school district or one reported in the literature had used the technique rather than because of knowledge of interaction theory. John Dewey had not fully come into his own, and little attention had been given to his contention that

theory is in the end . . . the most practical of all things, because the widening of the range of attention beyond merely purpose and desire eventually results in the creation of wider and farther-reaching purposes and enables us to make use of a much wider and deeper range of conditions and means than were expressed in the observation of primitive practical purposes (1929, p. 17).

## WHAT THEORY IS NOT

In the early days of theory development in education it seemed expedient to explain theory by making clear what it was *not*. Griffiths (1959) unequivocally eliminated a few popular misconceptions of theory, and others have been added to this list.

*Not a rule of thumb.* Frequently a style or pattern of operation is mistakenly called a theory: "We operate on the theory that student government is necessary to build morale."

*Not a brainstormed flight of fancy.* Thoughts tossed around in bull sessions are sometimes labeled theories: "My theory is that schools will someday use the daily newspaper as the entire curriculum."

*Not an "ought to."* A personal point of view, value statement, or set of "oughts" is sometimes called a theory: "My theory is that individualized instruction systems can be successful in every subject field."

*Not a taxonomy.* A taxonomy is a classification of data according to order, natural relationships, or governing principles that can be used for description of a subject matter or for diagnosing a problem. Taxonomies both summarize and inspire descriptive studies. Descriptive and taxonomic studies have been popular in educational investigations, and the information yielded is useful in building a theory. These sources are not theory, however.

*Not the literature.* Theory is not a term synonymous with classical works. Neither is it synonymous with the literature of educational criticism. However, these are also sources that are useful in developing a theory.

## WHAT THEORY IS

Theory is here defined as a set of propositions derived from data and creative thinking, from which constructs are formed to describe interactions among variables and to generate hypotheses. Theory describes, explains, goes beyond the data, predicts, and leads to new knowledge.

Characteristics of theory are stated by several writers, and these aid in clarifying the definition. Interrelatedness of a set of statements or events is a characteristic commonly noted. Fred Kerlinger brought together several dimensions when he wrote (1965, p. 11), "a theory is a set of interrelated constructs, definitions, and propositions that presents a systematic view of phenomena by specifying relations among variables with the purpose of explaining and predicting the phenomena."

The power of theories to generate new knowledge is another characteristic that is generally accepted. For example, theories summarize and inspire not descriptive studies but rather verificational studies—studies constructed to test specific hypotheses "generated from the theory" (Zetterberg 1965, p. 28). Zetterberg explains (pp. vii-viii) that a theory may

coordinate many methodologically imperfect findings into a rather trustworthy whole in the form of a small number of information-packed sentences or equations. Moreover, some of the bits and pieces coordinated into this trustworthy whole can be the challenging insights of the classics . . . [of a field] . . . and the celebrated writers of literature; in short, far from trivial propositions.

The relationship between hypotheses and theories is explained by Deobold Van Dalen (1966, p. 172), who says that a theory may contain several logically interrelated hypotheses. Van Dalen notes that hypotheses and theories are alike in that they are both conceptual and they both seek to explain and predict phenomena; but a theory usually offers a more general or higher-level explanation than a hypothesis. Van Dalen emphasizes that a theory usually presents a comprehensive conceptual scheme that explains diverse phenomena, and considerable empirical evidence is therefore needed to support it; however, no matter how wide a variety of confirming data is obtained, the theory is not established as an absolute truth.

This point is also made by Griffiths (1959, p. 11), who comments:

The instability of theory has caused many to suspect the whole notion of theory, yet this is not a necessary deterrent. Theories are not built for eternity. Theories are developed to help in the identification and clarification of problems here and now and in the immediate future. They are also constructed so that better theories might be built in the future. Theory building might be construed as a pyramiding task. Present theories rest on those of the past. When one examines past theories, even in the physical sciences, one notes the theories which were demonstrated to be untrue.

## DEFINITIONS

### Data

Information given as a basis for reasoning or inference is a general definition of data. Data may be expressed qualitatively, that is, using verbal symbols (word descriptions) such as the verbal observations of factors that hinder or foster change in the curriculum; or they may be expressed quantitatively, in mathematical symbols, such as numerals used to describe the frequency of occurrence of a given condition or to measure achievement on a given test, scale, or instrument.

Data used in this investigation were more qualitative than quantitative and were derived from experimental studies, observations and surveys of practices, generalizations in philosophical and historical works, and theory development in related fields.

## Construct

A construct is something (in this case a matrix and narrative interpretation) formed or created by a process of mental synthesis and/or by assembling parts or elements into an abstract creation.

## Hypothesis

A hypothesis is a provisional or possible explanation that implies given consequences, which the researcher seeks to confirm by providing factual evidence. It is an if/then tentative explanation: if $x$, then $y$. This temporary working principle requires testing to determine its worth.

## Facts

A fact is a piece of information presented as having objective reality. It may be any experience, change, occurrence, or event that is sufficiently stable and supported by enough evidence to be counted on in an investigation. Facts do not possess everlasting validity; they are subject to reinterpretation or revision when better insight is gained into phenomena.

## Assumption

An assumption is a statement taken for granted—a supposition that something is true.

## Phenomena

Facts or events of scientific interest that are capable of description and explanation are phenomena as the word is used in theoretical contexts.

## Model

The terms *model* and *theory* are sometimes used interchangeably; however, models are not theories. A model is an analogy, whereas a theory is a conceptual system that attempts to describe facts, relationships, and the interaction among the variables under consideration. Models are ways of representing given phenomena, although they are not the phenomena. Models may be drawings or graphic presentations that represent the real thing, or they may be more abstract, such as mathematical equations, verbal statements, or symbolic descriptions. They are tools that may be used in theory construction. A model may also be used to interpret a theory. The term *paradigm* is frequently used in theoretical literature as a synonym of model.

## Proposition

A proposition is a major premise on which subsequent meaning rests—a formal statement proposing something for development, discussion, testing, and verification. Hans Zetterberg (1965) distinguishes between "ordinary" and "theoretical" propositions. The higher the informative value of a proposition, the greater the variety of events for which it can account. Propositions of low informative value are ordinary propositions. Propositions of high informative value deserve to be called theoretical propositions. Ordinary propositions are of micro dimension or quality, while theoretical propositions are of macro dimension or quality. Ordinary propositions are used and subsumed in developing theoretical propositions. Part II of this book shows how numerous studies, findings, and observations have been drawn together into seven theoretical propositions.

### SOCIAL THEORY AND SCIENTIFIC THEORY

Although some disagreement exists among researchers about how scientific theory, that is, theory in the physical and biological sciences, applies to social theory, or theory in education, there is substantial support for the view that the mode of inquiry developed in these sciences can be transferred smoothly to the social fields of inquiry including education. An important difference requiring caution is stressed, however: social theories deal with humanistic or "raw" content, while biological and physical theories deal with symbols. Physical scientists, for example, hypothesize and look for underlying order through observations and experiments and note certain regularities, which when combined, become theories. From theories of physics, engineers then have created technological inventions in the fields of aerodynamics, optics, etc.

In social theory, an example cited by Zetterberg (1965, pp. 14-16) is Pitirim Sorokin's (1937-41) theory of social and cultural change, first developed in the 1930s. By translating historical events, from the earliest civilization on, into symbols representing "sensate" data and "ideational" data, Sorokin established basic lawlike generalizations, showing a rhythmic pattern through various periods of civilization and a correlation of the rhythm among fields of art, science, law, religion, and ethics. That is, society seemed to swing from sensate to ideational and back. No particular field led out each time, but fields seemed to move together. Sorokin's continuing explorations seek to show that, if a phase of a civilization can be located on a master curve of superrhythm, we should be able to tell a good deal about its art, drama, revolutions, etc. Although the theory is controversial, it has stimulated theory development in other social fields, e.g., the theory of cognitive dissonance by Leon Festinger, Catherine Bauer, and Robert Woods Kennedy (1950), and George Homans's (1950) theory of elementary social behavior.

Researchers and theorists in education and other social fields must face the difficulties of dealing with a great complexity and variety of phenomena that continually interact and are difficult to isolate. Influences of home, culture, community, government, peer groups, teacher behavior, etc., all bear on educational matters. Frequently, in attempts to be scientific, efforts have been directed toward maximum precision and minute areas of study, which have led to trivial conclusions having little if any effect on the larger problems in education.

Overworship of precisely measured and recorded data in social analyses tends to inhibit and narrow the field of theory construction, states Zetterberg. He points out that, in terms of confirming a theory, questions or indicators that have counterparts in definitions of cause and effect are worthwhile. Zetterberg also asserts that theorists should be more courageous about using the abundance of ordinary propositions to develop theoretical ones without first gathering the maximum evidence to support them. He notes that the surest way to discredit any research report seems to be to compare it with the ideals of science, and yet, even in science, theoretical propositions make claims that go far beyond the data scientists cite to support them. Obvious illustrations of his point are the theory of relativity, the use of probability theory in microphysics, and the existence of undemonstrable proofs in mathematical theory. Theorists in science as well as in social fields need to look for what is possible, for, if knowledge were limited or almost limited to summaries of what was observed, it would have very little informative value and would permit a very limited range of prediction.

James Macdonald (1967), in an insightful discussion of curriculum theorizing, speaks of scientific theory as "technological rationality" and social theory as "aesthetic rationality." While recognizing the power and usefulness of technological rationality, he warns against mechanistic uses. A theory involves objects in interaction with each other in systems, but a curriculum theory must be an open system as opposed to a mechanistic or closed system.

If educators become overenamored of the "systems" approach to human behavior, in the interests of efficiency and effectiveness, they risk losing contact with reality. Macdonald illustrates this point with the concept of instructional systems. It is conceivable that, to achieve maximum quality of learning in minimum time with least cost, learners, instructional goals, and media and materials could be organized systematically and controlled by computer processes, so that the pupil could receive instruction at home. Such a curriculum plan, developed in an industrial context, could be programmed in terms of individual variables and fed directly to the student at home, which would rid our present system of two expensive items: teachers and school buildings. Effectiveness and efficiency are obviously uppermost in this imagined situation, rather than the human condition.

Macdonald draws a parallel example from weapons delivery, suggesting that it is possible to feed hypothetical enemy actions and projected losses into a computer, which then calculates the weapons potential and probable loss of life before the "enemy" is knocked out. This "game" would be a fantastic display of technological rationality—the integrated use of mathematical reasoning, systems concepts and technical hardware—but the irrational end (destroying millions of persons) is totally repelling.

Curriculum theory should be committed to human fullness in creation, direction, and use, emphasizes Macdonald (1967, p. 169):

> Curriculum theorizing calls for immersion in the concrete data of curriculum experiences; awareness of general ideas and developments in such areas as psychology, sociology, anthropology, biology, philosophy, and theology; knowledge of the historical and contemporary developments and theories in curriculum; and a willingness and ability to utilize both aesthetic and technological rationality in the process of theorizing.

## ELEMENTS OF THEORY

All theory-building starts with observations of some sort or other. Griffiths (1964) asks, does a formulation have to be tested to be called a theory? He feels the answer is probably no. What is needed is that the theory be logically capable of proof or disproof, whether or not the tools for testing are available at the time of its formulation.

### Criteria

A similar view is expressed by Ira Gordon (1968), who drew on studies of instructional theory in identifying criteria to assess the quality of a theory. The criteria Gordon would apply to the analysis of a theory are: explicit limitations, interrelationships, congruence with empirical data, capability of generating hypotheses, generalizations that go beyond the data, verifiability (e.g., data obtained from studies of animals may not be applicable to humans), possibility of collecting data for disproof, provision for explanation of past events, capability of predicting future events, and representation of qualitative syntheses as opposed to quantitative relationships among variables.

### Propositions

Propositions are the central elements of a theory. The definition of proposition provided by Zetterberg (1965) for social theory building is used, since curriculum development theory also involves people, society, and knowledge. Propositions may be research findings or may be lawlike generalized statements that are supported empirically and are consistent with existing findings, observations, or other accepted propositions, such as those from classical works. Lawlike propositions can be combined into systems, that is, theories.

To check a theory, the theorist examines how well each of the propositions conforms to the evidence and how well several propositions in conjunction with each other lead to a major construct.

Propositions relate variates (variables) to one another, and two variates are needed at a minimum to have one theoretical proposition (Homans 1950; Zetterberg 1965). One-variate statements are not theoretical propositions; they are ordinary propositions or descriptive statements, e.g., "x varies." An example is "modern children spend excessive amounts of time looking at television." A two-variate statement must point out that "if x varies, then y varies." The illustrative statement might be expanded into a two-variate statement as follows: "If the time children spend looking at television increases, then their reading ability decreases."

When we speculate that "the more children look at television, the lower their reading ability," we have related the variates television and reading to each other. Television is designated as a *determinant* (cause or independent variable) and reading is designated as a *result* (effect or dependent variable). The cause and effect relationship indicates the direction in which the variates influence each other. In this example, poor reading is said to come from excessive television, not excessive television from poor reading.

Propositions with two variates are acceptable as intermediate steps in theory construction even if they do not tell the whole story. Once formulated, they lend themselves to further development. In a complex field such as curriculum development, propositions may be multivariate.

In applying analysis to the elements of propositions in theory-building, Zetterberg refers to Andrzej Malewski's (1968) work and points out (1965, p. 153):

Theoretical knowledge is considered here not as a set of infallible and absolute truths, but rather as a system of hypotheses which present a challenge to other investigators who through gradually modifying them make somewhat more adequate hypotheses. Accordingly, the process of building up a science is one where the various hypotheses and their systems, while offering an approximate picture of regularities of human behavior, inspire further investigations which lead to the formulation of more and more adequate systems of hypotheses.

Propositions may form a chain pattern if a result in one reappears as a determinant in another. For example, knowledge of attitudes of a group may lead to prestige for a person; prestige may lead to authority for him or her; and authority may lead to centrality in the group. Studies can be cited showing that all of these variables are positively correlated (Hopkins 1964).

A matrix is another form for presenting propositions and specifying their interrelationships. The matrix is more useful than the chain pattern for searching out relationships, as the chain pattern is restricted to sequential propositions. In chapter thirteen of this study, the theoretical propositions are arranged on two axes of a matrix. Possible interrelations between these variables, identified at points of intersection on the matrix, become the basis for constructs from which hypotheses for testing are derived.

## Rules for Theorizing

George Beauchamp (1972) has provided some clear and concise rules for curriculum theorists to follow:

1. Define the technical language, including unique or specialized terms, and use those definitions consistently throughout the theoretical work.

2. Identify the principal ingredients essential to the field of concern; that is, classify the accumulated information and describe the circumstances and conditions under which the sets of events occur.

3. Identify relationships among the various parts or the theoretical statements, and explain the character of those relationships. Defining, describing, classifying, and relating are fundamental to the more general process of explanation, which is essential in theory building.

## Steps in Constructing Theory

Several investigators are essentially in agreement about the steps in constructing a theory: (1) make systematic observations or make use of systematic observations provided by other investigators, (2) invent or use propositions and constructs to represent relationships among things or events, and (3) derive hypotheses on the basis of the constructs and their relationships (Beauchamp 1968; Griffiths 1959; Ryans 1965; Silverman 1967).

## Functions of Theory

Coordinating many clues, findings, educated guesses, segments of information, and insights of distinguished analysts and writers into a reliable, comprehensive whole from which new knowledge may be generated is an important function of theory. Theory is also useful as a guide to the collection of facts, not only in the process of building further on the concepts of the original theory, but also in the process of validating the theory. One of the most useful functions of theory is serving as a guide to new knowledge by suggesting testable hypotheses and inspiring further research.

Another use of theory is as a guide to choices of actions in terms of their consequences. An adequate theory should prepare students and practitioners for further growth by helping them avoid over-simplified explanations of actions that seem to be successful and making them aware of changing conditions that might call for changed behavior patterns. Such a guiding theory should help keep them alert to unanticipated consequences of their actions as well as providing economical ways of planning experiences (so that they do not "reinvent the wheel").

## REFERENCES

Beauchamp, George A. "Basic Components of a Curriculum Theory." *Curriculum Theory Network*, fall 1972, pp. 16-22.

―――. *Curriculum Theory*. 2d ed. Wilmette, Ill.: Kagg Press, 1968.

Coladarci, Arthur P., and Getzels, Jacob W. *The Use of Theory in Educational Administration*. Stanford, Calif.: Stanford University Press, 1955.

Dewey, John. *Sources of a Science Education*. New York: Liveright, 1929.

Festinger, Leon; Bauer, Catherine; and Kennedy, Robert Woods. *Social Pressures in Informal Groups*. New York: Harper, 1950.

Gordon, Ira J., ed. *Criteria for Theories of Instruction*. Washington, D.C.: Association for Supervision and Curriculum Development, 1968.

Griffiths, Daniel E. "The Nature and Meaning of Theory." In *Behavioral Science and Educational Administration*, part II, pp. 95-118. Sixty-third Yearbook of the National Society for the Study of Education. Chicago: University of Chicago Press, 1964.

―――. *Administrative Theory*. New York: Appleton-Century-Crofts, 1959.

Halpin, Andrew W., ed. *Administrative Theory in Education*. Chicago: Midwest Administration Center, 1958.

Homans, George C. *The Human Group*. New York: Harcourt, Brace and World, 1950.

Hopkins, Terence K. *The Exercise of Influence in Small Groups*. Totowa, N.J.: Bedminster Press, 1964.

Kerlinger, Fred N. *Foundations of Behavioral Research*. New York: Holt, Rinehart and Winston, 1965.

Macdonald, James B. "An Example of Disciplined Curriculum Thinking." *Theory into Practice* 6 (October 1967): 166-71.

Malewski, Andrzej. "Levels of Generality in Sociological Theory." In *A Symposium on Theoretical Sociology*, edited by Hans L. Zetterberg and Gerda Lorenz. Totowa, N.J.: Bedminster Press, 1968.

Moore, Hollis A., Jr. *Studies in School Administration*. Washington, D.C.: American Association of School Administrators, 1957.

Ryans, David G. "A Model of Instruction Based on Information System Concepts." In *Theories of Instruction*, edited by James B. Macdonald and Robert R. Leeper. Washington, D.C.: Association for Supervision and Curriculum Development, 1965.

Silverman, Robert E. "Theories and Models and Their Utility." *Educational Technology* 15 (October 1967): 1-7.

Sorokin, Pitirim A. *Social and Cultural Dynamics.* 4 vols. New York: American Book, 1937-41.

Toffler, Alvin. *Future Shock.* New York: Bantam Books, 1970.

Van Dalen, Deobold B. *Understanding Educational Research.* New York: McGraw-Hill, 1966.

Zetterberg, Hans L. *On Theory and Verification in Sociology.* Totowa, N.J.: Bedminster Press, 1965.

## ADDITIONAL READINGS

Bruner, Jerome S. *Toward a Theory of Instruction.* New York: W. W. Norton, 1966.

*Curriculum Theory Network,* various issues. Journal published by the Ontario Institute for Studies in Education, Toronto, Canada.

Homans, George. "Contemporary Theory in Sociology." In *Handbook of Modern Sociology,* edited by Robert L. Faris. Chicago: Rand McNally, 1964.

Kaplan, Abraham. *The Conduct of Inquiry.* San Francisco: Chandler, 1964.

Kuhn, Thomas S. *The Structure of Scientific Revolutions.* Chicago: University of Chicago Press, 1962.

Lewis, Ralph W. "Implosions of Knowledge." *Intellect* 102 (April 1974): 428-29.

Marcuse, Herbert. *One Dimensional Man.* Boston: Beacon Press, 1964.

Merton, Robert K. *Social Theory and Social Structure.* Rev. ed. New York: Free Press of Glencoe, 1957.

Parsons, Talcott, and Shils, Edward, eds. *Toward a General Theory of Action.* Cambridge: Harvard University Press, 1959.

CHAPTER FOUR

# Curriculum Development in a Responsive Context

Contextual factors affecting curriculum development are many, varied, complicated, interconnected, and constantly changing. A given model for curriculum development may be suitable in one setting and inappropriate in another. Thus, a theory of curriculum development that can be responsive to individual and social needs in a complex, changing society cannot be built around linear or single-principle concepts. In addition to the many environmental factors involved, the participants must be considered. Also, wisdom does not stand still; it is constantly being revised, extended, replaced, and interpreted differently from varying points of view.

Even the definitions related to curriculum vary from one source to another. George Beauchamp (1972) comments that people who use different meanings of curriculum fall into three groups: one group thinks of a curriculum as a plan for subsequent action; another views curriculum and instruction as synonyms or a unified concept; and a third group sees curriculum as a very broad term, encompassing the learner's psychological processes as she or he acquires educational experiences. Since there is a lack of agreement on the definitions of *curriculum, instruction,* and *curriculum development* among people in the field, it is important to set forth the definitions on which this discussion is based.

*Curriculum* here means a plan for achieving intended learning outcomes; it is a plan concerned with purpose, with what is to be learned, and with the results of instruction.

*Instruction* is the process of providing learning environments that offer students a wide range of interactions with other people, things, places, and ideas, through which the curriculum is delivered.

*Curriculum development* is a process of assessing needs, identifying the desired learning outcomes, planning and preparing for the instructional alternatives to achieve the outcomes, and using the cultural, social, and personal interests that the curriculum is to serve.

Each of these terms is further developed in the following sections.

## CURRICULUM

The definition of curriculum as a plan for achieving intended learning outcomes is a departure from the definition of curriculum as "all the experiences a learner has under the guidance of the school," which prevailed in the literature from the 1930s until about 1960, according to Arthur Foshay (1969). Another common definition of curriculum is programmatic—"the curriculum is the program of school subjects"—emphasizing coverage of textbook material and subject matter. Foshay concludes that such definitions do not invite inquiry and may well block it. Mauritz Johnson (1967) defines the curriculum as a structured series of intended learning outcomes, and John Goodlad (1967) says that a curriculum is all the learnings intended for a student or group of students, which implies that there must be a plan specifying and justifying what they are to do and learn. Some assumptions about curriculum follow.

Curriculum is comprised of several elements: learning outcomes, selection, and structure. Criteria for the evaluation of a curriculum, like those for instruction and curriculum development, must be used cooperatively by the persons involved, particularly teachers and students, to assess educational quality and appropriateness. Learning outcomes include knowledge, attitudes, and skills. Knowledge includes facts, information, principles, and generalizations that help an individual understand his or her world better. Skills are techniques, processes, and abilities that enable the individual to be versatile in using knowledge and physical resources effectively to extend the horizons of his or her world. Attitudes include values, beliefs, interpersonal feelings, creative thinking, appreciations, self-esteem, and other aspects of affective growth.

Questions to be asked in making curriculum decisions are: Does this knowledge help the individual understand his or her world better? Are attitudes developing that enable individuals to be more humanly and humanely mobile and versatile in the world? Are individuals developing skills that enable them to extend the limits and horizons of their world? Are they becoming increasingly competent in coping with their concerns about their inner selves and the outer world?

Selection is an essential element of curriculum. Traditionally, adults selected curriculum content, which was drawn from the disciplines and organized in keeping with adults' views of the most functional division of information. Newer curricula are organized according to areas of investigation selected by adults and students together. This in no way implies an incidental curriculum. Selection is made from many sources of curriculum in the world around us, including people, materials, travel, and ideas. Selection recognizes the interrelatedness of knowledge, attitudes, and skills; it recognizes that concepts and generalizations do not occur singly or in isolation, but rather form clusters, and that the motivation for learning is derived from the significance of the content selected. Selection recognizes that modern communication media make cultural content available in many new dimensions. It also recognizes the distinction between skill training and education as a process of equipping an individual to cope successfully with the unpredictable needs of a changing world. Emphasis is on the quality of the learning environment in which experiences develop.

Structure identifies order or sequence or notes that order is immaterial. Structure for an individual may develop from his or her interests and motivations, when a range of alternatives is available.

Jerome Bruner's widely publicized statement in *The Process of Education* (1960) that anything worth teaching can be taught in some intellectually honest way at any level has conveyed the impression to a wide audience that there is some definite pattern of construction or organization of the subject matter of the separate disciplines that should be known by curriculum-makers and used in sequencing information to impart it to children in an efficient and effective way. This point of view influenced the curriculum "reforms" of the 1960s, which did not in actuality reform curriculum. John Dewey (1916) would probably not have advocated a rigid or set structure as an intellectually honest way to introduce children to life and experience.

Knowledge, of course, must be integrated to be meaningful, and curriculum structure can be constructed not only within the separate disciplines but also across disciplines or interdisciplinary areas of social, cultural, or personal interest.

Criteria for evaluation of the curriculum are provided when intended learning outcomes are identified. Evaluation examines the extent to which actual outcomes compare with intended outcomes and provides a means for constant revision and improvement of the curriculum.

The curriculum can be thought of as encompassing three general areas. One includes subject matter content and information, which have historically absorbed most of the curriculum development efforts. Concepts and relationships, communication of ideas in many modes and media, individual discovery, examination of values, and the creation of new knowledge stem from experiences with substantive content.

A second area is concerned with social development, group inquiry, social issues, political and economic problems, international understandings, peer relationships, and current concerns of the participants, e.g., ecology, race, and urbanization. The behavioral sciences are useful here.

Personal development and self-actualization are the focus of the third area. Experiences for increasing the level of self-actualization include activities for developing communication skills such as listening to others and understanding nonverbal communication, guided self-analysis using audio and video recordings, role-playing of conflict situations, practice in goal-setting and performance assessment, and seminars for identification and discussion of personal values. Other experiences may be sought in the real world, including participation in problem-centered projects, work experiences, and use of the arts as modes of expressing personal feelings and experiences.

## INSTRUCTION

Instruction is the process of providing learning environments that offer a wide range of alternatives through which the curriculum is delivered. Instruction consists of interactions between the student and an environment that has been strategically devised by the teacher so that intended learning outcomes can be achieved.

The learning environment may include books, printed materials of other kinds, films, television programs, self-instructional packages, tape recordings, and the many other media that comprise the technological support system. The environment includes people with whom to interact and the world both inside and outside the school. The teacher is no longer viewed as the mere transmitter of information but rather as the mediator of the environment—a person who must have competence in using the growing body of technical knowledge about artifacts and procedures, who must be able to move effectively within the environment as a helper to the instructional process, and who must know and use many alternatives in implementing the curriculum. Teacher-student interaction is an important part of instruction. It is motivational, and it assists in the integration of knowledge and the generation of new ideas. Interaction, however, must be distinguished from a "recitation" methodology, as underlined by Edmund Amidon and Ned Flanders (1963) as well as other interaction analysts.

Interpersonal relations between teachers and students and between students and students form the social system of the school. This social system may have a greater influence on the learner than many of the other aspects of the learning environment. James Coleman's (1963) research indicates that students form values and norms that substantially affect the behavior of their fellow students; for example, where students approved intellectual activity, their peers tended to achieve more academic learning, in studies of both the most able students and less able students.

## CURRICULUM DEVELOPMENT

Curriculum development is a complex process of assessing needs, identifying desired learning outcomes, planning and preparing for instruction to achieve the outcomes, and using the cultural, social, and personal needs and interests that the curriculum is to serve. Curriculum development involves many kinds of decisions on several different levels. At the classroom level, teachers—in conjunction with students, administrators, resource personnel, and lay citizens—are responsible for developing a curriculum that is relevant to local situations. At governmental levels, district school board members, state legislators, and federal officials make policy decisions that support some aspects of curriculum development and restrict others. At the institutional level, administrators, teachers, and students determine the specific curriculum sequences or outlines or ways of relating the various kinds of knowledge, choices of materials and equipment, and other decisions that influence curriculum development.

## Models

Three models for the curriculum development process, described by James O'Hanlon (1973-74), can be found in operation in various schools, school districts, and classrooms. Eclectic models that draw from all also exist. O'Hanlon says that the three models—management, systematic, and open-access curriculum development—might well be used in a growth pattern, moving from the one of greatest control to the one of greatest humanistic or autonomous value.

### The Management Model

In the management model, there is a hierarchy of authority for curriculum decision-making. The school administrator, a single manager, or an administrative team, with final decision-making authority, is at the top of a hierarchy designed to increase the consistency of decisions. The manager recognizes, however, that others, particularly teachers and principals, must go along with the decisions if they are to be implemented effectively. He or she therefore engages others in curriculum development activities, while retaining final authority over major decisions in the matter. Work groups, curriculum committees, advisory groups, and individuals may develop proposals for curriculum changes (based on the general goals of the institution) and submit them through a series of processes for disposition.

In this model, curriculum goals are usually stated in terms of what the school will do for the student, and evidence of accomplishment is sought by comparing students' standardized test scores with national norms, following up the achievements of graduates in college, and comparing the school's program with those of other schools thought to be exemplary. Curriculum evaluation also includes opinions about acceptance of the curriculum by teachers, citizens, and students of the school community. Curriculum guides and scope and sequence charts are prepared to indicate to teachers what and how they are to teach. In-service education programs are developed to support the curriculum plan, materials are purchased that are consistent with it, and new teachers are hired who have or are willing to acquire the skills needed to implement it.

### The Systematic Model

The systematic model of curriculum development borrows from systems approaches in industry and is frequently described as a performance-based program. The first step in this approach is to establish the goals of the curriculum. Then the planners develop a series of tasks that can be diagramed in a flow chart, indicating their relationships to each other. At this point a procedure begins that O'Hanlon (1973-74) calls "feedforward." It consists of a series of directives for moving from one task to another in the curriculum development process. One type of directive is to compose objectives in terms of the observable student outcomes to be produced, with each objective divided into subobjectives that are reanalyzed into successively smaller units, until the classroom lesson plan level is reached. Another aspect of the feedforward process is the establishment of guidelines that provide a rationale for decisions, such as how the curriculum matter should be organized, what content should be selected, and what instructional method should be used. During the curriculum development process, some sort of monitoring must be carried on to determine whether each task in the system has been accomplished on time and adequately, so that the succeeding tasks may be undertaken.

Carried to an extreme of control, this model may become a closed system, with instruction restricted to carefully identified objectives. Thus the systematic model might conceivably be "guaranteed" to produce the student learning, and ultimately the effect on society, for which it is designed. This strict behavioristic interpretation underlies some of the "accountability" efforts described elsewhere in this book.

It is also conceivable that a systematic model may become an open system, based on humanistic and democratic values, in which students, teachers, and others concerned with the immediate learning environment cooperatively plan general goals, specific objectives, and tasks around a mutual organizing center of interest and, by self-monitoring, determine whether they are reaching their goals and how those goals, objectives, and tasks should be revised.

### The Open-Access Model

In the open-access model, decisions are made on the basis of their consistency with humanistic values. A principal premise is that this consistency is accomplished when the decision-making process is based on open inquiry. This means that persons involved in or concerned with the curriculum are free to participate in its development in ways that are meaningful to them. Current information about the curriculum and about decisions being considered is made available to all, all decisions are open for reconsideration at any time, and all decisions are based on a humanistic rationale.

The open-access model does not imply a lack of leadership. However, leadership is carried out on a situational rather than a continuing basis, and responsibility is decentralized, with decisions being made by the group or subgroup closest to the persons affected by the curriculum. The general outline of the curriculum is often sketchy at the outset, and parts are filled in as they are tried out in actual practice. Open inquiry receives a high priority, and the model is based on the assumption that the curriculum will provide learning experiences that students find significant to them as individuals.

The open-access model is illustrated in numerous alternative schools, open classrooms, and other forms of open education around the country. The systematic model has been developed, extended, and interpreted through the work of regional educational laboratories and research and development centers. The management model is probably more commonly used than the other two, however. Advocates of any model need familiarity with the others to continue their growth in taking responsibility for curriculum development.

## The Process of Curriculum Development

Curriculum development is far from being a simple, rational process. Hilda Taba's (1962) insights into curriculum development more than a decade ago have relevance today. She describes the development process as a coherent stream within which flow the demands and needs of the culture, the growth and development of children, the principles of learning, the fundamental ideas in various content areas, and the unique modes of thought represented in these areas. This stream must yield a development of ideas, forms of thought, feelings, habits, and skills to be integrated by the learner. Curriculum development is further complicated by the philosophies and value orientations of the participants, which make some plans seem of greater worth than others.

James Macdonald (1971) points out that curriculum development is not a simple rational process but rather a complex political and ethical phenomenon. Curriculum development, he says, has been influenced over the past several years by such factors as Sputnik, federal funding, television programs, inner-city problems, racial strife, alienated students, Bruner, Piaget, environmental problems, and Head Start. Since curriculum development is oriented toward the goal of a systematic organization of cultural beliefs, expressive symbols, and values, it must select from all cultures and needs to create the pattern of encounters that will be internalized most meaningfully by the learners. Macdonald's position is that curriculum development should be designed to help learners create culture as well as assimilate culture, meet and maintain social relationships, and develop personally; but above all, it must reflect a moral commitment to human freedom, worth, and dignity.

It is obvious that curriculum development must be a responsive process, constantly extending, expanding, and revising the curriculum. This requires continuous planning of learning outcomes that will help individuals draw effectively on growing realms of knowledge, develop new skills in a rapidly changing world, and develop insights into and constructive approaches to unresolved problems. The process of curriculum development must continue to be responsive to needs and problems and to generate alternative means for reaching desirable ends.

## CONTEXTUAL FACTORS

Curriculum development may seem deceptively simple and acceptable at face value, but it becomes highly complicated when applied to theory building. Some of the settings, aspects, and factors operating within the context of curriculum development are discussed in this section. The participants in curriculum development are also a contextual factor and are discussed in chapter five.

Curriculum development may be directed toward a great variety of educational settings and populations—those of early childhood, elementary, middle school, secondary, college, postgraduate, vocational, and other specialized types of education. Curriculum development may be micro or macro; that is, it may refer to a very small unit, such as a teacher and ten students, or to a statewide or national group. It may refer to a specific subject field or to an interdisciplinary area of investigation. The clientele may have pluralistic backgrounds or a homogeneous culture; may be oriented toward rural or urban interests; may be handicapped or normal; and so on.

Other dimensions of unlimited variation enter into considerations of context. Such aspects as needs, diagnoses, objectives, processes, knowledge, future thinking, technological support, cultural pluralism, creativity, personal responsibility, teaching competence, student perceptions, school buildings, and community resources are among the contextual topics requiring attention. This is by no means an exhaustive list, but it illustrates the possibilities for responsiveness in curriculum development, particularly when considered in light of the great variety of educational and cultural settings already mentioned. Questions about each of these factors must be considered in the process of curriculum development.

### Needs

Curriculum development assumes, explicitly or implicitly, that the learner needs something that can be met through the curriculum and instructional processes that are being planned. Needs are sometimes thought of as the psychological needs of the students, the need of the school district to produce a quality product, the needs of the subject matters as measured by the discrepancies between students' scores on standardized tests and the national norms, the parents' needs, the community needs, or the national needs. Suffice it to say at this point that this is a most important consideration in curriculum development. It is further developed in chapter ten.

### Diagnosis

The concept of diagnosis implies that curriculum development seeks the alternatives that are most appropriate to each person who uses the curriculum. Tasks, styles of learning, materials, and experiences must be designed to encourage the individual to move at his or her optimum rate and to develop his or her fullest potential. Each person who uses the products of curriculum development should experience success without being labeled or typed.

## Goals and Objectives

Goals and objectives for curriculum development are formulated at various levels, ranging from the broad societal goals to specific objectives for the classroom level. Since life is always changing, and at present is changing rapidly, and since objectives for curriculum development grow out of experience as well as guide experience, they cannot be constructed once and for all. Objectives must recognize human values as well as technical quality.

## Learning Experiences

*How* students learn should be emphasized in curriculum development as well as *what* students learn. Responsive curriculum development should lead to processes of instruction and dynamic living experiences in which individuals learn how to draw effectively on knowledge, act constructively when faced with conflicts or dilemmas, interact and work with others across cultures and classes, and develop respect for those of differing needs and concerns. Processes of instruction should help the learner assume responsibility for assessing how far the agreed objectives have been met.

A common thread that should run through teaching-learning experiences is the spirit of inquiry, which seeks to capitalize on the learner's curiosity and the excitement of the search. Methods of inquiry must teach students to formulate questions, bring questions into a productive order, search in a variety of places and a variety of ways for answers, organize ideas into principles and concepts, and test the reliability of their judgments.

## Evaluation

Evaluation is essential in the decision-making processes of curriculum development. Curriculum development cannot be responsive if there is not a constant stream of feedback about what is going on in the instructional process and how it is working. A test of an evaluation system is the question, "Does it deliver the feedback that is needed, when it is needed, to the persons or groups who need it?"

Self-evaluation, assessment by and of the learner, is a fundamental outcome of the evaluation of instruction, in addition to continuing feedback on the larger questions of curriculum development. Evaluation must facilitate learning and teaching; it must not be confused with the processes of grading, sorting, and screening out students. Evaluation must include a great variety of feedback data beyond the usual standardized tests and paper-and-pencil work. It must encompass attitudes and values as well as cognitive skills.

The evaluation process is a tool for finding alternative ways of achieving an effective curriculum and appropriate instruction. It also helps to detect needed improvements in the curriculum development process itself.

## Knowledge

Curriculum development demands the use of a broad scope of knowledge. Skills and understandings that are important in curriculum development include knowledge of facts, information, principles, and methods; comprehension, expressed by interpretation, explanation, and paraphrasing; application of concepts or abstractions to new situations; analysis of elements and relationships; synthesis of ideas, plans, and operations; and evaluative uses of knowledge that show judgment based on criteria.

For curriculum to be meaningful, content is needed. Six fundamental realms of meaning designated by Philip Phenix (1964) provide a broad map of content: symbolics (language, mathematics, gestures); empirics (observation and experimentation in the natural and social sciences); aesthetics (music, visual arts, movement, literature); synnoetics (personal knowledge, meditative thought); ethics (moral meanings, obligations, perceptions); and synoptics (integrative meanings, including history, religion, philosophy).

## Future Thinking

Curriculum development must anticipate the rate and direction of social and technical change. Given further acceleration, knowledge may become even more temporal than it now is; information may quickly become obsolete as new knowledge emerges. Students will need skills of adaptation; they will need to learn how to continue learning for a lifetime.

Curriculum development needs to attend not only to space, but also to time. For example, students need to study maps, charts, and globes to assimilate spatial relationships on the earth and in the universe. They need to study contemporary events and issues and relate these to past history to gain new insights into the changing condition of mankind. These are all common subjects now. But does time stop with the present day in the curriculum? What redirection is needed to include a focus on the future and the problems that must predictably be faced by present and future generations?

## Technological Support

In curriculum development, technology can provide an array of materials and equipment that will meet the needs and learning styles of individuals responsively. On the other hand, technology can control the curriculum mechanistically if it is viewed as a program that must be transmitted without regard to individual needs. Materials, media, and equipment can provide varied alternative routes for reaching goals. In selecting technological resources, criteria should include: recognition of the need to foster search, creativity, and open-endedness; recognition of the need to provide materials that vary considerably in complexity and that allow each student to move at his or her optimum pace; and recognition of the need to use multi-sensory experiences to capitalize on multiple modes of learning. Books and other printed materials, videotape and audiotape libraries, films, language laboratories, programmed instruction, television courses, self-instructional packages, simulations, and complex multimedia systems can support curriculum development and provide recipients with broad access to information.

## School Buildings

Important among the contextual factors in developing a curriculum is the school building itself. Curriculum developers should recognize that the hundred-year reign of the boxlike school and the batch processing of students is rapidly coming to an end. It seems to be the nature of box forms or "egg crate" designs to invite the use of drab colors for walls and woodwork and the use of hard, echoing materials for floors and ceilings. Sterile physical surroundings seem to be accompanied by a grimness of organizational tone, expressed in a lockstep hierarchy, uninspired materials, and an undemocratic attitude. Such schools seem to be sorting students into those who should go on to college and rejects who are not able to keep up with the uniform requirements.

The newer open-concept school buildings reflect new realizations about learning: that learning is enhanced by discovery, exploration, and joy, that learning comes from many sources, and that there are many diverse and individual ways to learn. Schools (old and new) can be arranged to provide places for individuals to work by themselves, for twos or threes to work together, for ten to twenty students to form a group for a specific purpose, or for hundreds to meet together for a more general purpose. Curriculum development should push toward greater adaptive uses of buildings and their space.

## Community Resources

Possibilities for adding a community dimension to curriculum and instruction are almost unlimited. Schools-without-walls, now common, build a curriculum that may operate in any part of a city—its businesses, its industries, its museums, its transportation systems, its government, and unlimited other resources. Curriculum plans in a school *with* walls may include arrangements for individuals and groups to make learning forays into the city or other areas outside the building; to gain real-world work experiences of an apprentice nature; or to have exploratory, observational, or hands-on experiences in many types of surroundings.

The community may also come into the school, and more and more opportunities are being arranged for adults to mingle in classes, either as fellow learners or as resource persons and tutors. Schools and communities are mingling in evening classes, year-round programs, and other modes. All of these influences affect the context of curriculum development.

## Cultural Pluralism

Cultural change and pluralism demand constant adaptations of the curriculum through curriculum development processes at all levels. Learning about people, respecting differences, and recognizing commonalities are among the ramifications of this area. Stereotyped superior-inferior views on sex, race, age, and provincial differences. among others, may creep into the curriculum unless curriculum developers are aware of and alert to bias in materials and cultural differences in learning styles, learning readiness, and competences.

Respect for cultural pluralism extends into the area of student rights as well as that of student self-realization. Opportunities can be created to develop interracial and intergenerational trust and understandings. Pluralistic cultures have varying traditions, customs, beliefs, institutions, sciences, arts, and commonsense ways of thinking and doing things; these are part of the life of the people, and they must be reckoned with in curriculum development.

## Student Perceptions

Curriculum developers must recognize that in the final analysis each student makes his or her own curriculum. The past experiences that the individual brings to the situation, his or her personal thoughts, feelings, and meanings, are all part of the context in which the curriculum operates. Both intended and unintended learning outcomes occur. Students constantly perceive hidden messages in communications by the teacher or other students that tell them whether the sender is transmitting warmth, love, and respect or prejudice, hostility, and contempt.

What students learn in school and what they eventually become are significantly influenced by how they feel about themselves and the world outside. A positive self-image is a necessary condition for learning. Students need a variety of ways to recognize and express feelings about themselves and the world.

It is the responsibility of curriculum development to lead students toward full functioning, full use of their potential, self-knowledge, and realistic, socialized, and appropriate behavior, recognizing that students are ever changing, developing, and discovering themselves. Development of student potential requires that a high priority be given to respect for human worth.

## RESPONSIVENESS IN CURRICULUM DEVELOPMENT

Much has been said and implied in the preceding pages about the desirability of responsiveness in curriculum development. What, then, is this responsiveness? What is responsive curriculum development as opposed to unresponsive? What are the philosophical values of responsiveness?

Responsive curriculum development implies the ability to meet diverse human needs, to receive new ideas, and to adapt to new situations, new knowledge, and new uses of knowledge. It is a process of continuing renewal of the curriculum, through which new forms are created to fit new conditions of the environment.

Unresponsive curriculum development implies that the ends are fixed and unyielding—that there is rigidity in principle and practice, inflexibility in opinion and judgment. An unresponsive process of curriculum development is a process that reflects undeviating conformity to contents, standards, and requirements that may be obsolete.

Involvement by individuals and referent groups is a precondition of responsiveness in curriculum development. It is a process that requires responsibility and sharing. A fixed curriculum, the output of unresponsive curriculum development, requires less complex involvement, does not require democratic decision-making processes, and operates chiefly by directive, coercion, or manipulation, rather than by group inquiry.

Unresponsiveness in the curriculum development process is revealed when there is a lack of sensitivity or adaptability to pluralistic values and cultures, to local needs and differences, to the changing national or international scene, to humanistic values, to student needs and concerns, to teacher needs and concerns, to the potential contributions of various referent groups, and to fields of knowledge or disciplines that have been ignored in the past.

Rigidity in curriculum development may be particularly harmful for unsuccessful students. Benjamin Bloom (1971, p. 7) draws from several research studies to make this point:

Education has for centuries been thought of as a pyramid, with all or most of the younger age groups attending school at the bottom and very few ever reaching the apex. . . . Education has been viewed as having a fixed curriculum, a graded set of learning tasks, and a mixed group of learners to be classified at each major time unit in the system. Examinations or other evaluation procedures are used to make critical and often irreversible decisions about each student's worth and his future in the education system. These decisions and classifications frequently affect his entire career. . . . The result of this method of categorizing individuals is to convince some that they are able, good, and desirable from the viewpoint of the system, and others that they are deficient, bad, and undesirable. . . . To be physically (and legally) imprisoned in a school system for ten or twelve years and to receive negative classifications repeatedly for this period of time must have a major detrimental effect on personality and character development.

The National Education Association (1971, p. 46), addressing the question of responsiveness in curriculum development, asks what relationship exists between a student's course of study and his or her present and future life:

What content is important to him now? What content will be important to him in the future?

There are few lasting answers to any of these questions. Indeed, much of student, teacher, and parent dissatisfaction with curriculum stems from the schools' and colleges' clinging to the answers that earlier decades offered. Curriculum revision, especially in a society as fast-paced as ours, must be constant; it will never be completed.

Ole Sand (1970), reviewing the work of another NEA committee, points out that it has recommended that the curriculum undergo close and continuing reevaluation in the light of new knowledge and that everyone contribute to this herculean task—the teacher, the school administrator, the scholar, the informed citizen, and the student. These recommendations have been slow in reaching fruition, however.

Rejection of unresponsive models for curriculum development is implied by Archibald MacLeish (1951, p. 17) when he states that, in the American concept of freedom, man and his conscience come first, and established opinions and official views come later:

Our reliance in this country is on the inquiring, individual human mind. Our strength is founded there: our resilience, our ability to face an ever-changing future and to master it. We are not frozen into the backward-facing impotence of those societies, fixed in the rigidness of an official dogma, to which the future is the mirror of the past. We are free to make the future for ourselves.

The urgency of the need for responsiveness is expressed by Amitai Etzioni (1971), who stresses the limitations of the schools and hypothesizes that financial shortages, riots or strikes, and alienation of citizens, parents, and students will severely constrict the very ability of schools to function unless they rapidly and broadly increase their responsiveness to changing conditions.

Alvin Toffler (1970, pp. 405, 402) calls for a future-responsive movement in curriculum development:

It would be a mistake to assume that the present day educational system is unchanging. On the contrary it is undergoing rapid change. But much of this change is no more than an attempt to refine the existent machinery, making it ever more efficient in pursuit of obsolete goals. The rest is a kind of Brownian motion, self-canceling, incoherent, directionless . . . [whereas] the technology of tomorrow requires not millions of lightly lettered men, ready to work in unison at endlessly repetitive jobs. It requires not men who take orders in unblinking fashion, aware that the price of bread is mechanical submission to authority, but men who can make critical judgments, who can weave their way through novel environments, who are quick to spot new relationships in the rapidly changing reality.

Solon Kimball (1967, p. 8) also deplores a curriculum development stance that sets itself aside from social and cultural contexts and emphasizes transmission to the young of a fixed body of knowledge from the past.

Under conditions of rapid change, we can no longer assume that the knowledge or the practices that served us adequately in the past are sufficient for either the present or the future. Hence, we must rethink what we mean when we speak of education as the transmission of the cultural heritage . . . [and] we must consciously reconstruct an educational system to serve a society that is in a state of continuous emergence.

Achieving responsiveness, however, is not easy in itself and may create other difficulties and problems. Taba (1962) endorses cooperation and the widest possible participation in planning and evaluation by all persons—professional and lay—who are affected by policy and action decisions, but she notes difficulties inherent in wide participation. In her firsthand observations and searches of the literature she found examples of various participatory combinations of the public: students, teachers, administrators, supervisors, specialists in curriculum development, and child psychologists. She noted, however, that there was an absence of definition of the role for each participant and of distinctions between decisions that involved general wisdom and those that required expertise. Difficulties also arose because of faulty division of labor. Since curriculum development entails many different tasks, the division of labor may produce group work that fails to relate the various elements of the curriculum to each other, that develops a piecemeal curriculum, or that seems to be based on an oversimplified notion of the task. Taba found examples in which one group was working on objectives while another group was working on content, with no apparent relationship between the two elements.

John Dewey's (1916) philosophy of democracy advocates group inquiry—a necessity for responsive curriculum development. Dewey views the good society as one in which community is constantly deepened and perfected by the sharing of pooled resources. In a progressive society these resources are not merely replenished from generation to generation but reconstructed by the method of intelligence.

Harry Broudy (1971) observes that "by equating the good society with democracy and with shared intelligence Dewey created a model not only for social organization, but for teaching and learning as well. Despite certain limitations as a formula for schooling, it remains the most original and fruitful paradigm of education in modern times." Broudy also observed that Dewey's view, while powerful as a concept of the democratic person and the democratic school, is not widely implemented in practice. The sort of collective problem-solving that Dewey envisioned is limited to circumstances in which small groups of individuals can carry on face-to-face collective inquiry. Such circumstances still exist, but they are not the circumstances in which the great societal problems of our time are attacked. Representative democracy was installed because the average voter cannot collect the data he or she needs to vote intelligently on the mass of daily issues in government. Political power struggles result, and economic factors lodge power in large interest groups. Broudy, however, finds it possible for referent groups to grow in rationality, and he advocates the Dewey formula as an avenue for increasing responsiveness in curriculum development.

D. B. Gowin (1969), reviewing research on philosophy of education in the 1960s, raises questions concerning the relation between fixed ends for education and indoctrination. Gowin generalizes that, when educational ends are thought of as fixed, final, and justifiably achieved by any means, the charge of indoctrination is pertinent. He cites the military ends of Spartan education, the prescriptions of piety, and the racial superiority doctrine of the Nazis as fixed educational ends that were achieved all too well under some circumstances. However, criticism of fixed ends seems to pose a paradox, in that any new end that replaces an objectionable end becomes a fixed end itself in turn.

Critics of fixed ends seem to be forced to advocate no ends, hence aimlessness, and observers may conclude that the price to pay to avoid rigidity, narrow direction, and authoritarianism in education must be inefficiency, drift, and incoherence. This raises the philosophic question of the relation of the individual to the established order in curriculum and instruction. If the teacher selects the subject matter and the pupil has no choice of material, lack of freedom and lack of respect for the individual are possible. The teacher is faced with the dilemma of sharing power with immature and uninformed students or making deliberate ethical and scientific decisions unilaterally even though they may be exceptionally important in the life of the student. The teacher inevitably influences the students, as education is an intervention in their lives. Thus, teaching must be based on considerations of freedom, equality, authority, choice, and respect for the individual as well as the techniques of instruction and the structure of knowledge underlying the curriculum.

The philosophy of values basic to theory construction for responsiveness in curriculum development is captured by Dewey's concept of growth as constant expansion of horizons and consequent formation of new purposes and new responses. This concept can meaningfully shape our educational goals and offer us guidance in building programs so that every student can develop the attitudes, knowledges, and skills that are essential for a democratic life in a complex society.

## REFERENCES

Amidon, Edmund J., and Flanders, Ned A. *The Role of the Teacher in the Classroom*. Minneapolis: Paul Amidon, 1963.

Beauchamp, George A. "Basic Components of a Curriculum Theory." *Curriculum Theory Network*, fall 1972, pp. 16-22.

Bloom, Benjamin S.; Hastings, J. Thomas; and Madaus, George F. *Handbook on Formative and Summative Evaluation of Student Learning*. New York: McGraw-Hill, 1971.

Broudy, Harry S. "Democratic Values and Educational Goals." In *The Curriculum: Retrospect and Prospect*, part I, pp. 113-52. Seventieth Yearbook of the National Society for the Study of Education. Chicago: University of Chicago Press, 1971.

Bruner, Jerome S. *The Process of Education*. Cambridge: Harvard University Press, 1960.

Coleman, James S. *The Adolescent Society*, Glencoe, Ill. Free Press, 1963.

Dewey, John. *Democracy and Education*. New York: Macmillan, 1916.

Etzioni, Amitai. "Schools as a 'Guidable' System." In *Freedom, Bureaucracy, and Schooling*, pp. 29-48. Yearbook of the Association for Supervision and Curriculum Development. Washington, D.C.: ASCD, 1971.

Foshay, Arthur W. "Curriculum." In *Encyclopedia of Educational Research*, pp. 275-80. 4th ed. Toronto: Macmillan, 1969.

Goodlad, John I. *Planning and Organizing for Teaching*, pp. 5-31. Washington, D.C.: National Education Association, 1967.

Gowin, D. B. "Philosophy of Education." In *Encyclopedia of Educational Research*, pp. 946-51. 4th ed. Toronto: Macmillan, 1969.

Johnson, Mauritz, Jr. "Appropriate Research Directions in Curriculum and Instruction." *Curriculum Theory Network*, winter 1970-71, pp. 24-37.

———. "Definitions and Models in Curriculum Theory." *Educational Theory* 17 (April 1967): 127-40.

Joyce, Bruce R. *Alternative Models of Elementary Education*. Waltham, Mass.: Blaisdell, 1969.

Kimball, Solon T. "Culture, Class, and Educational Congruency." In *Educational Requirements for the 1970's*, edited by S. Elam and W. P. McLure. New York: Praeger, 1967.

Macdonald, James B. "Curriculum Development in Relation to Social and Intellectual Systems." In *The Curriculum: Retrospect and Prospect*, part I, pp. 97-112. Seventieth Yearbook of the National Society for the Study of Education. Chicago: University of Chicago Press, 1971.

Macdonald, James B.; Wolfson, Bernice J.; and Zaret, Esther. *Reschooling Society: A Conceptual Model*. Washington, D.C.: Association for Supervision and Curriculum Development, 1973.

MacLeish, Archibald. "To Make Men Free." *Atlantic*, November 1951, pp. 17-30.

National Education Association, Center for the Study of Instruction. *Schools for the 70's and Beyond: A Call to Action*. Washington, D.C.: NEA, 1971.

O'Hanlon, James. "Three Models for the Curriculum Development Process." *Curriculum Theory Network* 4, no. 1 (1973-74): 64-71.

Phenix, Philip H. *Realms of Meaning*. New York: McGraw-Hill, 1964.

Sand, Ole. *On Staying Awake: Talks with Teachers*. Washington, D.C.: National Education Association, 1970.

Taba, Hilda. *Curriculum Development: Theory and Practice*. New York: Harcourt, Brace and World, 1962.

Toffler, Alvin. *Future Shock*. New York: Bantam Books, 1970.

## ADDITIONAL READINGS

Association for Supervision and Curriculum Development. *Curricular Concerns in a Revolutionary Era*. Washington, D.C.: ASCD, 1971.

Bellack, Arno A., and Davitz, Joel R. *The Language of the Classroom*. New York: Bureau of Publications, Teachers College, Columbia University, 1963.

Berman, Louise M. *New Priorities in the Curriculum*. Columbus: Charles E. Merrill, 1968.

Firth, Gerald R., and Kimpston, Richard D. *The Curricular Continuum in Perspective*. Itasca, Ill.: F. E. Peacock, 1973.

Frymier, Jack R. *A School for Tomorrow*. Berkeley: McCutchan, 1973.

Guttchen, Robert S., and Bandman, Bertram, eds. *Philosophical Essays on Curriculum*. Philadelphia: Lippincott, 1969.

Joyce, Bruce R. "The Curriculum Worker of the Future." In *Curriculum: Retrospect and Prospect*, part I, pp. 307-56. Seventieth Yearbook of the National Society for the Study of Education. Chicago: University of Chicago Press, 1971.

Neagley, Ross L., and Evans, N. Dean. *Handbook for Effective Curriculum Development*. Englewood Cliffs, N.J.: Prentice-Hall, 1967.

Saylor, J. Galen, and Alexander, William M. *Planning Curriculum for Schools*. 2d ed. New York: Holt, Rinehart and Winston, 1974.

Tyler, Ralph W., ed. *Educational Evaluation: New Roles, New Means*, part II. Sixty-eighth Yearbook of the National Society for the Study of Education. Chicago: University of Chicago Press, 1969.

Weinstein, Gerald, and Fantini, Mario D., eds. *Toward Humanistic Education: A Curriculum of Affect*. New York: Praeger, 1970.

Wilhelms, Fred T. "Evaluation as Feedback." In *Evaluation as Feedback and Guide*, pp. 2-17. Yearbook of the Association for Supervision and Curriculum Development. Washington, D.C.: ASCD, 1967.

CHAPTER FIVE

# Roles and Responsibilities
# of Participants

If involvement in curriculum development, which requires responsibility and sharing, is a precondition of responsiveness, who should be involved? Who are the participants and referent groups? What inputs, competencies, and types of responses should be expected from each individual and group? To what extent should they be directly involved in cooperative decision-making as contrasted to advisory roles? What degrees of responsibility can be expected from each in order to avoid irresponsibility? What factors must influence decisions on curriculum-planning and on priorities with curriculum-planning? This chapter is addressed to these questions. For development of a proposition on links among the participants, see chapter eleven.

Participants are those who have a direct share in curriculum development at some level: policy-making, producing, or using. Referent groups are those who should be consulted about curriculum development but have more indirect relationships, interests, and concerns. A number of writers have identified "publics" that should participate and interact in the curriculum development process if it is to become responsive. These include students; teachers, curriculum specialists, and administrators of elementary and secondary schools; lay citizens; school board members; members of state education departments and other governmental agencies related to education; university professors of education and related fields; and professional staff members of regional laboratories, research and development centers, and commercial developers of curriculum materials and methods.

Although publics may be categorized by groups, their roles and responsibilities are not neatly differentiated. Responsibilities are interlocking; for example, at the local level new roles for students and lay citizens are made possible by new roles for teachers and administrators, and responsibilities for change in curriculum are shared at several levels. Cooperative action in curriculum development requires a willingness on the part of school officials and local policymakers to share decision-making power.

Levels of decision-making in curriculum planning, types of decisions, and factors affecting curriculum-planning are illustrated by Galen Saylor and William Alexander (1974) in figure 2. Although the diagram is like a ladder, there is no assumption that curriculum plans are uniformly passed up and down. The fifty states vary in the extent to which state requirements control local planning by prescribing subjects to be taught, graduation requirements, time allotments, special programs and emphases, and other factors. At the national level, curriculum studies supported by the federal government (e.g., career education and innovations funded under the Elementary and Secondary Education Act and Right to Read), various national organizations (such as the National Assessment of Educational Progress), and the national curriculum projects of the 1960s continue to affect curriculum content. Curriculum-planning at the local level, especially that of the individual teacher, is nearest to the actual learning situation. From the state authority to the federal initiative and the individual teacher there is much latitude, and great variation in control exists. At all levels—national, state, and local—there is evidence of a desire on the part of officials to include other citizens in decision-making processes. The United States Office of Education and the state departments of education have established a number of advisory committees.

At the local level, community involvement is frequently invited

# FIGURE 2

## Decision-making Levels in Curriculum-Planning

*Legal Structures and Agencies that Directly Affect Curriculum-Planning*

*National* — national guidelines, projects, systems, etc., influencing curriculum planning

U.S. government grants, Supreme Court decisions

*State* — state education authority, curriculum commissions, advisory groups, etc.

state legislative acts
state board regulations,
state department of education standards and policies

*School District* — curriculum councils and committees; advisory groups, etc.

local board of education regulations

*School* — faculty, curriculum committees

*Teaching Group* — grade level, departmental teams

*Individual Teacher* — students and parents

*Data considered*
major sources—students, society, knowledge, learning process, goals

*Additional elements*
legal structures, resources and facilities, research, other factors

*Types of decisions made*
curriculum policies, selection of curriculum content, technical development of the curriculum, arrangement of learning opportunities

*Extralegal Factors that Affect Curriculum-Planning*

*Forces*
accreditation, knowledge industry, philanthropic foundations, preparatory syndrome, public opinion, special-interest groups, testing programs, tradition

*Externally developed plans and systems*
textbooks, national curriculum projects, instructional packages and systems, performance contracts, alternative schools, networks, leagues

From J. Galen Saylor and William M. Alexander, *Planning Curriculum for Schools* (New York: Holt, Rinehart and Winston, 1974), in determining priorities among school goals, new programs of study, evaluative processes, etc. Communities have frequently initiated curriculum-planning and provided lay leadership, especially when important areas of study, such as black studies, have been omitted from the curriculum or when the curriculum has become seriously irrelevant, such as in the New York City schools that have come under community control. Community interests have also been known to wrest a subject out of the curriculum, such as sex education or theories of evolution.

Frequently when lay citizens become involved in curriculum decisions, they deal chiefly with school administrators and school board members. Less frequently are teachers and students directly involved with lay citizens. However, in more and more instances students, teachers, parents, administrators, and others are working together for improvement of the educational program in one way or another. Cooperative efforts for involvement are not without problems, and we might well ask, Are we ready for involvement? What education do we need for the involvement of diverse interests in decision-making?

## PROBLEMS OF COOPERATIVE (DECISION-MAKING )

Most persons have little or no past experience in cooperative decision-making about curriculum development. Students, teachers, many citizens, and even administrators are accustomed to top-down decisions, particularly those concerning the curriculum. The most that many hope for is a chance to complain. When invited to become seriously involved, participants may be "too busy," skeptical, or even suspicious of the motives of the board, superintendent, or other persons who are trying to initiate true cooperation.

There is a reluctance on the part of the general public to put in the time needed for serious decision-making. Long meetings in which nothing seems to happen and nothing is really decided are discouraging to persons not accustomed to working through and around bureaucratic structures. Feelings are likely to erupt into heated accusations that the authority structure is deliberately blocking or delaying the particular outcome that was hoped for by one individual or another. Participants may then resort to devious methods, concluding that the best way to influence decisions is to talk informally with one or more board members if one is a citizen, or with a principal if one is a teacher, or with a teacher if one is a student, and "let them fight it out in their meetings."

Communication problems usually arise. Information about the time and place of meetings, the agenda, and the status of decisions and processes frequently appears to be missing. Lack of information cannot always be attributed to failure to transmit it. Recipients may mislay the mail, be oblivious to purple ditto sheets, not notice an announcement on a cluttered bulletin board, or not catch an item in the newspaper. Many tune out announcements over the school's public address system. Perhaps in this multisensory age communicators will be able to find more effective means of communication.

Related to the communications problem is the matter of unequal access to resources. For example, the superintendent and the principal have secretaries; the teacher and the student usually do not. It is much more difficult to issue communications from the bottom up than it is from the top down.

Particular problems arise when students are involved with adults in decision-making, not merely in offering advisory opinions. Some adults cannot believe that a student should have a share of the power to make decisions that affect others. An example that occurred in the organization of the Metro Experimental Alternative High School in Chicago is reported by Donald Moore (1972, p. 324). The director of the program, with the staff and students, had prepared a recommendation to be submitted to the next higher administrative level of the district for approval. The plan provided for equal representation by students and teachers, each having one vote, on significant matters pertaining to the organization and curriculum of the school. The director reported back to his group: "I showed the plan to the district superintendent. She couldn't stop laughing. 'Teachers and students have equal votes!' She showed it all around the office."

Another example occurred in a suburb of St. Louis in the early 1970s, when black students were demanding recognition of black studies in the curriculum. A large planning committee was organized, including lay citizens, teachers, administrators, and students. The students proved to be quite articulate in expressing their views and at one point asserted that white teachers could not teach black studies, whereupon some of the white teachers in the group walked out. A few minutes later the students suggested that some of the black teachers were Uncle Toms, and at that point some of the black teachers walked out. The committee reorganized itself, however, and accomplished its task through several months of intensive work. It demonstrated the need for participants to approach cooperative decision-making with a determination to rise above prejudices and attitudes that lack respect for human worth.

Recognition by a local planning group of the critical need for well-planned implementation is of extreme importance. Unless the curriculum decision includes a plan for implementation, the finest committee process in the world can fail. Usually it is relatively easy to carry out decisions that delegate work to a few people. For example, a large community advisory committee might plan an innovative project and assign three people to write a federal proposal. The three will probably get right to work and get the job done. But, when it falls back on the larger group to smooth the way for implementation, interest may wane, and there may be a tendency for participants to dodge further responsibility for successfully installing the new curriculum plan.

## THE PARTICIPANTS

### Students

The most common type of student participation in curriculum planning occurs at the teacher-student level, with students in advisory roles. Many teachers seek the opinions of students—even of very young students—through classroom meetings, opinion pools, evaluative discussions of instructional activities, and personal conferences. Planning and carrying out independent study programs, action learning projects in the community, student exchange programs with other schools, and field trips are examples of teacher-student curriculum planning in which students assume responsibility with teachers for accomplishing a joint agreement. Less frequent is the involvement of students in developing basic curriculum plans for a school, department, division, etc., although high school students are occasionally invited to sit in on curriculum-planning groups, and their contributions may be sincerely sought by teachers and curriculum specialists.

*Practical Examples*

A number of school districts offer students either pay or high school credit for participating in summer work groups or courses during the school year that prepare new curriculum plans. Those described here and similar programs are reported by Glenys Unruh and William Alexander (1974). The school districts of Buffalo, Atlanta, and San Diego have paid stipends to students for working as members of curriculum writing and review teams during the summer. In Pasadena, California, one high school has a student-parent-staff curriculum committee that meets once each month to gather student and parent reactions to the present curriculum and to curriculum plans being developed. Several classes of American history students in Lubbock, Texas, were involved in rewriting an American history course by responding to the survey question, "What do you think is worth knowing about American history?" Using the students' ideas, teachers worked with librarians to organize themes and related units. Students then assisted the teachers and librarians in searching out materials and readings that they considered desirable for the course. Student enthusiasm for this type of participation was reported to be high, and the cooperative effort of students, teachers, and librarians seemed to bring about unusually positive attitudes toward the American history course. Students are not always ready to assume responsibility for curriculum development, however.

One of Chicago's Metro Experimental Alternative Schools is specifically designed to involve students in decision-making, not only about such matters as dress, grooming, and attendance rules, but also about the planning, selection, and evaluation of the curriculum. Although before the opening of alternative schools student underground papers and rap sessions had regularly criticized the establishment for excluding students from this type of planning and decision-making, Stephen H. Wilson, a participant observer who spent two years in the Metro school, reported (in Moore 1972, pp. 324-28) that when the opportunities were fully provided students made little use of them. At staff-student meetings organized for the purpose of planning, students seemed to be interested chiefly in making sure that their rights about freedom of dress, movement, expression, and association were fully guaranteed, that they could complain to the staff about activities they disliked, and that they had the right to opt out of any activity, including curriculum-planning, any time they wished. Decision-making about curriculum offerings soon fell almost entirely to the staff, although staff members continued to urge students to take part.

Conclusions of the study were that schools should not drop the idea of student involvement in decision-making about the curriculum and organization of the school, but that participation in decision-making might be better regarded as a skill to be developed than a right to be granted. Students having no previous experience in decision-making at their former schools were not suddenly converted into enthusiastic participants in a process that placed new demands on them for learning skills, collecting information, weighing causes and effects, and spending time in deliberation.

*Action Learning*

Many students are assuming a great deal of responsibility for individual and group curriculum-planning in various types of action learning programs in their communities. The Experience Based Career Education program, sponsored by the National Institute of Education, is demonstrating in several cities that there are profitable ways in which students can engage in curriculum development with adults and draw from a wide range of community resources. High school students in the EBCE program in such widely diverse settings as Philadelphia, Pennsylvania, Charleston, West Virginia, Oakland, California, and Tigard, Oregon, are exchanging ideas and learning in the everyday world from and with adult technicians, social workers, trial attorneys, auto mechanics, doctors, printers, teachers, architects, union stewards, museum directors, and others. Action learning is a part of a comprehensive curriculum that includes fundamental skills in reading, writing, and mathematics and process skills of inquiry, decision-making, and problem-solving. Students plan and replan constantly and cooperatively with the teaching faculty of each EBCE school and with the members of a research and development team attached to each program.

In the Experience Based Career Education program, "career" is defined broadly to mean life path or life-style, not just a particular nine-to-five job segment. "Experience-based" is not synonymous with on-the-job training and is far removed from traditional vocational education concepts, which focus on learning an immediate job-entry trade. In this program, students rotate from one site to another to learn about as many career possibilities as they can while working collaboratively with adults in the school and in the community to develop a personalized curriculum. Both adults and students are constantly learning from each other, growing, and changing in beneficial ways.

## Teachers

Essential to responsive curriculum development are responsive, sensitive teachers. These are the participants who daily face groups of students of all ages and who are responsible for the instructional process. Charles Silberman (1970) and Mario Fantini (1973) suggest that teachers are frequently victimized by the ways in which schools are currently organized and operated, that they are unable to deviate from rigid curriculum-related specifications developed at the top for an entire school system. If teachers continue to comply with that situation, they are abdicating their responsibility as teachers.

Customarily, societal-level decisions are the function of local and state boards of education and deal with broad goals for all students. Institutional-level decisions usually encompass selection of more localized goals, materials, and methods of evaluation for a school system or an individual school. At the classroom level, specific decisions are made within the general policy framework and carried out largely through teacher leadership. For teachers or their informed representatives to avoid involvement in decision-making about curriculum objectives is professionally irresponsible. At the state and district levels, teachers' voices can be heard even though boards and administrators convene the meetings. Not only should teachers seek involvement in curriculum-planning but they should also assume responsibility for involving students in goal-setting, planning alternative means for reaching educational goals, and evaluating progress. That goals can be formulated wholly by one level, group, or individual and assigned to others to carry out without question was condemned by John Dewey (1938, pp. 67-69):

Plato once defined a slave as the person who executes the purposes of another, and . . . a person is also a slave who is enslaved to his own blind desires. There is, I think, no point in the philosophy of progressive education which is sounder than its emphasis upon the importance of the participation of the learner in the formation of the purposes which direct his activities in the learning process. . . .

The formation of purposes is, then, a rather complex intellectual operation. It involves (1) observation of surrounding conditions; (2) knowledge of what has

happened in similar situations in the past, a knowledge obtained partly by rec-
ollection and partly from the information, advice, and warning of those who
have had a wider experience; and (3) judgment which puts together what is
observed and what is recalled to see what they signify.

Dewey implies that the learner must be involved, but that mature
judgment from other sources is also needed.

Part of teacher responsibility for responsive curriculum development is teacher recognition of the complex nature of curriculum
development and the need for expertise of many varieties. If teachers
themselves cannot contribute the competences that are needed in the
process to express their point of view, it is their responsibility either
to develop these skills collectively or to invite other competent persons into the curriculum dialogue.

Teachers can stimulate dialogue about human values; they can
teach the relationship of knowledge to decision-making and purpose-
fully extend curriculum-planning to include a much wider range of
resources.

Hilda Taba (1962) has many suggestions of timely merit regarding
the teacher skills needed for curriculum development, in addition to
the face-to-face experiences of teachers with students: teachers must
know how to mobilize groups, initiate them into curriculum work,
diagnose concerns, develop problems and plans from the concerns,
formulate objectives, project hypotheses from local or general research, and translate these hypotheses into curriculum possibilities.
Sufficient familiarity is needed with the content of specific fields to
guide the process of selecting valid core ideas and samples of content.
Knowledge about learners and learning processes is needed to guide
the selection of learning activities and their sequences. Competence is
needed in the choice of diagnostic and evaluation devices and in
interpreting data. Ability is needed in diagnosing human factors and
interpersonal relations, recognizing blocks to overcome, discrimi-
nating levels of perception, and understanding attitudes of the participants. Familiarity with group processes is also needed.

Continuous self-improvement in the competences required for curriculum development is a responsibility of teachers. The roles and
responsibilities of teachers for curriculum development include
reaching into new fields, such as futures research, anthropology,
philosophy, and others not usually included in the teacher-education
curriculum; making contacts with persons at all other levels of

decision-making; and developing the mode of inquiry as a process of curriculum development.

Teachers are behaving irresponsibly in curriculum development if they are preoccupied with the content to be covered, overemphasize information and facts, and rule out student feelings, nonverbal communication, and intuitive expressions of current thought. Omission of controversial issues and questions from the curriculum is also irresponsible, as Newmann and Oliver (1970) emphasize. Neither value indoctrination nor bland objectivity about values is desirable. A difficult role for the teacher, but one of responsibility in curriculum development, is that of stressing valuing as a complicated, continuing process, always incomplete but never in opposition to the mainstream of morality. Intelligent discussion and legitimate scholarship can infuse students with the desire to examine their beliefs in dialogue with others, to concede or modify their views in the face of challenging evidence, to seek clarity in and attention to empirical findings, and eventually to value human dignity, pluralism, and rational consent.

## Curriculum Specialists

The quality of curriculum development in a school district depends heavily on the leadership quality and vigor of the local curriculum specialists. These are the "official" curriculum leaders in the schools. Their titles include curriculum director, curriculum associate, assistant superintendent for curriculum and instruction, and similar terms. The position may be either line or staff ("management" or "labor"). How these specialists approach the task of curriculum development is a critical factor in determining the degree of responsiveness of the process to changing knowledge, needs of learners, and societal changes. Whether the curriculum specialist is considered to be line or staff, he or she needs leadership ability with both groups. The chief measure of leadership is the specialist's ability to stimulate participation, ad hoc leadership, growth, and contributions of ideas from all participating groups and individuals.

### Competences Needed

While teachers must be cognizant of the array of competences needed for curriculum development and alert to the availability of these abilities among their members, it is the curriculum specialist's responsibility to make sure that all needed skills are available in the curriculum development working group and to contribute needed abilities personally or to recruit persons from outside the working group who can supply these resources.

Curriculum development abilities needed by curriculum specialists, in Taba's (1962) view, are skills in identifying problems, planning strategies for change, constructing a conceptual framework for curriculum development that will lead toward a comprehensive curriculum rather than a piecemeal approach, and relating curriculum development to the fundamentals of child development and the requirements of culture. The specialist must also have a technical understanding of diagnosis and evaluation.

Included in the responsibilities of the curriculum specialist are interpreting the research of others, stimulating local research, and seeking new knowledge related to curriculum development in traditional fields and in new fields such as sociology, urban problems, and youth culture.

An example of incompetence or irresponsibility on the part of curriculum specialists was a widespread custom during the 1940s and early 1950s: curriculum committees of local school systems, composed of teachers and curriculum specialists, wrote numerous "curriculum guides" that were mainly outlines of content and activities lifted from several textbooks. The textbook publishers in turn collected these curriculum guides and published more textbooks, setting up a cycle of mediocrity in curriculum development that lasted for more than a generation. Curriculum specialists are also acting irresponsibily if they view curriculum development with tunnel vision and neglect the complex variety of humanistic, moral, philosophical, and scientific aspects of the process.

Personal characteristics needed by the curriculum specialist are discussed by Adolph Unruh and Harold Turner (1970). They include versatility, perceptiveness, sensitivity, patience, and skill in working for and with others in a team approach to problems. The curriculum specialist sees worth in others, shares authority and decision-making responsibilities, generates leadership in others, stimulates interactive processes and curriculum dialogue, and discovers and develops ideas.

*Scope of the Task*

The roles and responsibilities of curriculum specialists are many and varied. They participate with and involve others in collaborative and leadership functions so that the following interrelated tasks can be accomplished:

1. Defining goals and objectives at the several levels of decision-making.

2. Identifying needs and problems by both objective and subjective means.

3. Developing a conceptual model for curriculum development, in the situational context, that can open new patterns of thought. This may be a model adapted from elsewhere, a model produced from a systematic collection of ideas and alternatives from participants, or a model developed empirically as experiments are tried.

4. Developing plans, strategies, and procedures that invite the trust of people within and around the work of curriculum development, that spark responsiveness, that maintain integrity, and that elicit cooperative decision-making.

5. Developing interrelationships and comprehensiveness in curriculum development through interaction among subject field interests, learning theory, media and materials development, and other resources.

6. Involving people of different as well as like interests, ages, and backgrounds in discussing issues, developing plans, and working together on effective action programs.

7. Finding ways to communicate and use feedback both inside the school and with external referent groups.

8. Increasing professional outreach and sophistication through contacts with other curriculum development centers, contacts with consultants and other professional resources, and use of research findings, current literature, and new knowledge on subject matter content, learning processes, instructional materials, and technology.

9. Planning a time-phased implementation schedule that will be feasible for moving the curriculum developed into the mainstream of the school system.

10. Using evaluation processes, both formative and summative, so that the curriculum development system can constantly trigger new plans and produce continuing change and renewal.

## School Administrators

The school administrator's philosophical outlook must be humanistic, democratic, and consistent with that stated for teachers and students. The administrator must play a supportive role in relation to teachers and students if responsive curriculum development is to occur. Serious regard for the worth of the learner's views, which leads to inclusion of students in curriculum-planning, is a necessary attitude for the school administrator. While educators need to extend their knowledge of *how* the learner thinks, it is equally important for them to determine and respect *what* the learner thinks about. Student preoccupations and aspirations should be known, considered, and understood, as they apply to curriculum-planning.

Distrust, hostility, fear, and insecurity will be created between teaching personnel and administrators if administrators tend toward rigid authoritarianism. The administrator who recognizes the teacher as a valuable source of data for curriculum development expands the teacher's role and the teacher's effectiveness in the development process. Charles Silberman (1970) discovered in his visits to schools across the country that, when teachers were placed in an atmosphere of freedom and trust by administrators and treated as professionals and as people of worth, they behaved like the caring, concerned people they would like to be. Silberman also observed the converse.

Beyond compatibility with teachers and students, however, lie even greater responsibilities for administrators to exercise vision and statesmanship. Sharing power over curriculum development with teachers, students, experts, scholars, parents, and other lay citizens entails risks. Whether the participation and interaction of these various groups leads to responsive curriculum development may depend on the willingness of school administrators to view the new constituents in education not as competitors for a limited and static amount of power but as previously untapped sources of leadership in the expanding field of education.

Effective communication with those involved in curriculum development is essential. The administrator must be responsible for clarifying the decision-making structure from the beginning of the task, so that participants do not become disappointed with the organization or charge that it was deliberately contrived to keep out certain interests. The administrator is irresponsible unless he or she makes efforts to ensure inputs from all the diverse elements of the community.

Another difficult role falling within the responsibilities of the administrator is that of opening philosophical dialogues concerned with human values, comments Craig Wilson (1971). Because the various approaches to human dignity lead to diverse conceptions and interpretations, it is the administrator's responsibility to arrange enough contact among differing groups for them to become aware of each other's views. The administrator has it within his or her province to initiate dialogue on significant policy and program alternatives. It is irresponsible for him or her to abdicate this role and settle for political power-bargaining with dissenters or to go to the opposite extreme, in which law-and-order ranks tighten to defend unchanging values and culture-free standards.

## Lay Citizens

In general, some of the principles stated for students apply to parents and other lay citizens. Persons who are apathetic toward curricular matters or who choose to remain ignorant of the complex nature of curriculum development are as irresponsible as those who misuse power to exclude interaction among referent groups that could lead to cooperative decision-making. Apathy and ignorance are revealed by George Gallup (1974a, 1974b) in a series of annual polls in which the parents interviewed were more interested in items peripheral to the central purposes of education, such as discipline, than in curriculum development or humanizing concepts.

In some instances, parents have roused from a state of apathy to question why children in great numbers continue to "fail" in school, asking whether it is their children or the schools that are failing, and popularizing the cry for accountability—on the part of teachers and principals, that is. The concept of accountability, however, means that the school, at all of its decision-making levels, shares with parents the responsibility previously charged to children for their own success in school or failure to take advantage of educational opportunities.

With accountability comes responsibility by all parties involved. Citizen participation is needed at three levels: societal, institutional, and instructional. At all these levels citizens can be involved in goal-setting, in finding alternative learning opportunities, and in evaluation. Emphasis at the societal level may be on legislation; at the institutional level it may be on the goals of education in relation to a changing culture and technology; and at the instructional level it may be on a shift from failure orientation to success orientation for children in the schools. These responsibilities are not discrete; there is a need for citizen involvement at all three levels and across levels, and involvement may be initiated at any level.

### Rationality and Responsibility

Responsibilities of citizens, then, must include recognition and respect for the roles of other groups, protection of the professional educators' rights, and determined efforts to increase competence in selecting representatives and charging them with responsibilities for improved curriculum development possibilities.

The concept of respect for human dignity underlies the role of citizens in keeping the policymakers "honest." To accomplish the task is not easy and requires much time and attention. Citizen participation that influences curriculum development and respects the value of rational consent may be direct involvement (e.g., in town meetings, in referenda on bond issues, through membership on curriculum committees, and through service as resource persons in instructional activities); delegation of decision-making power to elected representatives (e.g., in elections to school boards and state and federal government offices); and consent to procedures that define the consent process itself (e.g., constitutional conventions that define the criteria for selection of public officials or the nature of governmental power.

Fred Newmann and Donald Oliver (1970, p. 20) stress the need for involved citizens to respect the value of rational consent:

Loyalty to the vague ideal of human dignity is not sufficient to prevent conflicting interests from destroying each other. In addition, we believe men must develop a process for arriving at collective decisions, a process that affirms the right of each person to have voice in the public decisions that affect him and favors a method of reasoned discussion and free exchange of views through which each person decides what his position will be. We combine these ideas in the value *rational consent,* which we consider equal in significance to freedom of choice (pluralism) as a requisite to individual human dignity.

It is the citizen's responsibility to influence policies that affect him or her, and the "rational" aspect of this value emphasizes reasoned discussion rather than brute force, random choice, or subtle forms of coercion. A rational position takes account of the factual consequences, supports its claims with reliable evidence, and states qualifications of value judgments. Rational discussion allows consideration of diverse viewpoints, regardless of their source. It encourages mutual inquiry into problem-solving rather than trickery, combat, or deceit to win a point. It values development of unique personal positions rather than dogmatic consensus to a party line. Citizens can improve their skills in productive discussion by referring to relevant literature as well as by testing views in oral dialogues in the home, office, school, or bar.

Although parents and other citizens are not generally as well organized for selecting representatives as are teachers and students, they have the right to be represented meaningfully and the responsibility to become informed and actively involved. Citizens' advisory committees, appointed at the national level by the president and at the state level by the governor, are becoming more and more numerous in connection with curriculum projects. "Grass roots" voices can be heard in the process of appointing persons to these committees. It is the responsibility of the public at large and of its representatives to conduct rational problem-solving inquiries even though needs have arisen from irrational or emotional situations and hostile confrontations.

## School Boards

The responsible involvement described for lay citizens also pertains to school boards, who represent the people. Citizen apathy or powerlessness is illustrated in the toleration by American parents of authoritarianism of partisan boards of education. In large cities and the large consolidated school districts of suburban or rural areas, a board of six to nine persons, usually from the white middle class, often makes major policy decisions for children of other ethnic groups. An Urban Education Task Force of the U.S. Department of Health, Education, and Welfare (1970) concluded that school boards in urban centers are not representative of the people they serve. Members generally come from and reflect the attitudes of upper- and middle-class cultures. In many cities where a large majority of the school children are Negro or Spanish-speaking, board members are nearly all whites or Anglos. Where school boards do have minority group representatives, they are generally middle-class men and women who have escaped from the slums and often have as little in common with the ghetto dweller as the rest of the board. As a result, the boards are frequently unresponsive to the needs of the ghetto schools.

Some cities have not yet heeded George Counts's advice (1928, p. 357), although more and more are going in this direction:

Let the groups, the working classes, the women's clubs, the more important religious sects, and other groups have their representatives on the board. Recourse to the methods of indirection would then be unnecessary, and genuine differences would be brought out in the clear sunlight of discussion.

School boards, as policymaking bodies, have the power to make it possible or impossible to open a curriculum dialogue among participant groups. The competences required of lay citizens are more intensely needed in school board members. The school board has far more access to information that can bring understanding of the contributions of the various participants. Drawing on this knowledge, it is the board's responsibility to initiate processes that involve others in formulating comprehensive statements of educational purposes. From these, in turn, the professional staff must formulate more specific curriculum and instruction plans. The school board is also responsible for following the priorities, based on the educational goals, that were established through interactive processes. Commitment to priorities involves allocation of financial resources, allotment of time for dialogue with various publics, and employment of teaching and administrative personnel who support the concept of constant growth and development in keeping with changing environmental conditions.

## State Departments of Education

If local school boards and administrators are the gatekeepers at the entry to responsive curriculum development for a local school district, state departments occupy that position for an entire state. The state department of education includes the state board of education, the chief state school officer, and the professional staff of the department.

The United States Constitution is silent on federal responsibilities for education and thus vests control of education in the states. For generations, few states took the responsibility seriously enough. Few paid homage to research and development on the quality of the curriculum development process, the curriculum plan, or the instructional process in the classroom. Frequently underfinanced and understaffed, state departments of education devoted their energies to regulatory functions: how many minutes a student should sit in class, how many days should be included in the school year, what textbooks should be put on approved lists, and similar matters. Textbooks, an influential source of curriculum, often were selected by a few state officials, sometimes with the assistance of small, hand-picked committees of educators, and frequently under the promotional pressures of publishers.

In recent years, federal legislation has forced state departments to administer funds appropriated to stimulate innovation in curriculum and instruction and to implement procedures to improve human rights in the schools. Irresponsibility at the state level is sometimes more a matter of actions omitted than of narrow descriptions of functions and circumscribed possibilities for change.

State boards are frequently composed of distinguished lay citizens and university professors. They present an excellent opportunity for wider cross-group representation, possibly also including students and teachers (at least in an advisory capacity) so that the interactive process could begin at the state level. Several states are moving in 'this direction.

It is assumed that members of a state board will act in ways compatible with the philosophical statements made cooperatively by themselves and the groups they represent. The chief state school officer and his or her professional staff should be guided by the humanistic, democratic values described for school administrators and teachers.

Inputs of the state department into the process of curriculum development can cover a much wider area than mere regulatory functions. These should be reshaped to serve the needs of people and society rather than merely fulfilling quantitative statistical functions. Using resources for innovation, curriculum development, and child development provided by the federal government and augmented by state funds, state departments of education have a major responsibility for setting the stage in each state so that curriculum development can be responsive.

## University Professors

"University professors" is used in this context to include professors of education, other teachers of teachers in higher education institutions, and professors of other disciplines. Persons referred to in the literature as "scholars" are also included in the university grouping. The university has two roles in curriculum development: (1) to sponsor inquiry, experimentation, and research that contributes to curriculum planning; and (2) to interact with other participants in the curriculum development process.

Contributions of university expertise to curriculum development, then, include not only the traditional subject matter fields of science, mathematics, history, English, and other languages, but also fields previously unrepresented in curriculum development for elementary and secondary students. The humanities, philosophy, anthropology, and psychology as well as education have major contributions to make to the continuing dialogue on cultural values and to development of significant policy and program alternatives.

Types of responses to curriculum development by university professors are listed here in descending order of probable effectiveness:

1. Serving as members of the working group for developing the curriculum.
2. Arranging for school-university cooperative workshops or cooperatively planned university courses.
3. Providing consultant help.
4. Supplying professional literature.

## Researchers and Developers

Included in the category of researchers and developers are the professional staffs of federally financed regional educational laboratories; research and development centers, usually associated with universities but generally funded by foundations or federal sources; institutions such as the Ontario Institute for Studies in Education; and commercial materials developers.

Research and development centers offer a potential source of significant input into the curriculum development process, and aspects of their work are evident. One is that the various centers and laboratories have developed a variety of methodological approaches for the study of curriculum development, including studies of the relationships between curriculum materials and classroom practices. Another positive aspect is the raising of questions about curriculum development: How can local needs be assessed and used by curriculum developers in arriving at decisions about priorities? What are the demands of local user groups, and how can the external developer not only respond to these demands but also know whether he or she has met the demands? What are the effects of the various aspects of curriculum programs on different groups of users? The inputs of researchers and developers (external people, academic experts) are valuable to schools by virtue of their general information and skills about society, knowledge, teaching, and learning. The responsibility of these people, however, is not to direct the curriculum development practice but rather to identify and elaborate concepts about curriculum, to specify reasonable curriculum alternatives, to estimate the practical curriculum consequences of each alternative, to develop illustrative or complete curriculum programs reflecting one or another alternative, and to assist local people in identifying and articulating local practical needs.

Researchers and developers need to provide not only scholarly resources but also instructional aids with the flexibility to vary according to the demands of a particular situation. Regional laboratories and nonprofit research and development centers frequently rely on commercial publishers and developers to market a product once it has been thoroughly field-tested by the professional agency.

## SUMMARY

This chapter has discussed the roles and responsibilities of the chief participants: those responsible for developing curriculum, making policy, making critical decisions, providing resource and advisory assistance, and actually using the curriculum that is developed. The student becomes not only the user but also a participant in the process. Chapter eleven develops a proposition concerning links among these publics.

## REFERENCES

Connelly, F. Michael. "Some Considerations on the Status, Relationship to Character, and Study of Curriculum Development." In *Elements of Curriculum*

*Development*, pp. 164-73. Monograph supplement of *Curriculum Theory Network*. Toronto: Ontario Institute for Studies in Education, 1971.

Counts, George S. *School and Society in Chicago*. New York: Arno Press, 1928.

Dewey, John. *Experience and Education*. New York: Collier Books, 1938.

Fantini, Mario D. *Public Schools of Choice*. New York: Simon and Schuster, 1973.

Gallup, George H. *The Gallup Polls of Attitudes Toward Education*, 1969-1973. Bloomington, Ind.: Phi Delta Kappa, 1974*a*.

————. "Sixth Annual Gallup Poll of Public Attitudes Toward Education." *Phi Delta Kappan* 56 (September 1974*b*): 20-32.

Goodlad, John I. *Planning and Organizing for Teaching*, pp. 25-50. Washington, D.C.: National Education Association, 1963.

Merriman, Howard O. "A Conception of Curriculum Evaluation involving Teachers, Parents, and Other Educational Decision Makers." In *Elements of Curriculum Development*, pp. 23-26. Monograph supplement of *Curriculum Theory Network*. Toronto: Ontario Institute for Studies in Education, 1971.

Moore, Donald R., ed. "Strengthening Alternative High Schools." *Harvard Educational Review* 42 (August 1972): 313-49.

National Education Association. *Schools for the 70's and Beyond: A Call to Action*. Washington, D.C.: NEA, 1971.

————. *Rational Planning in Curriculum and Instruction*. Washington, D.C.: NEA, 1967.

National Institute of Education. *The Community Is the Teacher: Experience Based Career Education*. Washington, D.C.: NIE, 1974.

Newmann, Fred M., and Oliver, Donald W. *Clarifying Public Controversy*. Boston: Little, Brown, 1970.

Pillet, Roger A. "Boundaries of a Curriculum Network." In *Elements of Curriculum Development*, pp. 7-11. Monograph supplement of *Curriculum Theory Network*. Toronto: Ontario Institute for Studies in Education, 1971.

Saylor, J. Galen, and Alexander, William M. *Planning Curriculum for Schools*. New York: Holt, Rinehart and Winston, 1974.

Silberman, Charles E. *Crisis in the Classroom*. New York: Random House, 1970.

Taba, Hilda. *Curriculum Development: Theory and Practice*. New York: Harcourt, Brace and World, 1962.

Unruh, Adolph, and Turner, Harold E. *Supervision for Change and Innovation*. Boston: Houghton Mifflin, 1970.

Unruh, Glenys G., and Alexander, William M. *Innovations in Secondary Education*. 2d ed. New York: Holt, Rinehart and Winston, 1974.

U.S. Department of Health, Education, and Welfare, Urban Education Task Force. *Urban School Crisis: The Problems and Solutions Proposed by the HEW Urban Education Task Force*. Washington, D.C.: National School Public Relations Association, 1970.

Wilson, L. Craig. *The Open Access Curriculum*. Boston: Allyn and Bacon, 1971.

## ADDITIONAL READINGS

Boyd, William L. "The School Superintendent: Educational Statesman or Political Strategist?" *Administrator's Notebook* 22, no. 9 (1974): 1-4. Newsletter published by the Midwest Administration Center, University of Chicago.

Duncan, James K. "The Curriculum Director in Curriculum Change." *Educational Forum* 38 (November 1973): 51-77.

Fantini, Mario D. *The Reform of Urban Schools*. Washington, D.C.: National Education Association, 1970.

Friedenberg, Edgar Z. "The Modern High School: A Profile." *Commentary* 36 (November 1963): 373-80.

Koerner, James D. *Who Controls American Education?* Boston: Beacon Press, 1968.

Leeper, Robert R., ed. *Supervision: Emerging Profession*. Washington, D.C.: Association for Supervision and Curriculum Development, 1969.

Lippitt, Ronald. "Roles and Processes in Curriculum Development and Change." In *Strategy for Curriculum Change*, edited by Robert R. Leeper, pp. 11-28. Washington, D.C.: Association for Supervision and Curriculum Development, 1965.

Lucio, William H., ed. *The Supervisor: New Demands, New Dimensions*. Washington, D.C.: Association for Supervision and Curriculum Development, 1969.

Mackenzie, Gordon N. "Curricular Change: Participants, Power, and Processes." In *Innovations in Education*, edited by Matthew B. Miles, pp. 399-424. New York: Bureau of Publications, Teachers College, Columbia University, 1964.

Mallery, David. *High School Students Speak Out*. New York: Harper and Row, 1962.

Merrow, John. "The Politics of Federal Educational Policy: The Case of Educational Renewal." *Teachers College Record* 76 (September 1974): 19-38.

Peterson, Paul E. "Community Representation and the 'Free Rider.'" *Administrator's Notebook* 22, no. 8 (1974): 1-4. Newsletter published by the Midwest Administration Center, University of Chicago.

Raths, James, ed. *The Supervisor: Agent for Change in Teaching*. Washington, D.C.: Association for Supervision and Curriculum Development, 1966.

Schaefer, Robert J. *The School as a Center for Inquiry*. New York: Harper and Row, 1967.

Summerfield, Harry L. *Power and Process: The Formulation and Limits of Federal Educational Policy*. Berkeley: McCutchan, 1974.

## PART II

# Propositions for a Theory of Responsive Curriculum Development and Action

CHAPTER SIX

# Freedom and
# Moral Values

**PROPOSITION:** If planning for the freedom of individuals is included, the curriculum development process will become more responsive to social, ethical, and moral valuing.

Planning for the freedom of individuals is a conscious, orderly commitment to human worth and individual dignity. Planning for freedom means planning in such a way that the freedom of the individual is deepened, not diminished. Freedom implies that choices are available for individuals to develop. Freedom implies that, by generating more human environments for all, one's own self-realization is strengthened and grows.

*Valuing* is a process of weighing the consequences of thought and action, appraising the worth of a situation, or assessing one's obligations in a given matter. *Moral values* are principles of right and wrong in behavior pertaining to truth, honesty, justice, freedom for oneself and others, and similar concepts. *Social values* relate to the welfare of human beings as members of society. *Ethical values* deal with

123

personal obligations stemming from moral and social values. In chapter two, four value systems were compared, and value-related problems of the changing social, economic, and technological scene that have been identified by futures researchers were described.

In the context of social, ethical, and moral values, planning for the freedom of individuals is a process in which caring, feeling persons are deeply concerned with the welfare of others and apply their concerns to social and moral problems in active human roles. Associated with this proposition are the concepts of human worth and dignity, respect, peace, love, equality, justice, brotherhood, health, and prosperity.

In the process of curriculum development, questions are raised about the nature of freedom and the place of social and moral values. What shall we do about apathetic students, ethnic studies, the quality of the curriculum in ghetto schools, examining unethical practices in government, studying causes of crime, developing skills of decision-making, learning about people of many cultures, relating diminishing world resources to starving people in Asia, investigating causes and effects of environmental problems, and making studies of alternative futures? The way questions such as these are answered will influence the participants' growth in social and moral valuing.

### FREEDOM IN THE SCHOOL

Freedom in school settings is frequently misunderstood and misinterpreted. With freedom comes added responsibility for developing self-direction, for sharing obligations to the group, and for ensuring the quality of the learning environment.

John Dewey (1938) addressed himself to the nature of freedom and of violations of freedom that were occurring in some chaotic situations mislabeled "progressive" education. The only freedom that is of enduring importance, Dewey said, is freedom of intelligence; that is, freedom of observation and judgment exercised in behalf of purposes that are intrinsically worthwhile. What one does with freedom is the most important question for education. What end does it serve, and what consequences flow from it? Dewey was particularly critical of the deliberate lack of adult guidance in the "child-centered" schools. Freedom, he counseled, is not something given at birth or bred of planlessness. It is something to be achieved, to be systematically wrought by students in cooperation with experienced teachers, knowledgeable in their own tradition.

Lawrence Cremin (1961) also discusses abuses of the essentially sound premises underlying the progressive education movement of the 1920s and 1930s and misinterpretations of the concept of freedom. Advocates of the child-centered school and interpretations of Freud seemed to shift the focus of some "progressive" schools of the day to antiintellectual concerns. Then, as Cremin observes, in too many classrooms license began to pass for liberty, planlessness for spontaneity, recalcitrance for individuality, obfuscation for art, and chaos for education—all justified in the rhetoric of expressionism and freedom.

Sylvia Ashton-Warner, whose book *Teacher* (1963) is widely known and respected by the "compassionate" critics of contemporary education and by persons who are currently developing free or alternative schools, was invited to the United States to participate as a teacher in an experimental free school—one in the early 1970s mode. She questions the interpretations of freedom and equality that were operative in the school, and her comments reflect Dewey's criticisms in an earlier era. Here (p. 206) she describes her reactions as a participant-observer sympathetic to the cause.

I can't stand closed doors where children are segmenting the family fluidity, and when I see the door of the math room shut I take the liberty of opening it. I'm not one to intrude or invade if I can help it but, "That's no way for big boys to behave." . . .

All being equal, he [the student] can say what he likes, and do what he likes too. I'm learning that reciprocal respect is not necessary to equality. On the other hand, am I respecting their right to release their imagery; who am I to criticize?

Ashton-Warner reports the following conversation with one of the other adults (p. 208):

"I'm trying to work out what you mean by freedom."

"What *I* mean by freedom, or the kids, or the parents, or the—?"

"Well, I mean . . . there's an intoxication . . . you know, it's not really what children are. It's . . . I don't want to use words like 'license' and 'anarchy,' but . . . ."

"What happened was," from Senta, who is head of the upper school, "the kids were told before we opened they could do what they liked."

"We lost before we started, then."

"No, not quite," accurately, with a steady respect for facts, "but you can't start a school like this on immediate unqualified freedom. Kids coming from structured schools should be given freedoms gradually. They should have brought the structure over to start with, then loosen up in stages. The kids are not used to it, not ready yet."

Dewey's comments in *Experience and Education* (1938, p.58) are apropos today:

It is absurd to exclude the teacher from membership in the group. As the most mature member of the group the teacher has a peculiar responsibility for the conduct of the interactions and intercommunications which are the very life of the group as a community. That children are individuals whose freedom should be respected while the more mature person should have no freedom as an individual is an idea too absurd to require refutation.

Dewey finds that, when pupils are a "traditional" class rather than a social group, the teacher acts largely from the outside and not as a director of processes of exchange in which all have a share. In Dewey's view, when education is based on experience, and educative experience is seen to be a social process, the situation changes radically. The teacher loses the position of external boss or dictator and takes on that of leader of group activities.

James Shields (1973), another participant-observer, describes the frustrations of attempting to free students by setting up a situation in which each student is expected to discover and pursue his or her own particular interests and work out an individual curriculum. Shields is a professor who experimented with a nondirective form of freedom in his classroom and kept a daily journal on the attempt. He recorded that the students seemed to be doing nothing, or at least not doing what he would have liked them to be doing. Success for most students seemed to mean the ability to complete a project, and they varied between manic activity, accompanied by various forms of busywork, and passivity. There was no sudden adoption of modes of inquiry in the group.

Shields also recorded the perceptions of a student (p. 20). Following the first term in which he had attempted to create a free learning environment, she wrote to him:

We spent the majority of the time getting acquainted with each other and taking advantage of our freedom away from lectures and required readings. In the beginning, our group behaved very much like the students at Summerhill who stayed away from classes on their arrival because they did not know how to handle freedom. This was because freedom and democracy require both responsibility and participation—two elements which are never asked of students. Dewey's idea of learning by doing is easier said than done.

I do not think the fault lies merely with the students; the fault lies in our authoritarian society that addicts you to consumption and indentures you to a corporation to pay off your addiction. It is a society in which if you don't dominate, you are dominated. Unfortunately, most students spent the semester keeping up with the authoritarians in society, that is doing things that would give them a position of authority in society. The students, myself included, neglected those things they would have liked to do in your course.

No changes in your course, indeed in the entire university, will have any meaning unless that big world beyond your course and the university changes. For this reason, I suggest that in the future you and your students apply your energies to the world rather than to the course.

James Macdonald, Bernice Wolfson, and Esther Zaret (1973) advocate liberation as a value directive for schooling but emphasize that the concept is in no way an unplanned curriculum. Liberating is contrasted to controlling, and they see the basic goal of schooling to be the development of autonomous, valuing human beings, not the impersonal development of role-oriented skills. For the curriculum to be liberating, both teacher and student must share in transactions about cultural realities and substantive issues within a context that has both a past history and a future orientation. These transactions require the continuous examination of values and commitments by each person in the process. Planning, in their view, is

the structuring of a living situation with a wide range of educative alternatives. The transactions that take place within this structure cannot be planned in the traditional manner. They are more in the nature of "planned accidents" .... The curriculum is the cultural environment which has been selected as a set of possibilities for learning transactions (p. 17).

When a range of educational alternatives is available, the principle of choice becomes an essential consideration in planning for freedom.

### CHOICE AS AN ELEMENT OF FREEDOM

It is necessary in considering "choice" to differentiate that term and "whim." Whim implies acting on impulse, on a sudden idea, a capricious notion, or a momentary desire. Choice implies the use of reasoned judgment, reflection, and prior consideration of the consequences.

The element of choice must be present if there is to be freedom; yet a paradox of responsibility and freedom exists, particularly in educational situations, Macdonald and his associates (1973) remind us. No matter how openly structured or free it may be, the educational situation influences or creates the limits of the learners' choices. Thus, planning is essential.

Howard Kirschenbaum and Sidney Simon (1974) point out that education must teach a process of making choices; that it is essential for the educational enterprise to assume responsibility for teaching young people to examine the consequences of the alternatives under consideration and, by illuminating the pros and cons of each, to increase the chances for good decisions. An important part of valuing is considering seriously the consequences of each alternative before making a choice, rather than just gravitating toward the alternative that seems most attractive at first glance. In the view of these writers, well known for their work in value education, schools must create environments in which young people can make choices about beliefs, behaviors, and the course of their own education. They must be given opportunities to look at alternatives, weigh consequences, make their own choices, look at the interim consequences, and then go through the whole process again. Kirschenbaum and Simon add, "there is no short cut. We can't teach people to make responsible choices unless they are given a chance to make real choices. All else is to impose values, which simply will not help them deal with the future" (p. 265).

In the course of creating learning environments that allow growth in making responsible choices, growth also occurs in the valuing process and leads to personal development of fundamental moral values. The future will offer new alternatives that demand choices made on a firmer basis than whim or conformity.

## SOCIAL AND ETHICAL VALUES

Mario Fantini (1974), known for his work in the humanist movement, relates humanism to social and ethical values. While central standards of humanism are individual freedom, dignity, and self-worth, humanists also advocate the freedom of each person to prosper. When faced with social realities, says Fantini, the genuine humanist will not retreat from ugly problems or change the ground rules to justify personal retreat. Nor will he or she reinterpret values to avoid the personal stress of working to convert negative environments into settings that support human dignity for others.

Schools, Fantini observes, could work toward a social renewal curriculum that deals directly with major community problems, e.g., pollution, safety, health, and housing. Although he sees only slight efforts being made in that direction by curriculum developers at the present, there are some worthy examples of persons working toward social and ethical values in the quest for freedom for others in American society.

The lawyers who are leading the struggle to increase the basic rights of citizens under the equal protection clause of the Fourteenth Amendment are using their legal expertise humanistically; for example, some lawyers have challenged the constitutionality of public school financing systems that discriminate against the poor by making the quality of a child's education depend on the socioeconomic resources of his or her community. Fantini also cites doctors who are working to reduce birth defects by helping to improve prenatal environments among the poor, television news commentators who use the media to help expose injustices such as intolerable conditions in institutions serving the mentally retarded and the elderly, and Ralph Nader and other consumer rights advocates who are working actively for social and ethical values.

An increasing number of persons in several professions are entering their careers not for status and financial security but rather for opportunities to work on social renewal problems such as relief of poverty, disease, slum conditions, racial and class discrimination, and other injustices. Fantini concludes that schools have the responsibility to provide leadership in expanding the boundaries of the humanist concept, so that new talents and energies can join in crucial tasks related to freedom and values.

## MORAL VALUES

In considering right and wrong, the boundaries of morality are not clearly and inflexibly defined. Psychologists Carl Rogers (1969) and Abraham Maslow (1967) are among those who have deplored the lack of attention to moral valuing and have proposed a "new science" that will recognize subjective as well as objective experiences—a discourse that will provide new means for obtaining consensus on value questions. In the view of these writers, a natural value system, which can identify boundaries of morality, will emerge through submitting value questions to the test of what is ultimately wholesome for the whole person.

Rogers and Maslow are quoted by Willis Harman (1970 pp. 44-46) in this context:

The new science bids fair to incorporate the most penetrating insights of psychology, the humanities, and religion. These developments will have profound impacts on the goal priorities of society, on our concepts of education, on the further development and use of technology, and perhaps (as in the case of the Copernican Revolution) on the distribution of power among social institutions and interest groups. . . .

The real significance of a science of subjective experience is that it is in this area that our individual and social values are experientially and historically rooted. The development of such a science would redress what in retrospect is a puzzling discrepancy between the audacity with which man has pursued the physical, biological, and social sciences and the timidity with which he has confronted the development of a moral science.

Philosophers and theologians as well as psychologists are recommending that more credence be given to social data, subjective findings, and common sense or "folk knowledge." Scientific, objective data are not sufficiently encompassing for advancing our knowledge about human freedom and social, ethical, and moral values.

Kenneth Boulding (1966, p. 7) emphasizes the importance of folk knowledge in carrying out humanistic relationships, and he distinguishes between folk knowledge and scientific knowledge in this way:

Folk knowledge is the process by which we acquire knowledge in the ordinary business of life and in ordinary relationships in the family, among friends, and in the peer group, and so on. Scientific knowledge entails the constant revision of images of the world under the impact of refined observation and testing.

Brian Hill (1973) maintains that it behooves educational theorists to give serious consideration to the contributions of philosophy and theology, to use "several complementary realms of discourse to discuss the nature and sanctity of the individual," and "to give due honor to the various spheres of life, knowledge, and education that correspond to them." While objectivity and the scientific method are valuable in the progress of human understanding, inclusion of the philosophical sphere is also essential in the study of man, says Hill. He provides the following analysis of the thinking of Martin Buber, Jacques Maritain, and Reinhold Niebuhr in relation to moral values in education and consequently in curriculum development.

In Buber's view, a prime purpose of education should be the formation of character. He finds such an education to be neither individualist nor collectivist, for "genuine education of character is genuine education for community." Buber expresses the belief that moral education depends on the promotion of freedom and dialogue. The teacher becomes more than an instructor; he or she must achieve a meeting with the student. Giving direct instruction in ethics is undesirable, in Buber's view, as it may produce the opposite result of what was intended. The teacher must submit to the more exacting labor of winning the confidence of the student, so that the student accepts the educator as a person—as someone who in turn accepts the student before desiring to influence him or her. Social education, says Buber, is more profound than mere adjustment, and he emphasizes that responsible behavior by the teacher in a valuing discussion means responding, not merely concurring. The teacher is "not the unobtrusive scene-shifter of progressive education any more than he or she is the authoritarian bearer of assured values of traditional education. The teacher is a person seeking a meeting with a person in the making" (p. 193).

Maritain sees the prime goal of education as the conquest of internal and spiritual freedom. He recommends that teachers shift their thinking from a focus on use of the curriculum syllabus to a focus on truth generated by the syllabus through processes of enlightened reasoning. As to the moral attitudes that all schools may properly promote, Maritain recommends the practical tenets of the democratic charter as a guide; however, in a pluralistic society many viewpoints will exist and can be brought out through discussion. While it is not the business of the school to shape the will and attempt to develop moral virtues directly in students, says Maritain, neutrality on the part of the teacher cannot be an option, if the teacher is to be a responsible member of the group.

Niebuhr distinguishes thinking and feeling in relation to freedom. The education of thinking, in his view, includes not only freedom from the thought of others but also freedom to think. The education of feeling involves achieving depth and sincerity of feeling and building a community of love in the school where moral education may take place. Niebuhr's sense of "community" does not belittle the important role of reason in moral education, but it gives precedence to love, meaning, dialogue, and responsibility.

Attention to moral valuing is increasing, and new centers for the study of values and the development of value education curricula are appearing at major universities (e.g., Harvard and St. Louis University). Robert Theobald heads a National Values Project whose work is reported in the journal *Futures Conditional* (1973–). Investigations into developmental aspects of values have been under way for some time by Lawrence Kohlberg and others.

## DEVELOPMENTAL ASPECTS OF VALUING

Kohlberg's (1972, p. 460) stages of moral development are applicable in the context of curriculum development. While he rejects the superficial translations of Dewey's teaching that appeared in some progressive schools in the 1930s, Kohlberg accepts certain of Dewey's key assumptions. These are: (1) intelligent thought about the education of social traits and values requires a philosophic concept of morality and moral development, which is very different from the concepts "social adjustment" and "mental health"; (2) moral development passes through qualitative changes or stages; and (3) the stimulation of moral development, like other forms of development, rests on the stimulation of thinking and problem-solving by the child.

In 1957, Kohlberg and his associates began testing the moral judgment of a group of seventy-two boys, aged ten through sixteen, by asking them questions involving moral dilemmas. From the answers, six basic types of moral judgments were found, and subsequent retesting of the group at three-year intervals showed growth proceeding through the six stages in the same qualitative order. The stages are:

1. Orientation to punishment and reward and to physical and material power.
2. Hedonistic orientation, with an emphasis on exchange of favors or trade-offs.
3. Orientation toward winning approval of one's immediate group, with morality defined by individual ties of relationship.
4. Orientation to authority, law, and duty, to maintaining a fixed order, whether social or religious, which is assumed as a primary value.
5. Social-contract orientation, with emphasis on equality and mutual obligation within a democratically established order.

6. Morality of individual principles of conscience that have logical comprehensiveness and universality and that place highest value on human life, equality, and dignity.

The stages are defined by ways of thinking about moral matters and bases for choices rather than by particular opinions or judgments. Stages 1 and 2, which Kohlberg sees as typical of very young children and delinquents, are described as premoral, since decisions are made largely on the basis of self-interest and material considerations. Stages 3 and 4 are group-oriented and are the conventional stages at which most of the adult population operates. Stages 5 and 6 are those in which choices are made on the basis of principle. Only at stage 6 is each life seen as inherently worthwhile, aside from all other considerations.

In another, related study under Kohlberg's direction, a moral education curriculum focused on a series of moral dilemmas, which were discussed by the instructor and the students. It was found that moral development could be stimulated by a teacher who bolstered and clarified arguments among children when the teacher supported arguments that were one stage above the lowest stage manifested by the children. For example, if the lowest level of the discussion among the children was at stage 2, the teacher supported stage 3 positions until that level of argument was understood by the students. The teacher then challenged that stage, using new situations and clarifying the arguments at the next higher level, stage 4.

The educational implications of these experiments are that teachers can help children consider genuine moral conflicts, think about the reasoning they use in solving such conflicts, see inconsistencies and inadequacies in their ways of thinking, and find ways of resolving them. To do this, however, the teacher must know the child's level of thought and must communicate at the level directly above it. Kohlberg concluded that if schools wish to foster morality, they have to provide an atmosphere in which interpersonal issues are settled on the basis of principle rather than power. They have to take moral questions seriously and provide food for thought instead of conventional "right answers."

In Kohlberg's studies the main experiential determinants or causal factors in moral development seem to be the amount and variety of the child's social experience and the opportunities he or she has had to assume a number of roles and to take other perspectives into account. Being able to put oneself in another's place is a source of principles; for example, when parents sought their children's views and elicited comparisons of views in dialogues, the children reached more advanced stages of moral development.

Kohlberg also refers to an Israeli study of disadvantaged adolescents, who underwent rapid moral development in a kibbutz through the stimulation of their peer group in school during a period when the teenagers had little direct contact with their own parents. Religion did not enter into this particular study, as the kibbutz mentioned was atheistic. In general, Kohlberg's studies indicate that variations in religious affiliation and attendance are unrelated to moral development. He recommends that planned moral education take place in the schools.

Studies and observations such as Kohlberg's reveal new insights into the necessity for us to make considered choices as a people; they also give us new insights into the questions surrounding values and beliefs and new insights for curriculum development. Inevitably these bring new responsibilities for the schools. What societal support will the school find for curriculum development that recognizes the valuing process as a concomitant of planning for individual freedom? Indications are that society is presently in a transition period—that major conceptual shifts in societal values and beliefs appear to be taking place.

### SHIFTS IN VALUE BASES

Contemporary futurists may differ in vision, but most agree on one thing: that man is now undergoing one of the few major transitions in history. Ken Davis (1974, p. 12) observes that our culture is now experiencing a breakdown of the industrial-age paradigm. Serious social problems of our day cannot be solved through applications of the industrial model and its accepted paths to success. Davis refers to the work of Willis Harman, who speaks for many future-oriented scholars when he describes the shift as a major conceptual revolution—an infrequent event in the history of man.

Studies of societal trends conducted by the Educational Policy Research Center of the Stanford Research Institute are analyzed by Harman (1970). Generalizations from the works of John Platt (1966), Kenneth Boulding (1966), Pierre Teilhard de Chardin (1964), Lewis Mumford (1965, 1956), F. W. Matson (1964), and

Ernest Becker (1969), and a comparison of recent events with such historic transitions as the Fall of Rome, the Reformation, and the Industrial Revolution, seem to Harman to indicate that significant changes are imminent. These historic transitions involved changes in basic cultural premises, the image of man in society, fundamental values, and social roles and institutions.

To illustrate his point, Harman compares events of the sixteenth century with those of the past decade or two. The Protestant revolt, the beginning of the Copernican scientific revolution, the age of exploration and discovery, the substitution of secular for religious authority, and the power generated by the printing press can be compared with modern student protest groups, the knowledge explosion, space exploration, the redistribution of authority in relation to urban growth, and the present technological revolution. Harman and others feel that society is at a point of choice; they emphasize that the philosophies of materialism and idealism need not take positivistic stances but rather may take relativistic positions in which they have a complementary relationship.

At this point of choice, Harman projects before us a continuum of alternative futures. At one extreme is a person-centered society; at the other is a garrison state; and midway between the two are various alternatives. The direction that society chooses, says Harman, depends largely on the capabilities of our educative processes.

## A Person-centered Society

The goals of the person-centered society include use of economic growth to meet human needs, control of social problems to increase individual self-fulfillment, achievement of knowledge, and aesthetic advancement. In the person-centered society, education is a valid occupation, and a diversity of educational paths and ways is available in which persons can win the esteem of others. Lewis Mumford (1965, p. 923) analyzes the basic attitude shifts required by the person-centered society:

The deliberate expression and fulfillment of human potentialities require a quite different approach from that bent solely on the control of natural forces. . . . Instead of liberation *from* work being the chief contribution of mechanization and automation, liberation *for* work, for educative, mind-forming work, self-rewarding even on the lowest physiological level, may become the most salutary contribution of a life-centered technology.

Harman sees this alternative as a planned society, but one planned through real participation by those for whom the planning is done and planned to enhance the freedom of the individual. Each person in it responds to human needs and works to lessen international tensions and internal animosities.

The person-centered society is a composite picture based on the views of many writers and analysts, including John Kenneth Galbraith (1967), Michael Harrington (1966), Erich Fromm (1968), Kenneth Boulding (1966), Robert Theobald (1968), John Platt (1966), and Abraham Maslow (1967, 1961).

## A Garrison State

The calamitous option among alternative futures, a garrison state, is characterized by violence and counterviolence, international strife, an escalating arms race, a militarized economy, continued subculture conflicts, and further alienation of segments of society, with major emphasis on the functions of law enforcement agencies.

## A Midway Alternative

An alternative midway between the two extremes—the person-centered society and the garrison state—is described compositely by Harman (1970, p. 18) from a weighted summation of the many trend projections, Delphi forecasts, and brave-new-world predictions that have been analyzed by the Educational Policy Research Center. He uses the *second-phase industrial society* to describe this alternative.

The operative goals of this society are continuing expansion of output (goods and services), a commensurate increase in consumption, technological advance, efficient use of resources toward these ends, and furtherance of the public images that sustain all of these goals. Individual lives are to be spent in the service of these goals. Human wants rate lower than, and thus must conform to, the needs of the industrial system. State policies, the educational system, and conventional morality are all molded to fit the requirement of the system.

In the second-phase industrial society, Harman predicts that a low priority will be given to abolishing slums, poverty, and racism, assisting poor nations, and attending to nature, beauty, aesthetics, history, and civility.

## Trends Toward a Person-centered Society

Within the past two decades several signs have appeared that support the view that societal values are moving more strongly toward the humane positions of the person-centered society. Fantini's (1974) observations were reported earlier in this chapter. Lynn White (1965) several years ago noted major shifts in four long-standing traditional canons of American culture. He describes these as:

1. The concept of European-American superiority has been displaced by a global canon with strong international influences from the nonwestern world.

2. The spoken word and printed symbols are not viewed as the only instruments of intellectual analysis and expression; they are rapidly being supplemented by the creation and use of new symbols, including the visual arts, dance, theater, and other forms of nonverbal communication.

3. The canon of reason and rationality, which was once assumed to be the supreme human attribute, must now also accommodate the canon of the unconscious, which includes intuitive hunches, serendipity, sudden insights, and intellectual structures or visions that seem to happen at times without following logical methods of rational problem-solving.

4. The canon of a hierarchical structure of values seems to be shifting to that of a spectrum of values; for example, mathematics, logic, and literature were formerly at the top of a hierarchy that ranged down in steps of status to working with one's hands at the bottom. This is changing to the concept of a spectrum in which every human activity has potentiality for greatness, with a blurring of the barriers between the "aristocrat" and the worker.

Theodore Roszak (1969) calls attention to indications in recent times that the youth culture is reinforcing demands for a person-centered rather than an establishment-centered education and for a society adapted to humane man rather than to economic man. This is exemplified by the rise of what he has designated the *counterculture*, the attempt by some young people to create alternative cultures that seem to offer them new ways to fulfill their own and other people's human potentials. Alternative person-oriented views find educational expression in alternative or "free" schools, open education class-rooms, and other modes (discussed in chapters one and eleven in this book).

Margaret Mead (1970) also sees a shift toward a person-oriented society and away from the hierarchical or authoritarian structures that were derived from industrialism and widely used in schools. Mead notes distinctions among three different kinds of culture: post-figurative, in which children learn primarily from their elders; co-figurative, in which both children and adults learn from their peers; and prefigurative, in which adults learn also from children. She sees a definite shift toward a prefigurative culture. The upsurge of student activity in politics, social issues, and educational criticism is an ex-pression of this concept. Mead also notes that all three kinds of culture may be operating simultaneously.

James Macdonald (1971) also recognizes the person-oriented cul-tural shifts described by Mead and adds that cultural change is not a linear shift from one culture to another but rather a shift from an acceptance of one "right" culture to acceptance of plural cultures that must be reckoned with in curriculum development.

## SOCIETY'S VALUES AND CURRICULUM DEVELOPMENT

That curriculum is much affected by society's beliefs and values is well substantiated. Conquering the dust bowl, controlling small pox, developing nuclear power, and exploring space are all examples of the use of education to achieve societal objectives. But just as the beliefs and values of a society determine the kind of education it chooses, so the educational system affects what beliefs and values are perpetuated or changed.

Harman (1970, p. 49) observes that

the United States is presently at a choice point in moving toward either the "second-phase" industrial society or the "person-centered" society. It is obvious that no one in the White House or anywhere else will actually make such a decision. But in effect, through a multiplicity of decisions, made by such groups as the Congress, the Pentagon, local school boards, and industrial management, the choice is being made.

Values and perceptions of values are critical factors in curriculum development. Individuals and groups will judge the adequacy of cur-riculum plans and instructional processes in terms of what these people believe constitutes effectiveness. Perceptions and understandings are influenced by the experiences and inputs available through wide access to sources of knowledge and by interactions with decision-making levels or groups other than one's own.

From value perceptions come policy decisions on which curriculum is based. Curriculum development, of central importance in the educative process, has the capability of influencing the present shift in societal values and beliefs toward a person-oriented society.

## SUMMARY

In support of the proposition stated at the outset of this chapter, the following points have been stressed.

Planning for the freedom of individuals is a conscious, orderly commitment to human worth and individual dignity. Valuing is a process of weighing the consequences of thought and action, appraising the worth of a situation, or assessing one's obligations in a given matter. "Freedom" can be misunderstood to imply irresponsible leadership and planlessness in a school. Choice, a necessary element of freedom, must be distinguished from mere whim; it must involve reasoned judgment.

Insights for curriculum development are woven throughout the documented discussions of social, ethical, and moral values; the process of valuing; and developmental aspects of moral growth. Evidence is provided to suggest that our society is at a point of choice in moving toward alternative futures, and educative processes in valuing can influence the shift toward a person-oriented alternative and away from disastrous alternatives.

## REFERENCES

Ashton-Warner, Sylvia. "Spearpoint." *Saturday Review of Education*, 24 June 1972, pp. 33-39.

——. *Teacher*. New York: Simon and Schuster, 1963.

Becker, Ernest. *The Structure of Evil: An Essay on the Unification of the Science of Man*. New York: George Braziller, 1969.

Boulding, Kenneth C. *The Impact of Social Science*. New Brunswick, N.J.: Rutgers University Press, 1966.

Cremin, Lawrence. *The Transformation of the School*. New York: Random House, 1961.

Davis, Ken. "Myth and the Future." *Futures Conditional* 2 no. 3 (March 1974): 12.

Dewey, John. *Experience and Education*. New York: Collier Books, 1938.

Fantini, Mario. "Humanizing the Humanism Movement." *Phi Delta Kappan* 55 (February 1974): 400-402.

Fromm, Erich. *The Revolution of Hope: Toward a Humanized Technology*. New York: Bantam Books, 1968.

Galbraith, John K. *New Industrial State*. Boston: Houghton Mifflin, 1967.

Harman, Willis W. "Nature of Our Changing Society: Implications for Schools." In *Social and Technological Change*, edited by Philip K. Piele, Terry L. Eidell, and Stuart C. Smith, pp. 1-67. Eugene: Center for the Advanced Study of Educational Administration, University of Oregon, 1970.

Harrington, Michael. *The Accidental Century*. London: Penguin Books, 1966.

Hill, Brian V. "Martin Buber, Jacques Maritain, Reinhold Niebuhr: Modern Religions and Educational Thinkers." *Intellect* 102 (December 1973): 191-95.

Kirschenbaum, Howard, and Simon, Sidney B. "Values and the Futures Movement in Education." In *Learning for Tomorrow*, edited by Alvin Toffler, pp. 257-71. New York: Random House, 1974.

Kohlberg, Lawrence. "Moral Education in the Schools." In *Curriculum and the Cultural Revolution*, edited by David E. Purpel and Maurice Belanger, pp. 455-78. Berkeley: McCutchan, 1972.

———. "A Cognitive-Developmental Approach to Moral Education." *Humanist*, November-December 1971, pp. 13-16.

Macdonald, James B. "Curriculum Development in Relation to Social and Intellectual Systems." In *The Curriculum: Retrospect and Prospect*, part I, pp. 97-112. Seventieth Yearbook of the National Society for the Study of Education. Chicago: University of Chicago Press, 1971.

Macdonald, James B.; Wolfson, Bernice J.; and Zaret, Esther. *Reschooling Society: A Conceptual Model*. Washington, D.C.: Association for Supervision and Curriculum Development, 1973.

Maslow, Abraham H. "A Theory of Metamotivation: The Biological Rooting of the Value Life." *Journal of Humanistic Psychology* 7 (fall 1967): 91-127.

———. "Eupsychia: The Good Society." *Journal of Humanistic Psychology* 1 (fall 1961): 1-11.

Matson, F. W. *The Broken Image: Man, Science and Society*. New York: George Braziller, 1964.

Mead, Margaret. *Culture and Commitment*. New York: Doubleday, 1970.

Mumford, Lewis. "Technics and the Nature of Man." *Nature* 4 (December 1965): 923-28.

———. *The Transformation of Man*. New York: Harper, 1956.

Platt, John R. *The Step to Man*. New York: John Wiley, 1966.

Rogers, Carl R. *Freedom to Learn*. Columbus: Charles E. Merrill, 1969.

Roszak, Theodore. *The Making of a Counter Culture*. Garden City, N.J.: Doubleday, 1969.

Shields, James J., Jr. "The New Critics in Education." *Intellect* 102 (October 1973): 16-20.

Teilhard de Chardin, Pierre. *The Future of Man*. New York: Harper and Row, 1964.

Theobald, Robert. *Futures Conditional*, various issues, 1973—. Wickenburg, Ariz.

———. *An Alternative Future for America*. Chicago: Swallow Press, 1968.

White, Lynn, Jr. "The Changing Canons of Our Culture." In *Contemporary American Education*, edited by Stan Dropkin, Harold Full, and Ernest Schwarcz. New York: Macmillan, 1965.

## ADDITIONAL READINGS

Baier, Kurt, and Rescher, Nicholas. *Values and the Future*. New York: Free Press, 1969.

Chagan, Barry I., and Soltis, Jonas F., eds. *Moral Education*. New York: Teachers College Press, Columbia University, 1973.

Hawley, Robert C. *Human Values in the Classroom*. Amherst, Mass.: Education Research Associates, 1973.

Heathers, Glen. "Education to Meet the Psychological Requirements for Living in the Future." *Journal of Teacher Education* 25 (summer 1974): 108-12.

Henderson, George, ed. *Education for Peace: Focus on Mankind*. Yearbook of the Association for Supervision and Curriculum Development. Washington, D.C.: ASCD, 1973.

Hoffman, John F. "Moral Navigation: From Puzzle to Purpose." *Teachers College Record* 75 (May 1974): 501-5.

Kahn, Herman, and Wiener, Anthony J. "Faustian Powers and Human Choices." In *Futures Conditional*, edited by Robert Theobald, pp. 56-64. Indianapolis: Bobbs-Merrill, 1972.

Kohlberg, Lawrence. *Stages in the Development of Moral Thought and Action*. New York: Holt, Rinehart and Winston, 1969.

Kuhn, Thomas S. *The Structure of Scientific Revolutions*. Chicago: University of Chicago Press, 1962.

Menninger, Karl. *Whatever Became of Sin?* New York: Hawthorn Books, 1973.

Park, Joe, ed. *Selected Readings in the Philosophy of Education*. 2d ed. New York: Macmillan, 1963.

Reich, Charles A. *The Greening of America*. New York: Random House, 1970.

Wilson, John; Williams, Norman; and Sugarman, Barry. *Introduction to Moral Education*. Baltimore: Penguin Books, 1967.

CHAPTER SEVEN

# Culture and
# Curriculum Development

**PROPOSITION**: If planners draw upon more of the total culture, the curriculum development process will respond to the needs and concerns of the persons served by the school.

## SCOPE OF THE TOTAL CULTURE

*Culture* is defined as the environment of ideas, experiences, beliefs, traditions, customs, institutions, sciences, arts, technologies, humanities, and commonsense ways of doing things that are part of the shared life of the people.

Culture is complex, it consists of many related modes, and it is constantly undergoing reconstruction. Thus, when curriculum development draws from the total culture and recognizes both ends and means, the process becomes more responsive and creates new culture.

The process of curriculum development . . . includes selection from the total culture and the creation of a pattern of encounter that will maximize the authenticity of the material and the probability of its being internalized by learners. As a system of ideas and beliefs, it includes aspects of the cognitive world isolated by disciplines and/or subjects in terms of facts, information, generalizations, principles, laws, and the like. It also includes awareness of and facility in the use of expressive symbols such as art, music, and language. Further, it includes systems of value orientations for action in the form of such things as modes of inquiry, seeking new knowledge, respecting the integrity and worth of individuals, being concerned for other peoples, using democratic procedures, and so forth. . . . Cultural systems are substantive aspects of social and personality systems and evolve in a constant interaction shaped and influenced by the dynamics of structures and actions in . . . culture, society, and personality (Macdonald 1971, pp. 97-98).

Origins of the proposition regarding culture and curriculum development can be traced back through the literature for more than a century and are found in the writings of anthropologists, philosophers, psychologists, social scientists, and others. For example, in 1837, Ralph Waldo Emerson (1966), in his address "The American Scholar," spoke of education by nature, by books, by action, and by duties. Similar thoughts appeared in the writings of Cardinal Newman and John Stuart Mill in the nineteenth century. In 1926, Harold Rugg noted that curriculum-making must be continuous and carried out with a comprehensive view of the whole, that the rift between curriculum and society must be bridged, for curriculum is constructed out of the very materials of American life. George Counts (1952) maintained that the responsibilities of the school included curriculum development directed toward constructive modification and development of the nation's economy, social structure, cultural institutions, and outlook on the world. Curriculum development should lead toward creating as well as transmitting culture, meeting and maintaining democratic social relationships, and increasing individual self-realization, Counts asserted.

Curriculum development can be approached through countless points of entry. Problems arise when developers rely on single or limited avenues and sources and ignore other significant dimensions of the culture. Curriculum development must recognize the importance of both process and product—of the process of developing curriculum, of the curriculum plan being developed, and of the instructional processes to be generated.

The scope of available culture is almost limitless. It involves societal conditions, knowledge from the academic disciplines, professional knowledge about learning and educative processes, philosophical and value bases, futures research, realities in the classroom, pluralistic ethnic backgrounds of the participants, and their needs and desires. Some of these areas have been discussed elsewhere in this book. Illustrations are given later in this chapter of other major areas of the total culture that contribute to responsiveness in curriculum development.

## DISTORTIONS

Some distortions inhibit our perceptions of the total culture. Irving Buchen (1974) illustrates several such distortions from the field of curriculum development in the humanities. He notes that planners of humanities programs that officially seek interdisciplinary relationships frequently exclude the physical sciences or bewail the dehumanization of man by technology. Yet these same persons consult concordances put together by computers, cite articles reproduced by copying machines, allude to rare manuscripts made available on microfilm, and listen to chants and folk rituals on audiotape cassettes. What is even more serious, in Buchen's view, such an attitude frequently jeopardizes communication with students, who are often quite comfortable with computers and communication machines, recognizing that they as human beings have not been mechanized as a result of using the products of technology.

Buchen also notes that even the best humanities programs generally have no contact or relationship with programs in other fields, with the result that students and instructors in discrete fields may confront each other in adversary roles and create wide cross-cultural gaps. Numerous gulfs are carried over into society, such as the conflict between environmentalists and businessmen.

Henry Winthrop (1974) draws on an article by John Fischer about a case study using a hypothetical proposal by a real estate corporation to build a fifty-story skyscraper in the most congested area of midtown Manhattan. The proposal appears on its face to be a sound investment judged by earlier accounting methods. The builders estimate that 90 percent of the office space could be rented at $12 per square foot, yielding a profitable enterprise.

In Fischer's analysis, however, students would investigate a broad range of other factors. For example, what would be the cost of moving 12,000 additional workers in and out of midtown New York during rush hours? This would entail the purchase of several million dollars' worth of new city buses. When these additional buses join other vehicles in already clogged avenues, the daily loss of man-hours in traffic jams could run to more millions of dollars. Fumes from additional engines would cause a sharp increase in New York's incidence of emphysema and lung cancer, thus requiring the construction of three new hospitals. To supply the hospitals as well as the new skyscraper with water, which is already in short supply in New York, a new reservoir would have to be built on the headwaters of the Delaware River, 140 miles away. Some of the dairy farmers pushed out of the drowned valley would move into the Bronx and go on relief. The subtraction of their milk output from the city's supply would lead to a price increase in milk. For a Harlem mother with seven hungry children, that could be the last straw—she might summon her neighbors to join her in a riot, causing seven blocks to go up in flames, and the mayor would demand higher taxes to hire more police.

This fictitious case study, albeit exaggerated, represents an example of the need for a total-culture orientation to curriculum development. The development process must attempt to discover relationships between certain kinds of information and to see how those relationships bear on the problems under study.

Another example is offered by Henry Winthrop (1974)—in this case, the result when planners fail to pay attention to the cultural customs of a people. He notes that, when missionaries distributed steel axes to Australian aborigines to replace their stone axes, the whole value system of the tribe was undermined and broke down. Among these aborigines, the only person who could own a stone axe was the father. But the missionaries distributed steel axes to men and women, old and young alike, creating a social breakdown. Similar examples have arisen in American schools, e.g., when middle-class Anglo teachers forbade children from Spanish-speaking homes to utter a single word of their native language in school and punished them in various ways if they did so, or when schools showed disrespect for the customs of immigrant or ghetto children with "strange" backgrounds.

## DISCIPLINES, INTERDISCIPLINES, AND MULTIDISCIPLINES

A major cultural source for curriculum is the academic disciplines, both individually and in combinations. The contributions of the separate disciplines, multidisciplinary approaches, and interdisciplinary approaches are all essential to responsiveness in curriculum development.

### The Disciplines

The curricular reform of the 1960s accomplished some significant successes, although it was later called into question because its proponents viewed it for a time as all the reform that was needed and therefore omitted work on societal and human problems. The academic disciplines underwent a searching analysis and received attention that they had rarely enjoyed in previous educational reform movements. Curriculum developers departed from the old concept of the discipline as a range of information to be "covered" in the classroom and entered a new era in which, to quote Herman Eschenbacher (1974, p. 507), "the academic disciplines are perceived as models or systems through which to assimilate the unknown into what we already know in order to make change comprehensible, and manageable." The discipline was viewed as providing a technique for ordering data, applying them to a question of some significance, and establishing the rules by which the answer is validated. The discipline, in sum, notes Eschenbacher, is a functional analytic tool that remains when the ephemera of content have evaporated.

The desired product, continues Eschenbacher, is a quality of mind, an intellectual independence or style, that expresses itself in ways of acting. It seems axiomatic that, if what people learn does not change them in some way, it makes little difference what they learn. Although the disciplines have rarely functioned in this way in public education, and teachers have expected students to receive information rather than to develop independent answers, the curriculum reform movement of the 1960s brought new perceptions to curriculum developers and introduced a concept, now basic in curriculum development, that the educative process should help students learn how to learn. Each discipline promotes its own interpretations of modes of inquiry and directs applications of its techniques to real problems.

## Multidisciplines and Interdisciplines

A multidisciplinary curriculum is distinguishable from an interdisciplinary curriculum. The former is a parallel approach to curriculum development, in which each discipline has something to contribute about a given problem while remaining a discrete entity. Interdisciplinary approaches make use of what Winthrop (1974) terms the *convergence approach,* in which each discipline methodologically complements and illuminates the other. A convergence problem is one whose solution—if one is possible—requires considerable amounts of information from a number of different but specialized fields, seeks relationships between the kinds of information, notes the intersections of relationships that apply to the problem under study, applies a method of analysis to a problem that cuts across several fields, and relates the solution to the values of the community or consumers and to the context within which the curriculum is being developed.

A critical difficulty facing curriculum developers is that some of the most pressing and complex problems—problems that the schools are expected to heed—cannot be contained within the boundaries of any one discipline or frequently, even combinations of them. Problem-solvers must draw on other aspects of the total culture to approach these questions. Examples abound: studies of war and peace, the environment, the social effects of science and technology, communication, the status of women, crime and rehabilitation, meeting the needs of developing countries, racism in America, and scenarios of the future.

Eschenbacher (1974, p. 508) uses the "urban problem" as an example of the necessity for interdisciplinary approaches to curriculum development:

One wishes to know the dimensions of the problem, to come to understand it, to do something to alleviate it, if only out of self-interest. The schools should offer help, not through exhortation or preachment, but by enabling each child to develop a perspective that will foster analysis and make some personal sense of the problem for him. The social sciences, it is supposed, provide the means to achieve this. The urban problem is historical because it has been a long time evolving and because it breaks the surface of the historical consciousness only when certain forces intersect. These can be identified and analyzed by involving the historical method, but the analysis, although it furthers understanding, is only partial. Another part of the problem is economic, and is concerned with the apportionment of wealth, products, job opportunities, and the like. Another part is political, and still another aspect concerns social-class assignments, mobility, values, and so on. No single discipline is sufficient to encompass the problem as a totality.

Eschenbacher emphasizes that a separate discipline or multidiscipline approach is not sufficient, because the analytic process—a characteristic of interdisciplinary or convergent approaches—is the desired outcome. Curriculum development cannot be concerned with the product of a discipline only; it must be concerned with the process, and to rest on content without considering technique is to confuse ends and means. Providing students with analytic tools for drawing from the several disciplines in an interdisciplinary convergence on problems recognizes the essential factor of responsiveness. The disciplines are then used for conceptualization and as powerful referents for interpretating experience. Eschenbacher concludes that such an approach represents our best available opportunity for promoting autonomy and fostering growth. Critically applied, the disciplines support intellectual discernment and independence, the ends most coveted in a free system.

## Interdisciplinary Approaches: Pro and Con

Although resistance to interdisciplinary approaches to curriculum has been strong, awareness of the advantages of these approaches is increasing. Biases against interdisciplinary work come from tradition and resistance to change. Both the public and academicians fear that the contribution of a particular discipline will be diminished, that specialists who venture outside of their subject fields will lose stature, and that no one can possibly master several fields.

In response to these objections, Winthrop (1974) notes that contributions to the solution of many of the gravest problems facing education will have to cross disciplinary boundaries, that the status feelings of a single-discipline scholar spring from an elitist oulook, and that such a view cannot be taken seriously in a era when mankind is hard pressed to seek solutions to problems. The claim that no one can master several fields is true, but no interdisciplinary scholar claims to be a master of several fields. Such a scholar is problem-oriented and acquires needed information from several areas relevant to the problem without having to become a master in each area.

Ronald Hyman and other writers collected in *Approaches to*

*Curriculum* (1973) make a case for an interdisciplinary approach to the curriculum and contend that the lack of vitality of the present high school curriculum is due to its failure to come to grips with many issues about which young people are highly concerned. Gordon Cawelti (1974) points out that numerous students have only the barest notion of the economics of private enterprise, inflation, recession, prices, and unemployment and that, until there is broader public understanding of the effects of a given corrective policy when it is instituted, tedious debates over union and management roles in private enterprise will probably continue, resolving nothing with comprehension of the values ultimately at stake.

Other examples can be drawn from the arts. Without broad interdisciplinary programs in humanities, the arts, and aesthetic education, students in this area have only limited opportunities. Consequences of this limitation are evident today in the garish architecture and unaesthetic community design of areas in many cities. Tastes in film are at such a low level that sex and violence seem to be the only topics able to draw wide audiences.

On the issues of our deteriorating environment and scarcity of resources, most schools do offer courses. But frequently environmental or population studies are free-floating courses or units here and there in which students are helped to become aware of environmental problems but not to know what they can do about them. They are left with a feeling of hopelessness and a conviction that disaster is inevitable, if not for this generation then for future generations. However, a number of interdisciplinary programs in some schools can be cited as exemplars.

Lawrence Paros (1973) describes a curriculum known as "The City Game," in which high school students focused on the issue of urban decay and social and political change in Providence, Rhode Island. Through problem-solving activities that searched out information, used simulation games, provided face-to-face contacts and interaction with businessmen and city officials, and involved students on decision-making city commissions, students worked in four major areas related to environmental and population problems: (1) health and welfare, including medical care, problems of the aged, drugs, mental health, retardation, social welfare, and ecology; (2) law and justice, including civil rights and liberties, juvenile justice, contemporary issues in law enforcement, and state and local government; (3) education, including early childhood development, alternative theories of child-rearing, problems in inner-city education, and explorations of "changing the system"; and (4) communications, including journalism, radio, television, and creative writing.

This interdisciplinary example is compatible with John Dewey's advice in *Experience and Education* (1938) that schools "break loose from the cut-and-dried material which formed the staple of the old education." The field of experience is very wide, he said, and it varies in its contents from place to place and from time to time. Dewey differentiated education based on experience from traditional education, in that conditions found in present experience are used as sources of problems. It is the educator's responsibility, Dewey asserted, to see that these problems arouse in the learner an active quest for information and for production of new ideas, which then become the basis for further experiences in which new problems are presented.

Another dramatic example of the necessity for interdisciplinary convergence on a problem is presented by Winthrop (1974) in an example pertaining to starvation and mass hunger in India. This problem, one worthy of study in the curriculum, is so complex that a team of outstanding agricultural experts from North America, sent to India in 1959 to study the food situation and make recommendations for averting or reducing impending starvation, reported that the country's food production problems involved relationships among more than seventy factors. The experts cited India's need to manufacture and import fertilizers and to improve the water facilities as especially important. Factors in meeting these needs include research, roads, capital, soil surveys, services to provide education, program coordinators, and publications. Other factors to be considered in the broader task of solving India's food problems are religious beliefs, forestry problems and needs, the development of markets for raw materials and finished products, and the need for revision of the land tenure systems. In addition, related problems had to be attacked, including soil conservation, plant breeding, political disunity, the shortage of foreign exchange, population control, unemployment, communication despite the diversity of languages, plant pests, and soil drainage.

The point is that most of our modern problems, social or otherwise, require an interdisciplinary convergence approach. Unless curriculum development draws from the total culture and the total context, it will be unresponsive to changing knowledge and social and personal needs and therefore ineffective.

## CULTURE AND THE HUMAN QUEST

Herbert Thelen (1970) emphasizes that curriculum must draw from a totality of culture. Culture is a way of life, including the symbols, manifestations, and values that are shared by its participants. Humane persons are involved in their culture, and their personalities incorporate its wisdom and compassion. Humane persons, continues Thelen (p. 29), also contribute to further refinement of their culture and must have "a strong feeling for the human quest, the universal questions that all generations of man must tussle with, the human potentials for good and evil inherent in human nature, the problem of availability of rights and distribution of advantages."

What goes on, then, in the broader universe of classroom and person, observes Thelen, will be the quest for enlightenment. The student is conceived as having the potential for development of the whole range of human attributes to an extent characteristic of his age, social milieu, and cultural belonging. The student is a whole person, but the overall quality of this "wholeness" is in a state of becoming. Therefore, continues Thelen (p.30),

to correspond with the view of the wholeness of the child, the environment is to be conceived in its wholeness as a micro-society, complete with such considerations as materials, laws, social relations, formal and informal structure, long and short-range goals, and values and aversions. All aspects of life should be available for examination, and the aspects most salient at any particular time should be faced.

Thelen emphasizes the relationship of responsiveness in curriculum development to a totality of culture, and he emphasizes that the experience of the student must be conceived as full, rich, and meaningful. The student relates his or her behavior as a means to personal purposes to be achieved and thus understands the consequences of a given behavior.

Specific illustrations can be given in which curriculum development draws on the total culture in the sense of Thelen's human quest. One example is a unit of study titled "Changing Neighborhoods," being developed for children ten to twelve years old by Harold Berlak and Tim Tomlinson (1974) of Washington University, in which students become aware of values in decision-making. A problem is defined, needed information is identified, and children learn how to secure the information. A decision about the problem is finally made on the basis of predictable consequences of a series of actions and by weighing the efforts and hardships that must be encountered along the way toward a desirable goal.

The problem centers around the conflicts of black-white integration in formerly all-white suburbs. The study opens with an introduction to members of a black family who live on the fringe of the black area of a large city. They are expressing a desire to live somewhere else where they can enjoy life more. They are also considering problems of finance, moving, and making new friends. Built into the unit are budget games, in which children learn how to figure costs of housing, moving expenses, and living expenses including variations in taxes in different neighborhoods. Through the use of films, filmstrips, tape recordings, and role-playing, conflict develops within the family and between the family and other blacks. Should the Davises move to a suburb?

Then the scene shifts to the white suburb and to various illustrations of the reactions of the white community. Negative attitudes and fears are brought out through neighborhood association meetings and other role-playing situations. A white liberal family finds that belief in equality, justice, and freedom is in conflict with fears of violence and fears that property values will decline.

As the children of the social studies class are faced by the dilemma, they are led to apply thought processes and to learn how to make decisions by looking at differences between arguments based on fact and arguments based on values. Concepts of moral considerations and shared power are faced squarely.

The total culture, in Thelen's view of the human quest, includes give-and-take, interactive communication with others, and shared communion in which people face experiences together. To enter into such liaisons with students is possible only for a humane person whose faith in the worth of all children remains steadfast. As this faith is internalized by the individual teacher it is transmitted from him or her to the student.

A similar view, and one that further supports the proposition advanced in this chapter, is expressed by several writers and synthesized by Clinton Collins (1974). The essays that substantiate Collins's views are found in David Denton's *Existentialism and Phenomenology in Education* (1974). The next section draws from these essays and other sources.

## REALITIES OF THE CLASSROOM

Perceptions of the total culture that are held by curriculum planners must include other dimensions as well as the contributions of
the academic disciplines, the applications of interdisciplinary approaches to complex societal problems, and the context of the particular setting. The multiple realities of the classroom are identified
in Collins's (1974) synthesis of collected essays as "first-person perspective, second-person perspective, and third-person perspective."

The first-person perspective yields the inner reality of the stream
of consciousness explored by William James in *Principles of Psychology* (1890), in which he developed the point that a person's sense of
what is real varies according to what he or she is attending to. As
James and others since his time (twentieth-century novelists, for
example) have observed, not only does the aspect of the world
change as an individual's involvement deepens, narrows, or broadens,
but also, to the extent that the individual constitutes his or her world
by personal perception of it, he or she may be constantly moving
from one world to another or from one perception of reality to
another.

Arthur Combs (1970) speaks to the same point and observes that
curriculum development is concerned not only with what goes on
outside the learner but also with what happens inside him or her in
the human discovery of meaning. In Combs's view (p. 180), "a humanized curriculum needs a humanistic psychology . . . . We need a
psychology interpretative of students' feelings, values, beliefs, understandings, and personal meanings."

Carl Rogers (1969), whose writings have had a subtle influence on
curriculum-building for several years, points to the futility of presenting material that has no personal meaning to students. Rogers
contends that for learning to be significant and meaningful it must
use feelings, personal involvement, and experience in which there is a
sense of discovery, of reaching out, of grasping and comprehending
that comes from within and acts on contact with the stimuli from
the outside.

The second-person perspective is that generated through dialogue.
Martin Buber is a leading analyst of the reality that comes through
dialogue, and his *I and Thou* (1958) is a frequent reference in this
regard. In dialogue, says Buber, two people continuously construct a

reality that is both shared and private, and that expands geometri-
cally, with each partner contributing a dimension, in contrast to the
linear increments occurring in the inner stream of consciousness.
Socrates is cited as an example of an ancient user of the dialectic
method, in which two people help each other to see, to think, and to
act.

After a dialogue, however, two people may take different perspectives to their relationships with others outside the dialogue—that is,
to third parties. When former discussants in a dialogue give discrep-
ant reports of their relationship to a third party, their objectivity
comes into question, and, in the multiple realities of the classroom,
other sources from the total culture are needed.

A third-person perspective is that of people engaged in institutional life who relate to each other on the basis of certain shared
expectations regarding roles. Collins observes that in institutional
life, such as the school, there is a part of the individual that remains
aloof from identification with any group. By restraining themselves
from total involvement in the institution, individuals establish a kind
of opposition between themselves and the institution. In essence, the
school is a form of social organization to be used by the student and
at the same time held at bay, so that it is not allowed to usurp his or
her individuality. In an extreme form, says Collins, the institution
becomes reified, that is, it is viewed as an object having an existence
apart from the lives of the people who participate in it. The individual may come to think of the school as an institution in which
people are powerless actors moving through typical performances
according to the role expectations of the institution. From this outlook stem student apathy and cries of irrelevance of the curriculum.
Students often perceive themselves or are perceived by others as
outsiders in relation to teachers as a group. The majority of teachers,
comments Collins, seem to want to maintain the concept of students
as outsiders, to deny admission to an in-group. Some teachers seem
to fear that friendly relationships with students would be viewed as a
relaxation of discipline in the classroom and thus weaken the teachers' position of authority.

Nevertheless, supported by an impressive array of documentation,
Collins stresses the importance of preserving dialogue within the
school, since it is through dialogue that each person expands his or
her sense of reality. The teacher in a group setting can maintain the

possibility of dialogue with each individual, although the necessities of the classroom demand that instruction be carried on in groups. Successful dialogue can be carried on in groups through experiences following formats that involve students as performers and catch them up in a "we" feeling somewhat like that of dialogue. These experiences reduce the student's sense of estrangement from the institution. Role-playing, panels, discussion groups, and numerous other techniques may be created out of the elements of dialogue and at the same time add the dimension of social experience, which contributes further to student growth.

A teacher may influence the education of a student on any of the three levels of classroom reality (first-, second-, or third-person) and thus plan environments conducive to the liberation of the individual. Liberation occurs as the individual becomes aware that "the world is many, as well as one," according to Collins.

## NATIONAL AND WORLD EVENTS

That curriculum development must be concerned with the rapidly swirling events of the world around us is inescapable. Margaret Mead (1970) calls to our attention the emergence of a world community. For the first time, human beings around the globe have become a community, united by shared knowledge and danger—a single interacting community that has never before existed on this planet within archaeological time. Worldwide air travel and television satellites have made events taking place on one side of the earth immediately and simultaneously available to people everywhere else. Although the world community still lacks the organization and sanctions by which a political community can be governed, the world is, nevertheless, a community, Mead asserts.

The younger generation, continues Mead, is like the first generation born into a new country. Its members are familiar with instantaneous communications flashed around the world by television. They have known almost continuous war. They understand the effects of continued pollution of air, water, and soil and the problems of feeding an indefinitely expanding world population. The older generation, states Mead, is still bound to the past—to the world as it existed in its childhood and youth. For this reason, adult curriculum planners need the direct participation of the young to free their imaginations from the past and allow them to look toward the future through the eyes of the adults of the future.

On the national scene, we can best understand the pace of events by looking back over the past dozen years. Most of us can recall quite vividly the year John F. Kennedy was assassinated, 1963. *Not* in the news that year were Woodstock, Watts, Wounded Knee, Kent State, Bangladesh, and Watergate. Eighteen-year-olds did not have the vote. There had not yet been men on the moon, space walks, sky labs, energy crises, talk of zero population growth, or serious attention to the rights of minorities and the status of women. In curriculum development circles that year, we were mainly concerned with introducing the new math, the new biology, possibly transformational grammar, and even foreign languages in the elementary schools. We had not yet begun to employ large numbers of security guards in city schools. We had not yet experienced the student riots of 1969 and 1970, nor had our attention been so sharply directed to turned-off students, who came to pose as great a problem as their militant counterparts. We had not yet experienced the events leading to impeachment proceedings and the resignation of a president. All these events, with new ones appearing daily in the media, are significant parts of the total culture to which curriculum development must respond.

## A UNIFYING PRINCIPLE

The challenge to curriculum development is considerable. The importance of drawing on the broad scope of total cultural sources and realities may be acknowledged, but a pitfall exists: the result may be a hodgepodge of miscellany. Harry Broudy (1966) speaks to this problem, asserting that the only defensible basis for educational decisions is a unifying principle. The unifying principle is a theory—in this case a theory of curriculum development—that rationally weaves together the objectives of the culture, life outcomes, school outcomes, a curriculum design to achieve the outcomes, a program of training teachers, specialists, and administrators, and the facilities and resources by means of which the whole enterprise proceeds or falters. Broudy argues (p. 18):

The consistency of this theory, its inclusiveness, and sophistication, its faithfulness to the demands of the culture, to social reality, to the facts of pedagogical life constitute criteria for curriculum decisions that transcend establishments. It is, I shall argue, the only rationally defensible basis for educational decisions.

## SUMMARY

In support of the proposition on culture and curriculum development, distortions are presented in which use of a single dimension as the sole source for curriculum development leads to inadequate and unacceptable processes and products. The total culture is defined as the environment of ideas, experiences, beliefs, traditions, customs, institutions, sciences, arts, technologies, humanities, and commonsense ways of doing things that are part of the shared life of the people. The total culture, in illustrations to support the proposition, includes contributions from the separate disciplines, from multidisciplinary approaches, and particularly from interdisciplinary approaches. The part played by our human quest for values, attitudes, knowledge, and skills that will equip us to live rightly and well in a free society is discussed, and the multiple realities of the classroom are described—the inner stream of consciousness and perceptions of the person, dialogue with others, and mutual obligations of the individual and the school to one another. National and world events with their inevitable impingement on curriculum development are daily brought sharply to our attention and, indeed, a developer of curricula for the future will do well to note the pace of change by observing the flow of national and world events over a few weeks or a few days.

The need for a unifying principle, a theory of curriculum development, is stressed as a basis for making curriculum-related decisions that avoid the superficialities of incidental or haphazard approaches to curriculum.

## REFERENCES

Berlak, Harold, and Tomlinson, Tim. *Changing Neighborhoods.* St. Louis: Washington University, Graduate Institute of Education, 1974.

Broudy, Harry S. "Needed: A Unifying Theory of Education." In *Curriculum Change: Direction and Process*, edited by Robert R. Leeper, pp. 15-26. Washington, D.C.: Association for Supervision and Curriculum Development, 1966.

Buber, Martin. *I and Thou.* New York: Charles Scribner's Sons, 1958.

Buchen, Irving H. "Humanism and Futurism: Enemies or Allies?" In *Learning for Tomorrow*, edited by Alvin Toffler, pp. 132-43. New York: Random House, 1974.

Cawelti, Gordon, ed. *Vitalizing High Schools: A Summary of Six National Pro-posals for Reforming Secondary Schools and a Curriculum Critique.* Washington, D.C.: Association for Supervision and Curriculum Development, 1974.

Collins, Clinton. "The Multiple Realities of Schooling." *Intellect* 102 (summer 1974): 528-36.

Combs, Arthur W. "An Educational Imperative: The Human Dimension." In *To Nurture Humaneness*, pp. 173-88. Yearbook of the Association for Supervision and Curriculum Development. Washington, D.C.: ASCD, 1970.

Counts, George S. *Education and American Civilization.* New York: Bureau of Publications, Teachers College, Columbia University, 1952.

Denton, David E., ed. *Existentialism and Phenomenology in Education: Col-lected Essays.* New York: Teachers College Press, Columbia University, 1974.

Dewey, John. *Experience and Education.* New York: Collier Books, 1938.

Emerson, Ralph Waldo. "The American Scholar." In *Emerson on Education*, edited by H. M. Jones, pp. 77-101. New York: Teacher's College Press, Columbia University, 1966.

Eschenbacher, Herman F. "Social Studies, Social Science, and School Reform." *Intellect* 102 (summer 1974): 507-9.

Hyman, Ronald J., ed. *Approaches in Curriculum.* Englewood Cliffs, N.J.: Pren-tice-Hall, 1973.

James, William. *Principles of Psychology.* New York: W. W. Norton, 1890.

Macdonald, James B. "Curriculum Development in Relation to Social and Intel-lectual Systems." In *The Curriculum: Retrospect and Prospect*, part I, pp. 97-112. Seventieth Yearbook of the National Society for the Study of Educa-tion. Chicago: University of Chicago Press, 1971.

Mead, Margaret. *Culture and Commitment.* New York: Doubleday, 1970.

Paros, Lawrence. "The City Game." In *Title III and Changing Educational Designs*, pp. 10-12. Washington, D.C.: George Washington University, 1973.

Rogers, Carl R. *Freedom to Learn.* Columbus: Charles E. Merrill, 1969.

Rugg, Harold, ed. "Curriculum-making: Points of Emphasis," and "The Founda-tions of Curriculum-making." In *The Foundations and Technique of Curricu-lum-making*, parts I and II. Twenty-sixth Yearbook of the National Society for the Study of Education. Bloomington, Ill.: Public School Publishing, 1926.

Thelen, Herbert A. "Comments on 'What It Takes to Become Humane.' " In *To Nurture Humaneness*, pp. 27-32. Yearbook of the Association for Supervision and Curriculum Development. Washington, D.C.: ASCD, 1970.

Winthrop, Henry. "The World We Have Wrought." *Educational Forum* 38 (January 1974): 163-70.

## ADDITIONAL READINGS

Frazier, Alexander. *New Insights and the Curriculum.* Yearbook of the Asso-ciation for Supervision and Curriculum Development. Washington, D.C.: ASCD, 1963.

Hass, Glen; Wiles, Kimball; and Bondi, Joseph, eds. *Readings in Curriculum.* 2d ed. Boston: Allyn and Bacon, 1970.

Henry, Jules. *Culture against Man*. New York: Random House, 1963.

Jones, Richard M. *Fantasy and Feeling in Education*. New York: New York University Press, 1968.

Miel, Alice, and Berman, Louise, eds. *Educating the Young People of the World*. Washington, D.C.: Association for Supervision and Curriculum Development, 1970.

Purpel, David E., and Belanger, Maurice, eds. *Curriculum and The Cultural Revolution*. Berkeley: McCutchan, 1972.

Rubin, Louis J., ed. *Life Skills in School and Society*. Yearbook of the Association for Supervision and Curriculum Development. Washington, D.C.: ASCD, 1969.

Sarason, Seymour B. *The Culture of the School and the Problem of Change*. Boston: Allyn and Bacon, 1971.

Short, Edmund C., and Marconnit, George D., eds. *Contemporary Thought on Public School Curriculum*. Dubuque, Iowa: William C. Brown, 1968.

Spindler, George D. *Education and Culture*. New York: Holt, Rinehart and Winston, 1963.

Thelen, Herbert A. *Education and the Human Quest*. New York: Harper and Row, 1960.

Whitehead, Alfred N. *The Aims of Education*. New York: New American Library, Mentor Books, 1929.

# CHAPTER EIGHT

# Democratic
# Goals and Means

PROPOSITION: If means are used that not only exemplify but also strengthen the nation's founding
goals, curriculum development will respond to and
embody the purposes of American democracy.

*Democracy* is defined as a state of society characterized by freedom
of expression, respect for the essential dignity and worth of the human
individual, and equal opportunity for each person to develop opti-
mally and freely, with emphasis on community and mutual responsibility, and without discrimination on the basis of sex, race, religion,
age, social or economic class, national origin, or handicap. In the
proposition stated above, we are basically concerned with democratic
goals, principles, and means as applied to curriculum development
and the educative process.

## DEMOCRATIC GOALS

The broad goals of democracy in the United States reflect the set
of values phrased in general, abstract language as an American creed

by Gunnar Myrdal (1962). They include the worth and dignity of the individual; equality; inalienable rights to life, liberty, property, and the pursuit of happiness; consent of the governed; majority rule; the rule of law and due process of law; community and national welfare; and rights to freedom of speech, press, religion, assembly, and private association. Other, less constitutionally oriented values include brotherhood, charity, mercy, nonviolence, perseverance, hard work, competence, expertise, rugged individualism, compromise, coopera- tion, honesty, loyalty, and integrity of personal conscience. Myrdal describes how values are proclaimed in American life (1962, p. 4):

The schools teach them, the churches preach them, the courts pronounce their judicial decisions in their terms. They permeate editorials with a pattern of idealism so ingrained that the writers can scarcely free themselves from it even if they tried. They have fixed a custom of indulging in high sounding generalities.

Myrdal makes some searching observations about different inter- pretations of this creed by conservatives and liberals, blacks and whites, rich and poor, the advocates of one interest and the backers of an opposing interest. He describes the American dilemma as the widespread tension between our high-level ideals and our actual practices, in which real power seems to be exercised by military, industrial, and political interests.

The problem of differing interpretations of the American creed is also examined by Fred Newmann and Donald Oliver (1970). They note that conflicting commitments are frequently manifestations of diverse interpretations and paradoxes in American culture—for example, the emphasis on competition and rugged individualism on the one hand and a profound contradictory concern for community cooperation and compromise on the other.

Both ends and means are included in the creed without categoriza- tion or order. However, a fundamental value that supersedes others is that of individual human dignity, Newmann and Oliver note. Such creed values as national security, separation of powers, property rights, and due process of law do not possess intrinsic goodness in themselves, but their implementation relates to the fulfillment of the fundamental value of individual human worth. This value emphasizes the integrity of each person because he or she is a person. Individual worth includes the ability to make choices that affect one's life (e.g., in career, religion, politics, or family relations), the guarantees of physical protection of life and property, equal treatment under the law, the ability to defend oneself against prosecution by the state, and other values.

To support a proposition focused on democratic goals and means as part of an approach to a theory of curriculum development requires further clarification of terms and concepts. While definitions of American democracy are almost nonexistent in high school textbooks, as reported in a survey by Benjamin Rader (1974), two types of definitions are distinguished by Doyle Buckwalter (1973) from other sources. In one sense democracy is a moral goal, and in another it is a form of government. Confusion results if the goal and the form are not differentiated from one another.

As Buckwalter observes, it is far easier to identify democratic moral goals than it is to describe the democratic form of government. The moral goal of democracy is to improve the general welfare of all humans, and the phrase "all men are created equal" means that each individual is infinitely precious. The emphasis on the individual implies that democracy is not selective but applies to all types of people—the obedient, the lawless, the wise, the illiterate, the rich, the poor, the white, the black, the capable, and the incompetent.

On the form of government, John Gardner (1973) observes that, if our Founding Fathers returned today, they would be surprised to find that, despite all our professed concern for individual freedom, we pay so little attention to the instruments of self-government. To the Founding Fathers, the idea that liberty and justice for the individual result only from suitably designed political and governmental institutions was a basic premise. A concern for freedom and an interest in government were inseparable in their view.

Too many citizens today seem resigned to accepting the limitations of politics and government as they now exist, states Gardner. Public opinion polls covering the Watergate affair cited shocking statistics on the extent to which Americans had lost confidence in their public institutions. At this point we can only speculate, but various signs indicate that, with the culmination of the Watergate investigation and the resignation of President Nixon, citizen attention to the public processes of government revived, and Americans had a feeling that "the constitution works," as expressed by Gerald Ford in his inaugural address.

Buckwalter notes that, unless there is a reassertion and diligent application of democratic principles to ever-changing conditions, American democracy faces a fundamental danger. It, above all other approaches to governing, must be continually practiced to be accepted, states Buckwalter, and he adds that no space program or foreign or domestic policy can substitute for the binding quality of faith—faith that people working together can eradicate problems.

Frederick Mayer (1973, p. 22) emphasizes the same point: "The actual process of democracy—with its party bickering, blatant advertising, crime and corruption, economic domination, fragmentation of interests, and public apathy—may cause a sense of revulsion. But democracy is an educative process capable of indefinite renewal."

Renewal in the process of democracy, whether applied to government or curriculum development, depends on people working together; it depends on committed involvement, not pseudoparticipation. Paulo Freire (1970) describes the educative process for citizenship based on the principles of democratic freedom as consisting of two dimensions, reflection and action. In the democratic process, every person can be engaged at the cross-point of reflection and action. Either dimension alone is empty, observes Freire. Reflection can degenerate into idle chatter, verbalism, or nothingness, for there is no transformation without action. On the other hand, if action is emphasized to the exclusion of reflection, it becomes activism. Action for action's sake makes the process of renewal impossible, Freire notes.

Mayer (1973) asserts that democratic principles differ from concepts of aristocracy on this very point. Democracy does not concede different standards for "thinkers" and for "ordinary individuals." In ancient times, Aristotle advocated excluding merchants from active government because he asserted that they did not have time for reflection. Both thinking and acting, one transforming the other, are characteristics of a democratic process and lead to the concept of freedom, another basic principle of democracy.

Freedom is defined by Archibald MacLeish (1951) as the freedom of the individual human being to think for himself or herself and to come to the truth by the light of his or her own mind and conscience. He continues (p. 28):

Our reliance in this country is on the inquiring, individual human mind. Our strength is founded there: our resilience, our ability to face an everchanging future and to master it. We are not frozen into the backward-facing impotence of those societies fixed in the rigidness of an official dogma, to which the future is the mirror of the past. We are free to make the future for ourselves.

Similarly, Erich Fromm (1968, p. 52) observes that freedom is not just freedom from oppression of various kinds but also "freedom to create and to construct, to wonder and to venture. Such freedom requires that the individual be active and responsible, not a slave or a well-fed cog in a machine."

To be active and to be responsible require effort and commitment. Harry Broudy (1971) reminds us that the most differentiating characteristic of democratic and nondemocratic societies is the belief in the former that all those whose interests are affected should have a voice—usually an equal voice—in influencing the decision in a decidable situation that involves a diversity of interests. Having a voice implies that democracy is a problem to be worked on and solved, not a spectator sport.

### DILEMMAS OF DEMOCRACY

Apathy of the citizenry toward government and politics, confusion over the meanings of pluralism and egalitarianism in American society, and discrepancies between the principles of democracy and the actual practices in many schools are disturbing dilemmas.

### Principles Not Practiced

Discrepancies between democratic principles and practices sometimes exist at governmental levels in relatively minor institutions. Mayer (1973) illustrates the point by citing a small college that at one time prided itself on having an excellent political science course on the principles of democracy, but its own structure was a living negation of democratic processes. The college was governed by a board of trustees that had no sense of responsibility toward its community. While the chief administrator of the college acted in public as a pillar of democracy, in his life as an educational leader he tyrannized his faculty and behaved toward his subordinates like a dictator. Clearly, says Mayer, there is a substantial difference between talking about democracy and actually living it.

We are reminded of Machiavelli's cynicism in *The Prince* when he advises heads of state that the *appearance* of goodness and acquiescence to conventional morality is sufficient. This model, taken seriously by countless rulers, has been disastrous in both ancient and modern times. Democracy depends on overcoming the gap between the professed ideal and the actual practice.

Discrepancies between democratic principles and practices are also observable in vast bureaucracies, both public and private. Such organizations as the Internal Revenue Service, the Postal Service, major television networks, manufacturing corporations, and urban school systems sometimes seem quite remote and unresponsive to their constituents' needs and concerns.

Different groups have unequal effectiveness in influencing public policy. For example, wealthy and powerful industrialists can afford to employ lobbyists to pursue special interests in legislatures, while volunteer groups with conflicting interests may have much weaker influence. Well-educated parents have frequently exerted more pressure on schools for special (sometimes expensive) programs to benefit their children than the poor and uneducated could exert.

## Citizen Apathy

The apathy of many citizens toward governmental affairs poses still another dilemma of American democracy. Having the right to vote brings with it responsibilities for studying the background of issues, discussing one's views with others of varying viewpoints, and applying critical thinking skills to public controversies. In recent years, however, the public has shown an increasing interest in governmental, political, educational, and social matters.

John Gardner (1973) observes that, with the close of the 1960s, we saw the end of a forty-year period in which most informed Americans had little interest in any level of government but the federal. State and local government seemed beneath the notice of even well-educated persons. Legislative reapportionment in the 1960s called new attention to state legislatures and to representation. Then, as billions of federal dollars passed through state governments in the social programs of the middle and late 1960s, further attention was directed to shortcomings at that level of government. Gardner believes that the United States is presently at the beginning of a period of lively citizen interest in state and local government. In Gardner's view, the realization is dawning that a free society cannot survive for long unless citizens believe that they are in touch with their political and governmental institutions and that they can play a creative and responsible role in governing. In a huge, intricately organized society, a strong national government is needed, but strong and responsible government is also needed at the grass roots—where the people are. Gardner suggests that access, responsiveness, accountability, and effectiveness are guiding concepts in the improvement of our democratic form of government.

## Pluralism and Egalitarianism

The value of pluralism also poses a dilemma for American democracy. Stemming from the principle of individual human dignity, pluralism assumes the right of different groups (e.g., a religious sect, a black organization, a women's liberation group, a sportsmen's club, a student rights group) to exist, protected from intrusion or domination by outsiders considered to have alien values. However, Newmann and Oliver (1970) emphasize that, if such pluralism is to invigorate the larger society by expanding alternative paths to dignity, group members and outsiders must have enough contact to become aware of each other's options. Then the group risks destroying its distinctive nature by intermingling with other interests. Discerning the fine line between enough contact so that each segment can be aware of and possibly adopt the other's approach, and enough isolation for each group to work toward its particular vision of human fulfillment, presents a dilemma in modern practice, both in schools and in the larger society.

Related to the dilemma between the ideals of cultural pluralism and the actual practice are quandaries about the concept of egalitarianism. Christopher Hodgkinson (1973) discusses the dilemma of a strict interpretation of equality, in which everyone is treated in the same way. He draws from sociological findings that, without exception, human societies structure themselves according to some system of class—that two people placed on a desert island will inevitably create a social structure in which one is superior to the other. Hodgkinson notes that humans differ from each other in many ways, both as individuals and as groups, and that small-group psychology has found that inequalities inevitably emerge in decision-making groups. Excellence and meritocracy, continues Hodgkinson, tend to be limited to a few persons in any given area. Thus, while we have no difficulty with the principle of meritocracy in choosing our surgeon or airline pilot, the problem becomes a dilemma if democracy is interpreted to mean that all persons are the same in interests, energies, nature, and skills and thus must be treated exactly alike.

A broader interpretation of egalitarianism is provided by Terryl Anderson (1973) in a response to Hodgkinson. Characterizing democracy as application of a single value (everyone treated the same) is troublesome in Anderson's view. More basic to conceptions of democracy is the notion of equality as appropriate treatment for each person, with emphasis on individual differences and talents. To contend that the democratic ideal means elimination of all dissimilarity or the assumption that all persons have the same interests, energies, nature, and skills, is a narrow view. Indeed, democracy seeks the cultivation of diversity, including varieties of excellence. Democracy is a complex of values, such as freedom, justice, and equality, that form a network of criteria for judging the potential of particular social arrangements for providing optimum opportunities for all persons. Democracy in the American ideal is different in very fundamental respects from a Platonic class society, in which most people are considered incapable of being full citizens, and only the intellectuals are fit to rule.

John Dewey's (1937) expression of a broader view of democracy can clarify confused thinking on these dilemmas. He believed that the participation of individuals in creating, managing, and forming the values that underlie their social institutions was an essential feature of a democratic way of life. Dewey emphasized that what a person can and will become as a human being, both individually and in association with others, is affected by the institutions of society; therefore, each individual must share in the development of those institutions. Lack of participation by the individual is detrimental not only to his or her personal growth but also to society as a whole, which is deprived of that contribution. As Dewey maintained, democratic forms are simply the best means yet devised for realizing democracy in the wider sense.

Democracy, notes Mayer (1973), can be appreciated more for its future possibilities than for its past failings. We must not abandon democracy because of its dilemmas but rather must make it a reality in our own lives and institutions, through active, problem-solving participation.

## DEMOCRACY IN THE SCHOOLS

For application in the school, Dewey provides an interpretation of democracy in his classic volume, *Democracy and Education* (1916). Liberty, equality, fraternity, and the assorted rights that go with them, in Dewey's view, are not absolute principles or rules for economic and political competition, but rather are means toward a collective reconstruction of experience and the criteria of success in achieving it. Instead of using the school to sharpen the individual's weapons for competition, Dewey proposes that the school be a community in which pupils develop the attitudes and skills needed for collective inquiry and cooperative action. Later, in *Experience and Education* (1938, p. 34), Dewey emphasized the desirability of democratic and humane arrangements as opposed to autocratic and harsh ones: "Does not the principle of regard for individual freedom and for decency and kindliness of human relations come back in the end to the conviction that these things are tributary to a higher quality of experience on the part of a greater number than are methods of repression and coercion or force?"

Harry Broudy (1971) attaches great importance to community and communication, both of which necessitate the formalizing of experience so that it can be made an object of thought, discourse, foresight, imagination, planning, and verification. In this way democracy requires almost a synonymity among the terms *human, inquiry,* and *community*. By equating democracy with shared intelligence, we produce a model not only for social organization, but for teaching and learning as well, notes Broudy. Nevertheless, even with these democratic ideals represented in our goals for American education, gaps can be found between the broad goals of democracy and actual practices in schools. Several surveys document discrepancies between ideal and actual.

## GAPS BETWEEN DEMOCRATIC PRINCIPLES AND PRACTICES IN EDUCATION

Among the conclusions of an extensive study of high schools and their students under Project TALENT in the 1960s (Flanagan 1967) were that schools failed to assist students in developing a sense of responsibility for their educational, personal, and social growth;

that they failed to develop decision-making ability in students; and that they lacked emphasis on preparing students for the responsibility of citizenship.

Charles Silberman (1970, pp. 10-11), after nearly four years of intensive study and travel, in which he and members of his team visited countless schoolrooms and conferred with educators and other persons in all walks of life, expresses his feelings with emotion:

> It is not possible to spend any prolonged period visiting public school classrooms without being appalled by the mutilation . . . of spontaneity, of joy in learning, of pleasure in creating, of sense of self. . . .Because adults take the schools so much for granted they fail to appreciate what grim, joyless places most American schools are, how oppressive and petty are the rules by which they are governed, how intellectually sterile and aesthetically barren the atmosphere, what appalling lack of civility obtains on the part of teachers and principals, what contempt they unconsciously display for children as children. And it need not be! Public schools *can* be organized to facilitate joy in learning and aesthetic expression and to develop character—in the rural and urban slums no less than in the prosperous suburbs. . . . What makes change possible, moreover, is that what is mostly wrong with the schools is due not to venality or indifference or stupidity, but to mindlessness. . . .If mindlessness is the central problem, the solution must lie in infusing the various educating institutions with purpose, more important, with thought about purpose and about the ways in which techniques, content, and organization fulfill or alter purpose. And given the tendency of institutions to confuse day-to-day routine with purpose, to transform the means into the end itself, the infusion cannot be a one-shot affair. The process of self-examination, of "self-renewal," to use John Gardner's useful term, must be continuous.

In John Goodlad's and Frances Klein's survey of 150 primary classrooms of sixty-seven schools selected from major population centers of the country, members of a team, using an orderly observation procedure and analysis, found that almost all the schools pursued a course of bland uniformity regardless of pupil population, school setting, or pupils' needs. Goodlad and Klein conclude that each school faculty should identify its most critical problems, engage in a sustained dialogue about alternative courses of action, take one or more of these alternative actions, and periodically appraise the results. Approximately 6 percent of the schools visited came close to following such a course, while 94 percent followed built-in prescriptions of uniformity at a time when local diversity and individuality are desperately needed so that curriculum and instruction can be tailored to children's needs.

At the preschool level, millions of children may be irreparably damaged by our failure to stimulate them intellectually in their early years. Benjamin Bloom (1964) concludes from an analysis of dozens of research studies that the years before age four are most critical for stimulating the child's intelligence and activating his or her functions for learning. Yet relatively few American children have preschool experiences.

High school and college students voiced concerns in an investigation conducted by the United States Office of Education and reported in *Task Force Report on Easing Educational Tensions* (1970). They viewed as basic problems dehumanization (loss of identity and personal touch) within the school as an institution, inequities in society, educational irrelevance, and racial and cultural discrimination. The report also concludes that fear of authority seems to be the key factor behind a series of negative effects produced by schools on students as human beings. Fears of poor grades, punishment by authorities, humiliation, ostracism, and failure are used by school personnel from elementary through high school as weapons to establish and maintain student order and obedience.

Several investigators have called attention to the need for a clearer specification of goals in education. From the standpoint of students, a serious consequence of vague, unspecified purposes is the possibility that faculty members may direct their efforts toward minor or misinterpreted goals. For example, Richard Carlson (1964) has suggested that teachers of lower-class children may substitute maintaining discipline and control for the goal of educating students.

Kenneth Clark (1965, p. 128) observes that grouping students in ghetto schools often has these consequences:

Once one organizes an educational system where children are placed in tracks or where certain judgments about their ability determine what is done for them or how much they are taught or not taught, the horror is that the results seem to justify the assumptions. The use of intelligence test scores to brand children for life, to determine education based upon tracks and homogeneous groupings of children, impose on our public school system an intolerable and undemocratic social hierarchy and defeat the initial purposes of public education. They induce and perpetuate the very pathology which they claim to remedy. Children who are treated as if they are uneducable almost invariably become uneducable. . . . Many children are now systematically characterized, classified in groups labeled slow learners, trainables, untrainables, Track A, Track B, the "Pussycats," the "Bunnies," etc. But it all adds up to the fact that they are not being taught; and not being taught, they fail.

The Coleman Report (1966), sponsored by the U.S. Office of Education, measured skills in reading, writing, calculating, and problem-solving through standardized achievement tests administered to 645,000 children in grades one, three, six, nine, and twelve in 4,000 schools in all fifty states and the District of Columbia. The tests were not intended to measure students' intelligence, attitudes, or character, but rather the technical skills needed to help a student along toward a career. On all the tests administered, students from minority groups—Indian Americans, Mexican Americans, Puerto Ricans, and Blacks—scored substantially below white students. The report also revealed that, while black and other minority students are shortchanged in school achievement, so are large numbers of white students.

Shortly after the Coleman Report (1969), controversy arose about the Jensen hypothesis that black-white IQ differences are largely genetic in origin. Considerable data have been amassed refuting Jensen's argument and substantiating the Coleman Report's high correlation between low socioeconomic position and low academic achievement (Kagan 1969; Hunt 1961, 1969; Elkind 1969). A typical study is that of Richard Cloward and James Jones (1964) in which the investigators concluded that slum youths share the same aspirations as other American youths but are blocked, by discrimination and other reasons largely beyond their control, from reaching these goals.

A New York State case study of two inner-city schools, *School Factors Influencing Reading Achievement* (1974), shows that school practices do affect reading and implies that children in low-achieving schools should have the opportunities available to children in high-achieving schools. The study compared two New York City elementary schools in depth. The schools were matched on socioeconomic factors, ethnic composition, second languages, and pupil mobility. The training, experience, and competence of the classroom teachers as well as equipment and resources were all comparable. Achievement in reading was the evaluative criterion. One school made much greater gains than the other. The school with higher gains had identified reading as a significant school goal, had developed a coherent plan of action to provide leadership to classroom teachers, and had succeeded in creating an atmosphere in which learning could take place. In the low-achieving school, administrative behavior, policies, and practices seemed to account for the difference. The study's conclusions (p. 21) emphasized that,

although nonschool factors cannot be ignored, school factors can be much more significant than [is] generally acknowledged. The stress on nonschool factors too often leads to a justification for failure which then leads educators to act as if the children cannot learn, which in turn produces an atmosphere in which the children in fact do not learn. Thus the prophecy that the children could not learn has become the means of fulfilling itself. It is important that educators look carefully at how schools can be used and changed to improve learning rather than to be pessimistic about their impact.

Ralph Tyler, who has been involved in assessment of American education since the 1930s, has observed (1968, p. 209) in a similar vein:

Our failure to educate most of these children is not due primarily to their inherent inadequacies but rather to the inappropriateness of the typical school program. . . . Most of the children who do not attain an education find the school alien to earlier experiences and a source of failure and rejection. Many children from minority groups have not had extensive experience with American standard dialect, they have not had parents read to them, they have not seen family or friends devoting major attention to reading. They find the school work in reading foreign to their home experience and frequently fail to carry on the tasks expected. In this way they lose the zest of learning and have an increasing sense of failure while in school. As they lose interest and confidence in the early months, they fall behind the majority of children more and more so that they finish school or drop out without reaching a level of education on which to base a constructive life. Until recently this state of affairs was, oddly, accepted and tolerated, as statistics on adult illiteracy revealed. Now that we see that an adult illiterate can find no constructive role in a modern society, we can no longer tolerate failure to teach children to read. Massive efforts are needed.

David Livingstone (1970, pp. 15-16) reviewed a considerable body of literature on goals, priorities, and means, and he concludes that the most indispensable activities needed in the field of education today are goal formation and determination of goal priorities, evaluation of the adequacy of existing or proposed means for attaining these goals, analysis of the influences on existing means, estimation of future influences on means, suggestion of desirable means to enable future goal attainment, and selection of the most practical, desirable future goals and actions to implement them. Democratic goals require democratic means.

## DEMOCRATIC MEANS

The philosophy of Paulo Freire (1970) offers insights in our search for democratic means in the educative process. Freire's conviction, supported by a wide background of experience, is that every human being, no matter how ignorant or submerged he or she may be, is capable of looking critically at his or her world in dialogue with others. The business of the school is to provide the proper tools for dialogue so that the individual can gradually perceive his or her personal and social reality and deal critically with it. Freire's writings have applications not only in the field of education but also in the struggle for national development. They emphasize that pedagogy— the learning experience—must be forged *with* not *for* individuals and groups. Thinking must lead to action, thus constituting an authentic praxis, which can be achieved only when the leaders believe in the ability of the people to reason. Freire says (p. 52):

> Critical and liberating dialogue, which presupposes action, must be carried on with the oppressed at whatever the stage of their struggle for liberation. The content of that dialogue can and should vary in accordance with historical conditions and the level at which the oppressed perceive reality. But to substitute monologue, slogans, and communiques for dialogue is to attempt to liberate the oppressed with the instruments of domestication . . . and transform them into masses which can be manipulated.

Throughout his writings, Freire stresses the importance of "generative themes"—the dialogue of education as the practice of freedom. Dialogue, in Freire's view, affords the participants the opportunity to discover generative themes and to stimulate their personal awareness in relation to these themes. Man has the ability to create culture, to transform reality, by drawing on ideas and concepts of the past, the present, and the future.

Frederick Mayer (1973) provides further philosophical insights into the construction of democratic means. He speaks of the "perennial pilgrimage of democracy," which is the "affirmation of man and his wider community." In the schools, democratic means are those that demand the most intense degree of rationality, the broadest humanity, and the most fervent participation. The school must set the climate for a democracy, asserts Mayer (pp. 24-25):

> Without genuine concern and humanitarian agitation, democracy is a pretense. This implies a constant reform of institutions so that the needs of the individual

are recognized and so that rules and standards do not become coercive. . . . Democracy does not start when one becomes an adult; it must be embodied as much in kindergarten as in graduate school, in the home as well as in other social institutions. . . . To be proficient in knowledge is not enough. A new society of genuine democracy requires active learning and autonomous motivation. It requires a missionary spirit without fanaticism. The joys of culture are to be universalized, the benefits of freedom are to be shared, the citadels of ignorance and regression are to be conquered, the deserts of physical and spiritual poverty are to be transformed.

Mayer emphasizes that democratic means in the educative process reach beyond the boundaries of the school to all ages. Learning has no limitation, and the social and political institutions have a responsibility for determining the effectiveness of learning; but, in Mayer's view, democracy requires the school, of all institutions, to be the main source of learning and social change.

## APPLICATIONS TO CURRICULUM DEVELOPMENT

Two factors emerge from the literature as critical for attaining the broad goals of American democracy through educational means that are consonant with democratic ideals: (1) the attitudes and behavior of the curriculum specialist (including the teacher and the administrator), and (2) the nature of attention given in the classroom to major social and political issues of our time and of the future.

Freire's (1970) sharp insights are again appropriate. Too many students today, he says, from kindergarten to university, view the educational system as their enemy. He attributes this attitude to the relationship between teachers and students. Education is suffering from "narration sickness," in which the teacher talks about the world as if it were motionless, static, compartmentalized, and predictable, says Freire; or else the teacher expounds on topics completely alien to the experience of the students. Coining the term *banking education*, Freire defines it as education that is an act of depositing, in which the students are the depositories and the teacher is the depositor. The scope of action allowed to the students is merely receiving, filing, and storing the deposits. Freire emphasizes that, unless the mode of inquiry is present, permitting creativity, transformation, and the emergence of new knowledge through invention and reinvention, schooling falls into the structure of oppression.

Michael Scriven (1972, pp. 168-69) sharply calls to our attention some current deficiencies in curriculum development in terms of democratic means and goals:

I do not know any public high school offering courses on comparative contemporary systems of ethics, or on moral argumentation, as part of their normal curriculum. The latter deficiencies are too often explained in terms of the separation of church and state, a remark so shocking as to constitute a one-item proof of the essential immorality and practical absurdity of American public education. If the educators themselves do not realize that the democratic commitment to equal rights is a *secular moral* commitment—indeed, [if they] think the italicized terms are incompatible—how can education hope to preserve that commitment?

John Fischer's (1973, p. 11) observations concerning education in relation to the Watergate episode, while deploring the quality of national leadership, remind us of curriculum responsibilities:

A matter more fundamental than character weakness in a few dozen individuals is the failure of our system of universal education to engender in our population as a whole a keener appreciation of moral values, a higher level of expectation toward our political system, and higher standards for judging our elected officials.

Lest we overstress the negative criticisms of the schools, we should move on to positive suggestions for the curriculum specialist. Michael Hinkemeyer (1974) emphasizes the necessity of providing opportunities for participation by the student in the process of shaping his or her own education, as opposed to the ironic situation in which the curriculum specialist or teacher selects "democratic objectives" for the student. Instead, Hinkemeyer proposes a different kind of objective altogether, encompassing both recognition of values and provision for participation by the student in the process of shaping his or her own education. The school, he suggests (p. 117), would be:

1. Offering the student a series of experiences, and the opportunity to develop his own experiences, which may lead to an understanding of the various forces contributing to the rights and responsibilities of American citizens.

2. Offering and developing experiences relating to the inception and evolution of law in human societies, of the function of law, intended and actual, and of its benefits and misapplications. Studying the use of law as a many-faceted political instrument.

3. Offering and developing experiences leading to a basis upon which to learn more of the various methods, or models, which men have used throughout history to solve their problems.

4. Offering and developing experiences which may lead to extrapolations

regarding the evolution and development of identity symbols among nations and peoples.

5. Offering and developing experiences in ideology and political conflict, based on the claims and counterclaims of rival philosophies.

Schools should create conditions in which students are encouraged to ask, debate, and discuss, said Alvin Toffler in an interview with James Morisseau (1973) regarding educating for the future. Students should explore such topics as politics, religion, sex, drugs, and the morality of different kinds of work. The nature of the future that is rapidly approaching demands variety, creativity, individuality, and a social consciousness with mutuality of responsibility for problem-solving.

These examples are given to illustrate the significance of the concept of introducing students (young and old) to critical forms of thinking about their world, and the concept of affirming people as beings in the process of becoming—constantly attempting to be more human not only individually but also in fellowship and cooperation with others.

Henry Steele Commager, in an address to a national audience of teachers (1974), called on the schools to restore faith in the viability of our democratic and constitutional institutions, to reassert standards of civic virtue, and to create an educational, social, and moral system that will discover and encourage the leadership we must have to solve our problems. The basic problem posed by Watergate and all its repercussions is moral, not merely constitutional or political. Democracy is inescapably a moral goal of the schools and hence of curriculum development.

## SUMMARY

Support for the proposition on democracy is drawn from philosophers, observers of democratic and undemocratic practices, and several investigative studies. Democracy is viewed as a moral goal of the educative process and of American society. The aim is to achieve a school and a society characterized by respect for each person's worth and by opportunities for each to fulfill his or her potential. Dilemmas of democracy are abundant, but they must not cause us to abandon democracy; rather we need to engage in cooperative study and action to move toward the ideals of democracy. In schools, both good news and bad news can be told about the status of democratic practices. Gaps have occurred between principles and practices, but democratic means and processes are available to us, and curriculum development, though only a part of the whole educational enterprise, can exercise a decisive influence on American education by exemplifying the use of democratic means to reach democratic ends.

## REFERENCES

Anderson, Terryl. "A Broader View of Democracy." *Phi Delta Kappan* 54 (January 1973): 319-20.

Bloom, Benjamin S. *Stability and Change in Human Characteristics.* New York: John Wiley, 1964.

Broudy, Harry S. "Democratic Values and Educational Goals." In *The Curriculum: Retrospect and Prospect*, part I, pp. 113-52. Seventieth Yearbook of the National Society for the Study of Education. Chicago: University of Chicago Press, 1971.

Buckwalter, Doyle W. "The American Dilemma." *Social Studies* 64 (January 1973): 3-10.

Carlson, Richard O. "Environmental Constraints and Organizational Consequences: The Public School and Its Clients." In *Behavioral Science and Educational Administration*, part II, pp. 262-76. Sixty-third Yearbook of the National Society for the Study of Education. Chicago: University of Chicago Press, 1964.

Clark, Kenneth. *Dark Ghetto.* New York: Harper and Row, 1965.

Cloward, Richard A., and Jones, James A. "Social Class: Educational Attitudes and Participation." In *Nurturing Individual Potential*, edited by A. Harry Passow, pp. 66-91. Washington, D.C.: Association for Supervision and Curriculum Development, 1964.

Coleman, James S., et al. *Equality of Educational Opportunity.* Washington, D.C.: U.S. Government Printing Office, 1966.

Commager, Henry Steele. "Watergate and the Schools." *Today's Education* 63 (September-October 1974): 20-24.

Dewey, John. *Experience and Education.* New York: Collier Books, 1938.

———. "Democracy and Educational Administration." *School and Society* 45 (3 April 1937): 457-62.

———. *Democracy and Education.* New York: Macmillan, 1916.

Elkind, David. "Piagetian and Psychometric Conceptions of Intelligence." *Harvard Educational Review* 39 (spring 1969): 319-37.

Fischer, John H. "Education and the Commonweal: Observations after Watergate." *Phi Delta Kappan* 55 (September 1973): 10-12.

Flanagan, John C. "Functional Education for the Seventies." *Phi Delta Kappan* 49 (September 1967): 27-32.

Freire, Paulo. *Pedagogy of the Oppressed.* New York: Seabury Press, 1970.

Fromm, Erich. *The Heart of Man*. New York: Harper and Row, 1968.

Gardner, John W. "Reordering National Priorities." *Today's Education* 62 (January 1973): 14-17.

Goodlad, John I., and Klein, M. Frances. *Behind the Classroom Door*. Worthington, Ohio: Charles A. Jones, 1970.

Hinkemeyer, Michael T. "Societal Values: A Challenge to the Curriculum Specialist." *Social Studies* 65 (March 1974): 114-18.

Hodgkinson, Christopher. "Why Democracy Won't Work." *Phi Delta Kappan* 54 (January 1973): 316-17.

Hunt, J. McVicar. "Has Compensatory Education Failed? Has It Been Attempted?" *Harvard Educational Review* 39 (spring 1969): 278-300.

————. *Intelligence and Experience*. New York: Ronald Press, 1961.

Jensen, Arthur K. "How Much Can We Boost IQ and Scholastic Achievement?" *Harvard Educational Review* 39 (winter 1969): 1-123.

Kagan, Jerome S. "Inadequate Evidence and Illogical Conclusions." *Harvard Educational Review* 39 (spring 1969): 274-77.

Livingstone, David W. "Alternative Futures for Formal Education." *Interchange* 1, no. 4 (1970): 13-27.

Machiavelli, Niccolo. *The Prince*. Edited by Lester G. Crocker. New York: Washington Square Press, 1963.

MacLeish, Archibald. "To Make Men Free." *Atlantic*, November 1951, pp. 27-30.

Mayer, Frederick. *Education for a New Society*. Bloomington, Ind.: Phi Delta Kappa Educational Foundation, 1973.

Morisseau, James J. "A Conversation with Alvin Toffler." *National Elementary Principal* 52 (January 1973): 8-18.

Myrdal, Gunnar. *An American Dilemma*. New York: Harper and Row, 1962.

Newmann, Fred M., and Oliver, Donald W. *Clarifying Public Controversy*. Boston: Little, Brown, 1970.

Rader, Benjamin G. "Jacksonian Democracy: Myth or Reality?" *Social Studies* 65 (January 1974): 17-22.

*School Factors Influencing Reading Achievement: A Case Study of Two Inner City Schools*. Albany, N.Y.: State Office of Education Performance Review, n.d. (probably 1974).

Scriven, Michael. "Education for Survival." In *Curriculum and the Cultural Revolution*, edited by David E. Purpel and Maurice Belanger, pp. 166-204. Berkeley: McCutchan, 1972.

Silberman, Charles E. *Crisis in the Classroom*. New York: Random House, 1970.

*Task Force Report on Easing Educational Tensions*. Washington, D.C.: U.S. Government Printing Office, 1970.

Tyler, Ralph W. "Investing in Better Schools." In *Agenda for the Nation*, edited by Kermit Gordon, pp. 207-36. Washington, D.C.: Brookings Institution, 1968.

## ADDITIONAL READINGS

Carnoy, Martin. *Education as Cultural Imperialism*. New York: David McKay, 1974.

Gartner, Alan, and Riessman, Frank. "Strategies for Large-Scale Education Reform." *Teachers College Record* 75 (February 1974): 349-56.

Gordon, Ira J. *On Early Learning: The Modifiability of Human Potential*. Washington, D.C.: Association for Supervision and Curriculum Development, 1971.

Longstreet, Wilma S. *Beyond Jencks: The Myth of Equal Schooling*. Washington, D.C.: Association for Supervision and Curriculum Development, 1973.

Mason, Robert E. *Educational Ideals in American Society*. Boston: Allyn and Bacon, 1960.

Newmann, Fred M., and Oliver, Donald W. "Education and Community." *Harvard Educational Review* 37 (winter 1967): 61-106.

Wasserman, Miriam. *Demystifying School*. New York: Praeger, 1974.

# CHAPTER NINE

# Future Awareness and
# Planned Change

PROPOSITION: If there is a commitment to planned change, the curriculum development process will become responsive to dynamic and futuristic technological and social developments.

Planning, as a means for reaching future-aware goals, has new significance for curriculum development in today's rapidly moving society. Planned change, effectively demonstrated in such fields as medicine, forestry, city planning, communications technology, air and space travel, and organizational development, has implications for education. Adaptations and learning from these fields can be used in curriculum planning.

*Planning* is defined as the art or process of making or carrying out plans by establishing goals, policies, and procedures. A *plan* is a detailed formulation of a program of action, an orderly arrangement of parts of an overall design for meeting objectives. The idea of a plan includes two elements: proposed goals to be achieved and arrangements decided on to achieve the goals. The key to successful planning lies in choosing among alternative methods for reaching a given set of goals. This requires selection and analysis of data about the optimum choices among courses of action.

*Planned change* involves mutual goal-setting and a conscious, deliberative, and collaborative effort to apply appropriate knowledge systematically to human affairs so that procedures can be designed for reaching the goals. Planned change forms connectives between theory and practice and between knowledge and action. Planned change in the context of this proposition emphasizes humanistic and democratic processes—freedom, creativity, and individuality through planning. Planned change is based on the concepts of open systems; this implies that the parts are related to each other in a manner that will lead to the achievement of goals. The tools of systems approaches, when used in open systems, are potentially powerful techniques for planning more humane, more farsighted, and more democratic futures. (For an extensive discussion of systems concepts in relation to responsiveness in curriculum development, see chapter twelve.)

Planned change, as conceived in this chapter, is essential if curriculum development is to become less subject to conflicting and competing pressures, if it is to progress beyond either/or approaches, and if it is to grow more responsive to social and personal needs. From an extensive analysis of the literature on educational change, Louis Maguire (1970, p. 11) concludes:

Planned change is emphasized in education because the alternative is to be buffeted about by the pressures and demands of a society that clamors for educational services of many kinds, because it considers the mechanisms of change and the techniques for guiding the process toward desired end results, and because it is the only viable alternative for producing the dramatic and startling changes that are needed in education today.

Unplanned change in education cannot bring about the major and massive improvements that are needed. Educators sometimes react to pressure for change as though any kind of change were certain to be beneficial. Roger Kaufman (1970) reminds us that, although change is inevitable and the concept of change surrounds us these days, with much being written about it in education, the question educators must face is whether we will help to shape change as participants or whether we will be swept along with it as spectators. Martin Engel (1974), speaking to this, notes that vocal assertions about the universal need for change and for appropriate responsiveness must first be met with several questions: Responsiveness to whom? Real fundamental change or merely the tinkering and tampering of annual cosmetic model changes? Greater efficiency in what is now being done, or the doing of something quite different? Alvin Toffler (1970, p. 486) emphasizes that change is essential to man, is life itself, "but change rampant, change unguided and unrestrained, accelerated change overwhelming not only man's physical defenses but his decisional processes—such change is the enemy of life."

## ATTITUDES TOWARD CHANGE AND PLANNING

A critical view of education is expressed by James Cass (1974), who says that education has sometimes been characterized as the third most authoritarian profession in society—outranked only by the armed services and the police. Cass asserts that "education clearly fosters an environment that does not encourage independent thinkers or creative individuals, nor can it be expected to welcome fundamental change in the schools." If this statement is accurate, planned change is a necessity in our educational programs, although it is not always welcome.

John Goodlad's five-year study of the process of change in elementary schools is being published in a seven-volume series. The first volume, edited by Carmen Culver and Gary Hoban (1974), reviews the difficulties of bringing about fundamental change and reform, either in institutions or in individuals. Schools must provide an environment in which the pervasive desire for improvement can be supported and the natural creativity of a high proportion of teachers can be released. In their survey, Goodlad and his colleagues found that virtually every school has a nucleus of teachers profoundly concerned with improving the educational process—teachers who are hungry for ideas and eager to learn what is going on around the country. But individual teachers or even small groups of teachers are not able to launch fundamental changes without specific support mechanisms to encourage them.

At the crux of this problem is the dilemma of bringing together knowledge and action, a dilemma noted in chapter eight. It is obvious that far greater use of knowledge is needed as well as far greater collaboration between practitioners and researchers. George Kelly

(1969) reviews the state of naiveté of educational and social planning, both presently and historically. He notes (p. 24) that persons in influential positions seem to resist the effort, involvement, and collaboration required for planning fundamental changes to meet critical and pressing problems in both school and society; instead they "seem to rely on God, or magic, or science, or politics for solutions."

Several other barriers to planned change are obvious. The resource limitations of a given school district or educational unit may prevent it from using adequate planning processes. As noted by Alan Thomas (1974), decisions based on systematically collected data are initially more expensive than ad hoc decisions based on the personal judgments of an individual or a group. Competition for slices of a fixed financial pie usually increases pressure to base decisions on the emotional appeal of or reaction to those who are most vocal in expressing their concerns and complaints. Planning by a group that disregards the total context may impose requirements or hardships on other groups. John Galbraith (1974), who also examines problems in planning, suggests that the solution is to recognize the logic of planning with its resulting imperative of coordination.

Toffler (1970), in his studies of futures research, found "a strange coalition of right-wingers and new leftists" calling for nonplanning and advocating a "hang loose" approach to the future. One teenage girl remarked, "If you stay anywhere very long you get into a planning thing . . . so you just move on." Her statement implies that planning imposes values on the future; but the antiplanners overlook the fact that nonplanning does so too—often with far worse consequences. Angered by the narrow, materialistic character of technocratic planning, they condemn systems concepts and similar methods related to planning. Toffler concludes (pp. 451-52):

When critics charge that technocratic planning is antihuman, in the sense that it neglects social, cultural and psychological values in its headlong rush to maximize economic gain, they are usually right. When they charge that it is shortsighted and undemocratic, they are usually right. When they charge it is inept, they are usually right.

But when they plunge backward into irrationality, antiscientific attitudes, a kind of sick nostalgia, and an exaltation of now-ness, they are not only wrong, but dangerous. Just as, in the main, their alternatives to industrialism call for a return to pre-industrial institutions, their alternative to technocracy is not post-, but pre-technocracy.

Nothing could be more dangerously maladaptive. Whatever the theoretical arguments may be, brute forces are loose in the world. Whether we wish to prevent future shock or control population, to check pollution or defuse the arms race, we cannot permit decisions of earth-jolting importance to be taken heedlessly, planlessly. To hang loose is to commit collective suicide. . . .

We can invent a form of planning more humane, more farsighted, and more democratic than any so far in use. In short, we can transcend technocracy.

## HISTORICAL PHASES OF PLANNING

Karl Mannheim's (1961) studies of man and society trace the stages of planning back to primitive man, relate growth in thinking to growth in planning, and indicate the significance of planning in advancing societies. The first traces of thinking were characterized by chance discoveries preceded by trial and error. A second phase in the history of thought Mannheim identifies as inventing, in which man has somewhat limited and immediate goals and sets himself tasks to reach his goals, but he depends on natural selection and social processes. In the stage of inventing, man rationalizes and suppresses according to both individual and societal necessities and adaptations, which in their turn were not created by the people affected.

Mannheim advocates advancement to another stage, that of planning or planned thinking, in which man and society move toward intelligent mastery of the relationships of a multidimensional environment. An essential element in the planning stage is that man not only thinks out individual aims but also attempts to grasp a whole complex of events and guide the cycle of events. Planning avoids the problem of static structures by continuously accommodating to change. Mannheim continues (p. 38):

Discovery and invention by no means lose their function on the emergence of planning. But problems in thinking which can be solved only by planning cannot be left to discovery just as, on the other hand, planning always must build upon the stages of discovery and invention. In the same way, thinking in terms of interdependence (which is one aspect of planning) does not supersede abstraction with its separation of spheres. But one must know precisely how each stage of thought is related to the others and how they supplement one another.

In recent years the literature on planned change has increased. Contemporary conditions of social and technical change and increasing demands on the schools make a planning approach to curriculum development a necessity rather than an option. The curriculum requires a planning approach that maximizes freedom and realizes human dignity as well as bringing into fruition goals that are desirable for society.

## CURRICULUM PLANNING FOR A FREE SOCIETY

Ronald Lippitt (1965) relates planned change to curriculum-related needs and emphasizes the complex nature of the processes of change. Individuals and groups must be helped to see their particular area of involvement and responsibility, to collaborate in action research that discovers common interests from among conflicting interests, and to draw on the best available knowledge related to the mutual goals, the social forces and other factors bearing on the situation, and the likely consequences of alternative actions. Involvement requires not only retrieval of knowledge from various sources but also skills in creating and supporting a problem-solving approach.

John Dewey's philosophy is also consistent with that of contemporary advocates of planning. He rejected routine plans and programs handed down from the past, but stressed that progressive education is not a matter of planless improvisation; that "the central problem of education is to select the kind of present experiences that live fruitfully and creatively in subsequent experiences"; and that "growth is not enough; we must also specify the direction in which growth takes place, the end toward which it tends" (1938, pp. 28, 36).

Planning involves creativity and leadership, it recognizes polarizations, and it recognizes and attempts to bridge such either/or viewpoints as sameness versus diversity, the interests of the small unit as opposed to those of the whole, simple or complex problems, and order versus confusion. Planning leads to action, and action is effective when the essence of a need is found, when goals are valid, and when detailed, open, and observable planning is taking place.

Planning for change in a free and open society demands a commitment to a system of values to serve as criteria. Warren Bennis's studies of organizational behavior (1969) reveal that any change program involves a set of core values. These values emphasize man as a proactive, growth-seeking, inquiring, confronting person. In addition, the value system features an influence process that is transactional, meaning that the influence is a two-way process and that, regardless of status differences, there must be reciprocity if the decision is to be "owned" by all parties concerned.

Bennis states that *value power* is the strongest of the possible sources of power. Values based on humanism—concern for other persons, experimentalism, openness and honesty, flexibility, cooperation, and democracy—are the underlying values of planned change in the concept advocated here. Other sources of power, says Bennis, are relatively weak in comparison. Coercive power, which depends on rewards and punishment, is less durable, except under conditions of vigilant surveillance. Power stemming from the authority and credibility of experts and specialists who are advising a given group is transient and tends to weaken rapidly with the passage of time. Values that work toward liberation of the spirit and potential of people are the values that provide the driving force for planned change.

Bennis (1969, p. 573) notes a series of growing and fundamental changes that seems to be taking place gradually in the basic philosophy underlying managerial behavior, in educational planning as well as in business and industry. These changes are:

1. A new concept of *man*, based on increased knowledge of his complex and shifting needs, which replaces the oversimplified, innocent push-button idea of man.

2. A new concept of *power*, based on collaboration and reason, which replaces a model of power based on coercion and fear.

3. A new concept of *organizational values*, based on humanistic-democratic ideals, which replaces the depersonalized mechanistic value system of bureaucracy.

These transformations are not unanimously accepted or even understood, Bennis cautions, to say nothing of being widely implemented in day-to-day affairs. However, his studies indicate that they have gained wide intellectual acceptance in enlightened quarters. They have stimulated rethinking and consideration for the persons involved and are being used as a basis for policy formulation by many large-scale organizations.

## INTERDEPENDENCE IN CURRICULUM-PLANNING

Planning decisions in curriculum development relate to various kinds of problems at many policy and operational levels, all highly interdependent. Four major divisions of educational planning, identified by Marvin Alkin and James Bruno (1970) are: (1) economic planning, dealing with the allocation of resources to education; (2)

educational policy planning, dealing with choices among broad educational goals; (3) internal educational planning, dealing with choices among methods, media, and technologies; and (4) operational planning, dealing with choices among methods of implementation and methods of monitoring success and failure.

Responsiveness in curriculum development assumes a high degree of interdependence of elements and persons and an orderly approach to planned change. The elements of responsive change—humanistic values; democratic processes, goals, needs, objectives, policies, action programs, and evaluative processes; and interrelationships among the groups concerned with curriculum development—require a systems approach to planning if change is to endure. Changes brought about because of a selfish interest, an emergency, pressure from one group or another, or merely the charismatic quality of a leader may soon fade if procedures to ensure coordination in the planning process have not been carefully worked out.

Planned change, in the context of this chapter, depends on the use of open systems concepts as opposed to closed ones. Closed systems approaches to problems analyze them in terms of some internal structure and ignore external environments; for example, in planning a social studies curriculum, no regard may be given to contemporary and future societal issues and concerns. Open systems concepts imply a constant state of self-renewal. Such systems continuously reorganize to meet new problems, to examine new complexities, and to use new ideas and information as a part of the planning and renewal process (see chapter twelve).

Margaret Mead (1969), examining the concept of planning, admonishes us to ask ourselves whether we are open ended in our planning as well as in our plans and whether we are willing to sacrifice some kinds of apparent efficiency in large-scale planning. She notes that if we are willing to include numerous steps and a broad range of persons we are more likely to develop new and satisfactory interrelationships and understandings that were unforeseeable at any early stage. A special area of concern is the communication among all persons involved. Mead finds (pp. 567-68) that

the surest guarantee of change and growth is the inclusion of living persons in every stage of an activity. Their lives, their experience, and their continuing response—even their resistances—infuse with life any plan which, if living participants are excluded, lies on the drawing board and loses its reality. Plans for the future can become old before they are lived, but the future itself is always newborn and, like any newborn thing, is open to every kind of living experience.

Planning anticipates some future state of being, and planned change in curriculum development envisions ideal conditions of some sort that motivate, guide, and direct present actions. The rapid rate of change in contemporary society has produced dynamics that make planning difficult for curriculum developers who fail to become cognizant of futuristic technological and social developments. Finding direction for the future by projecting the forms of the past is obviously inadequate; the future will inevitably be different from the present. Thus, it behooves curriculum-planners to establish new contacts. They can expect confrontations and disagreements as responsiveness in curriculum development expands to include the contributions, needs, and interests of social classes, races, subcultures, and nations whose interdependence has not previously been widely recognized.

Vast networks presently illustrate many types of interdependence: technological media for instantaneous worldwide mass communication, global transportation, multinational corporations, and international political and economic arrangements are indicative of a changing world view. Future-oriented curriculum development necessarily commits itself more and more to the idea of planning. The planning process, by involving the human quest for self-awareness, by using reason to achieve and stretch human potential and possibilities, can open organizational operations to self-inquiry and analysis.

Useful strategies for effecting change and new methods of planning are emerging with applications to curriculum development. Several planning aids now in use can be of assistance. These are described only briefly here, as information on each is widely available.

## PLANNING AIDS

Planning-programming-budgeting systems (PPBS) are an analytic technique used to a limited extent in educational planning. Successful implementation of PPBS requires the participation and support of persons throughout the organization. It also requires a large body of systematically collected data about the students, the school system, the community, and the wider society. These data are needed to formulate meaningful objectives, both short-term and long-term. PPBS describes the various objectives of proposed educational programs and classifies proposed expenditures according to each objective. By relating objectives, programs, and expenditures to one another, PPBS enables decision-makers to consider all aspects of the planning process together. It avoids separate consideration of one aspect, such as the budget.

Simulation models are occasionally used in the planning process. Basically a simulation model is designed to portray a situation in the real world and enable planners to reach tentative conclusions about it. Simulations range from miniature mock-ups to role-playing or games in which improvisations attempt to project the consequences of various alternative courses of action as a means of assisting the decision-making process.

Delphi techniques are frequently used for obtaining certain kinds of input data. The Delphi technique is a procedure in which judgments are solicited from the participants or potential consumers of a curriculum development process or product through a series of questionnaires that are then combined and recirculated among the participants, possibly in several rounds, to obtain additional information and to reach a consensus on needs and priorities.

Program evaluation review techniques (PERT) depict a number of steps in a graphic presentation or flow chart that shows individual tasks and the time limits necessary for completing a project. The use of PERT or similar techniques can make planning more specific about the time required to complete each activity and the sequence of activities in the general flow of the plan.

## STRATEGIES FOR EFFECTING CHANGE

Three general types or groups of strategies for change identified by Robert Chin and Kenneth Benne (1969) are useful in analyzing techniques for planned change in curriculum development. Chin and Benne designate these the empirical-rational, normative-educative, and power-coercive strategies. The three families are shown in figure 3, grouped with the names of persons associated with the development of component ideas, points of view, or strategies for change. In adapting these general categories to their corollaries in planning for for change in curriculum development, I have renamed the terms empirical-rational, normative-educative, and power-coercive, using the terms enlightenment, reeducative, and coercive strategies, respectively.

*Enlightenment strategies* assume that people will follow rational interests, once these are revealed to them. In this category, some person or group who knows of a situation proposes a change that is desirable, effective, and in line with the interests of those who will be affected by the change. This strategy depends on building knowledge, diffusing the results of research, using experts as consultants, and clarifying definitions in order to communicate better and to reason more effectively, so that a realistic common basis can be established for acting and changing. A utopian ideal is emphasized as a goal. Difficulties in getting new knowledge into practice are frequently attributed to the lack of fitness of the persons whose job responsibility it is to improve practice. Thus, there is considerable emphasis on personnel selection and replacement. The enlightenment strategy, as noted by Chin and Benne, has been highly successful in technologies related to things, scientific research, and engineering problems. This kind of strategy has been less successful in areas that demand attention to people's attitudes and values and to considerations of social and cultural diversity.

*Reeducative strategies* are committed to releasing and fostering growth in the persons who make up the system to be changed. This approach emphasizes that persons are capable of self-respect and respect for each other in their responses, choices, and actions. Improving the problem-solving capabilities of the group is a major objective in the reeducative family of strategies, and the persons involved are as committed to reeducation of the participants as they are to effecting change in the system. Emphasis is on norms of openness of communication, trust between persons, lowering of status barriers between parts of the system, and mutual responsibilities for planning change. It is believed that creative adaptations to changing conditions may arise from within the group that is planning for change and do not necessarily have to be imported from outside. Effective conflict management is a part of the reeducative process.

Intelligence in action—Dewey's conception—is basic to this strategy. Dewey believed that our best hope for progress was for people to learn to use a broadened and humanized scientific method in facing problem situations. Chin and Benne note the contribution to

## FIGURE 3
### Strategies of Deliberate Change

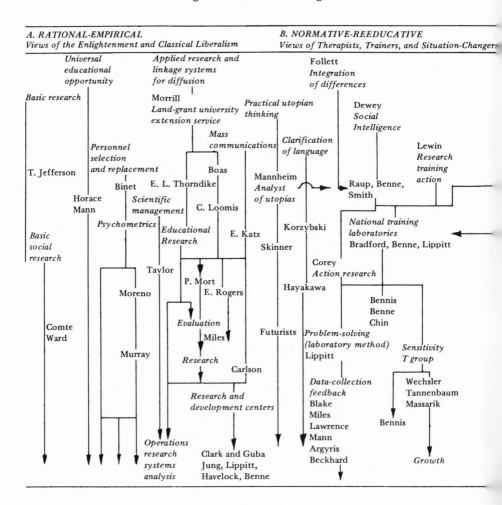

A. RATIONAL-EMPIRICAL
*Views of the Enlightenment and Classical Liberalism*

B. NORMATIVE-REEDUCATIVE
*Views of Therapists, Trainers, and Situation-Changers*

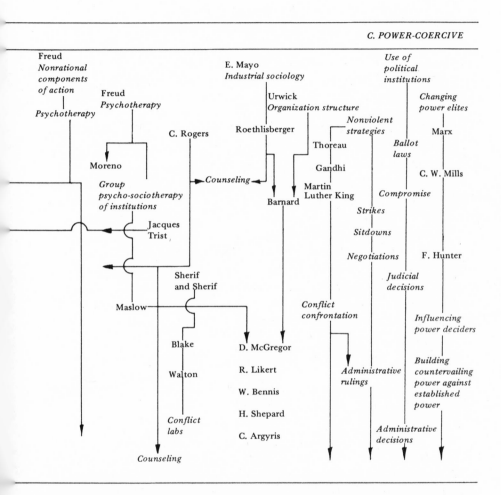

Freud
*Nonrational
components
of action*

*Psychotherapy*

Freud
*Psychotherapy*

Moreno

*Group
psycho-sociotherapy
of institutions*

C. Rogers

Jacques
Trist

*Counseling*

Maslow

Sherif
and Sherif

Blake

Walton

*Conflict
labs*

*Counseling*

E. Mayo
*Industrial sociology*

Urwick
*Organization structure*

Roethlisberger

Barnard

D. McGregor

R. Likert

W. Bennis

H. Shepard

C. Argyris

*Nonviolent
strategies*

Thoreau

Gandhi

Martin
Luther King

*Strikes*

*Sitdowns*

*Negotiations*

*Conflict
confrontation*

*Administrative
rulings*

*Administrative
decisions*

*C. POWER-COERCIVE*

*Use of
political
institutions*

*Changing
power elites*

Marx

*Ballot
laws*

C. W. Mills

*Compromise*

F. Hunter

*Judicial
decisions*

*Influencing
power deciders*

*Building
countervailing
power against
established
power*

From Robert Chin and Kenneth D. Benne, "General Strategies for Effecting Changes in Human Systems," in *The Planning of Change*, ed. by Warren G. Bennis, Kenneth D. Benne, and Robert Chin (New York: Holt, Rinehart and Winston, 1969), pp. 58-59. Reprinted by permission.

reeducative strategies of Kurt Lewin, who emphasized the interrelationships among research, training, and action in the solution of problems, in the identification of needs for change, and in the use of improved patterns of action in meeting these needs. The reeducative process would draw on research and knowledge, particularly through collaborative relationships among people.

*Coercive strategies* depend on the influence of one person or group on another. In the recent history of curriculum development, federal appropriations have exercised a coercive influence over the decisions of local school officials concerning various emphases in the school curriculum. Other examples of coercive power affecting curriculum development are judicial decisions supporting civil rights, legislative rulings regarding high school graduation requirements, and other administrative rulings on courses and programs to be offered. The coercive strategies depend on the management of power or the recomposition of a power group for change.

Curriculum workers, whether influenced by coercive strategies or by enlightenment strategies, still have considerable latitude for introducing democratic, reeducative methods of change. While curriculum developers must take account of actual concentrations of power wherever they work, reeducative strategies can find an appropriate place in the organizational arrangement.

## THE CURRICULUM WORKER AS CHANGE AGENT

The literature on planned change frequently uses the terms *change agent* and *client*. These terms may be traced back to *The Dynamics of Planned Change* (1958) by Ronald Lippitt et al. A change agent is the helper, leader, person, or group who is attempting to effect change. It may refer to a curriculum worker, a teacher, or a collaborative group of participants concerned with curriculum development in a given school district. The client is the person or group being helped, whether a student, teacher, group, organization, community, family, or other entity. In curriculum development, the clients are the consumers of the curriculum development products and processes. Change agents may also be members of the client system who have leadership responsibilities.

Bennis (1969) emphasizes that change agents (in this context, curriculum leaders) need more than energy and ambition. They must also have a professional attitude; be engaged in a self-educative process; be concerned with improvement, development, and measurement of organizational effectiveness; be highly interested in people and the process of human interaction; and be interested in changing the relationships, perceptions, and values of existing personnel, rather than replacing personnel as an expedient measure if problems arise.

The curriculum worker who aspires to become a change agent may find it useful to study models such as *The Managerial Grid* (1964) by Robert Blake and Jane Mouton. Through use of this analytic tool, a curriculum worker as change agent can estimate his or her approach to effective planning. At one extreme, the curriculum worker exerts minimum effort to get the required work done and maintain the status quo. At a more desirable extreme, work is accomplished by committed people whose interdependence in a common purpose leads to relationships of trust and respect. One area of the grid notes a style that mainly aims to keep people happy. While a leader may give thoughtful attention to the needs of people for satisfying relationships, a comfortable, friendly organizational atmosphere, and a relaxed work tempo, this style may be unproductive in the process of planning change to improve curriculum development.

Douglas McGregor (1960) describes and compares an authoritarian approach (Theory X) and a democratic and humanistic approach (Theory Y). Care must be taken to study these theories in depth and not translate them superficially to practice. Theory Y, for example, may be mistaken for a laissez-faire approach. Sheldon Davis (1969) describes a situation in which McGregor's intent was misinterpreted: A key person in an organization presented some work for approval to his supervisor; the supervisor did not like the quality of the work and said so; his subordinate pointed out that his people had worked very hard in producing the work and were highly committed to it; the supervisor then said, "Okay, in that case, let's go ahead." To Davis, this is an example not of McGregor's Theory Y but rather of soft, irrational human relationships that are not task-oriented.

An example of a different approach is also described by Davis: A department head discovered that a certain procedure hampered his effectiveness; he sought to get the procedure modified, but was told by his administrator that this was impossible—the procedure covered several departments and for that reason alone could not be modified. Furthermore, said the administrator, any change would be sure to raise the ire of at least one head of another division. The department head refused to accept the explanation and personally called a meeting of his administrator and three other heads of divisions. Within an hour the procedure was modified in the direction he had suggested.

These examples illustrate contrasting change agent approaches. The curriculum worker as change agent is confronted by a wide range of human problems that must be considered in planning for change: (1) problems of compatibility between individual needs and institutional goals, (2) problems related to the distribution of power, (3) problems related to managing and resolving conflicts, (4) problems of responding appropriately to changes in the societal environment, and (5) problems posed by future thinking versus status quo thinking.

## DYNAMICS OF CHANGE

Twentieth-century developments are contributing knowledge and conditions for positive change in a variety of ways:

1. The emergence of human sciences and greater understanding of human complexity are accompanied by rising aspirations and strengthening of the humanistic-democratic ethos.

2. Leadership studies and practices reveal not only an ethical component to the problem of power but also an effectiveness component: people tend to work more efficiently and with more commitment when they have a part in determining their own fate and have a stake in problem-solving.

3. Leadership is now viewed as too complex for one-man rule or omniscience; the increased need for interdependence enters into the need for professionalism in managing and resolving conflicts.

4. While external environments are more turbulent and less predictable, and rapid changes in technologies, tasks, manpower, raw materials, and norms can be expected, constant examination of the goals of society and education and general acknowledgment of the need for attention to the processes of change are engendering an attitude of constant revision and planned change (see Bennis 1969, pp. 574-75).

## SUMMARY

The proposition on planned change is supported more by rationality of argument and descriptions of related experiences than by carefully controlled research studies. Attitudes that form barriers to planning and the historical and philosophical arguments for planned change are discussed. Resistance to mechanistic systems approaches is noted, and closed systems are contrasted to open systems, which can make possible the humanizing of education. Curriculum-planning for a free society must systematically provide for creativity, leadership, freedom, and value development. Planned change is built on collaboration among people working toward mutual goals.

Strategies for planned change are analyzed in reference to three broad groupings, each of which draws on the work of distinguished specialists in related fields. The dynamics of change are shown to be logical sources of strength that can be directed toward curriculum development processes to match futuristic technological and social developments.

## REFERENCES

Alkin, Marvin C., and Bruno, James E. "System Approaches to Educational Planning." In *Social and Technological Change: Implications for Education*, edited by Philip K. Piele, Terry L. Eidell, and Stuart C. Smith, pp. 189-244. Eugene: Center for the Advanced Study of Educational Administration, University of Oregon, 1970.

Banghart, Frank W., and Trull, Albert, Jr. *Educational Planning*. New York: Macmillan, 1973.

Bennis, Warren G. "Changing Organizations." In *The Planning of Change*, edited by Warren G. Bennis, Kenneth D. Benne, and Robert Chin, pp. 568-79. 2d ed. New York: Holt, Rinehart and Winston, 1969.

Blake, Robert R., and Mouton, Jane. *The Managerial Grid*. Houston: Gulf Publishing, 1964.

Cass, James. "An Environment for Creative Teachers." *Saturday Review of the World*, 6 April 1974, p. 51.

Chin, Robert, and Benne, Kenneth D. "General Strategies for Effecting Changes in Human Systems." In *The Planning of Change*, edited by Warren G. Bennis, Kenneth D. Benne, and Robert Chin, pp. 357-70. 2d ed. New York: Holt, Rinehart and Winston, 1969.

Culver, Carmen, and Hoban, Gary, eds. *The Power to Change: Issues for the Innovative Educator*, vol. 1. 7 vols. New York: McGraw-Hill, 1974.

Davis, Sheldon A. "An Organic Problem-solving Method of Organizational

Change." In *The Planning of Change*, edited by Warren G. Bennis, Kenneth D. Benne, and Robert Chin, pp. 357-70. 2d ed. New York: Holt, Rinehart and Winston, 1969.

Dewey, John. *Experience and Education*. New York: Collier Books, 1938.

Engel, Martin. "Politics and Prerequisites in Educational Change." *Phi Delta Kappan* 55 (March 1974): 457-58.

Galbraith, John K. *Economics and the Public Purpose*. Boston: Houghton Mifflin, 1973.

Kaufman, Roger A. "System Approaches to Education: Discussion and Attempted Integration." In *Social and Technological Change: Implications for Education*, edited by Philip K. Piele, Terry L. Eidell, and Stuart C. Smith, pp. 121-90. Eugene: Center for the Advanced Study of Educational Administration, University of Oregon, 1970.

Kelly, George A. "The Expert as Historical Actor." In *The Planning of Change*, edited by Warren G. Bennis, Kenneth D. Benne, and Robert Chin, pp. 14-32. 2d ed. New York: Holt, Rinehart and Winston, 1969.

Lippitt, Ronald. "Roles and Processes in Curriculum Development and Change." In *Strategy for Curriculum Change*, pp. 11-28. Washington, D.C.: Association for Supervision and Curriculum Development, 1965.

Lippitt, Ronald; Watson, Jeanne; and Westley, Bruce. *The Dynamics of Planned Change*. New York: Harcourt, Brace and World, 1958.

McGregor, Douglas. *The Human Side of Enterprise*. New York: McGraw-Hill, 1960.

Maguire, Louis M. *Observations and Analysis of the Literature on Change*. Philadelphia: Research for Better Schools, 1970.

Mannheim, Karl. "From Trial and Error to Planning." In *The Planning of Change*, edited by Warren G. Bennis, Kenneth D. Benne, and Robert Chin, pp. 34-37. New York: Holt, Rinehart and Winston, 1961.

Mead, Margaret. "The Future as the Basis for Establishing a Shared Culture." In *The Planning of Change*, edited by Warren G. Bennis, Kenneth D. Benne, and Robert Chin, pp. 552-67. 2d ed. New York: Holt, Rinehart and Winston, 1969.

Thomas, J. Alan. "Educational Planning in School Districts." *Administrator's Notebook* 2, no. 7 (1974): 1-4. Published by the Midwest Administration Center, University of Chicago.

Toffler, Alvin. *Future Shock*. New York: Bantam Books, 1970.

## ADDITIONAL READINGS

Browder, Lesley H; Atkins, William A., Jr.; and Kaya, Esin. *Developing an Educationally Accountable Program*, pp. 106-27. Berkeley: McCutchan, 1973.

Clegg, Ambrose A. "The Teacher as Manager of the Curriculum." *Educational Leadership* 30 (January 1973): 307-9.

French, Wendell L., and Bell, Cecil H., Jr. *Organizational Development*. Englewood Cliffs, N.J.: Prentice-Hall, 1973.

Green, Thomas, ed. *Educational Planning in Perspective*. Guildford, England: IPC Science and Technology Press, 1971.

Henson, Kenneth T. "Future Education: A Systematic Approach?" *Educational Leadership* 30 (April 1973): 652-55.

Kaufman, Roger A. *Educational System Planning*. Englewood Cliffs, N.J.: Prentice-Hall, 1972.

Knezevich, Stephen J. *Program Budgeting (PPBS)*. Berkeley: McCutchan, 1973.

Miles, Matthew B., ed. *Innovation in Education*. New York: Bureau of Publications, Teachers College, Columbia University, 1964.

Miller, Donald R. *A Strategy for Planned Change in Education*. San Mateo, Calif.: County Board of Education, 1970.

Miller, Richard I., ed. *Perspectives on Educational Change*. New York: Appleton-Century-Crofts, 1967.

Morphet, Edgar L., and Ryan, C. O., eds. *Planning and Effecting Needed Changes in Education*. Denver: Publishers Press, 1967.

Ozbeckhan, Hasan. "The Emerging Methodology of Planning." *Fields within Fields* no. 10 (winter 1973-74): 63-80. Published by the World Institute Council, United Nations Plaza, New York.

Platt, John. "What's Ahead for 1990?" *National Elementary Principal* 52 (January 1973): 19-27.

Rippey, Robert M., ed. *Studies in Transactional Evaluation*. Berkeley: McCutchan, 1973.

Sarason, Seymour B. *The Culture of the School and the Problem of Change*. Boston: Allyn and Bacon, 1971.

Shane, Harold G. "Future Planning as a Means of Shaping Educational Change." In *The Curriculum: Retrospect and Prospect*, part I, pp. 185-218. Seventieth Yearbook of the National Society for the Study of Education. Chicago: University of Chicago Press, 1971.

Shostak, Arthur B. "Tomorrow's Reform Agenda." *Futurist* 7 (June 1973): 107-10.

Wolf, W. C., Jr., and Fiorino, A. John. "Some Perspectives of Educational Change." *Educational Forum* 38 (November 1973): 79-84.

# CHAPTER TEN

# Need as a Factor in Curriculum Development

PROPOSITION: If there is a more comprehensive assessment of needs, the curriculum development process will be more responsive to both individual and group concerns.

*Need*, as a fundamental consideration in curriculum development, is defined as the difference between existing actuality and envisioned ideal circumstances. *Needs assessments* are procedures, both structured and informal, for identifying gaps between the ideal and the real.

Need is a recent discovery in education—particularly needs of the participants most closely affected by curriculum development. Two kinds of needs must be encompassed in a responsive curriculum development process: educational needs and psychological needs. James Popham (1972) defines educational need as the difference between the student's current status and his or her desired status, and he defines educational needs assessment as a technique for identifying the most important educational objectives to be accomplished in a given instructional situation. The needs of society are generally reflected in educational needs as responses to immediate critical problems of education or in emerging problems that anticipate the future. Psychological need, in a composite definition drawn from Abraham Maslow (1970), Erik Erikson (1965), and Robert Havighurst (1953), includes the motivational factors that impel students in certain directions and repel them from others. Assessing psychological needs requires insight and knowledge about human emotions, growth, and development. Awareness of both educational and psychological needs is a prerequisite for curriculum development. Although necessarily concerned with the outcomes of a plan and with the processes to be used, curriculum improvement also depends on the driving forces—the needs—that determine whether a student's attention and effort are fully engaged. John Haysom and Clive Sutton (1974), in examining the importance of attention to need, observe that curriculum development has all too frequently been concerned with educational need as identified by "experts" and therefore has given little attention to student need as a motivational criterion, adopting a normative concept of curriculum.

### EDUCATIONAL NEED

A dominant influence on curriculum development since the early 1950s has been the Tyler rationale, set forth in Ralph Tyler's *Basic Principles of Curriculum and Instruction* (1950). The Tyler model asks:

1. What educational purposes should the school seek to attain?
2. What educational experiences can be provided that are likely to attain these purposes?
3. How can these educational experiences be effectively organized?
4. How can we determine whether these purposes are being attained?

These four basic questions have been elaborated on by numerous others who adhere to accepting predetermined needs from the educators' view of what is best for the student.

Tyler's questions are frequently credited with providing impetus for the behavioral objectives movement of recent years. Its advocates propose that instructional goals be stated in behavioral terms, with built-in criteria for measurement of outcomes. Selections are then made from alternative activities expected to help the student attain the desired behavioral objectives. Scope and sequence decisions follow, and evaluation is carried out. Various interpretations of this approach have led to highly technical procedures to develop a pre-planned program of behavioral objectives closely tied to subsequent measures of achievement.

Behavioral and other models adapted from Tyler seem to over-emphasize educational need and underestimate psychological need. Although Tyler was cognizant of the latter and referred to two types of need, he gave psychological need no more than a nod of recognition (pp. 7-8):

> It is well to keep . . . two meanings of the term "needs" distinct so that they will not be confused in our discussion. The first use of the term represents a gap between some conception of a desirable norm, that is, some standard of philosophic value and the actual status. Need in this sense is the gap between what is and what should be. The other use of the term by some psychologists represents tensions in the organism which must be brought into equilibrium for a normal healthy condition of the organism to be maintained.

The reference to tensions in the organism is not developed in succeeding pages of his text, and Tyler's discussion centers around establishing a curriculum in terms of educational needs. Consequently, the kind of curriculum ordinarily developed from his rationale is compartmentalized into subject fields with coverage of content and skills uppermost. Recognition of the personal needs of students is left to the ingenuity of those teachers who may be perceptive enough to recognize individual problems.

Two more questions should be added to Tyler's list, insist James Macdonald and his colleagues (1973, p. 3):

5. What is our view of the nature of man?
6. What are our value commitments?

These questions have only recently commanded serious attention in curriculum development. As psychological needs have a long history of neglect, they require our concerted efforts to bring them adequate recognition in line with our recognition of educational needs in curriculum planning.

Even as distinguished an authority on curriculum development as Hilda Taba (1962) seems to take the view that psychological needs are adequately dealt with in the various subjects of the curriculum, and that social and educational needs should move to the forefront in curriculum planning. She says (p. 287), "It is clear, for example, that needs representing psychological requirements are less focal to the curriculum of the public school than are the needs representing social demands and the requirements of educational objectives."

For two decades, interpretations of Tyler and Taba have led to the type of either/or thinking that Taba deplores at the outset of her volume on curriculum development. Curriculum materials producers have continued to emphasize the "needs" of the various subjects in the curriculum and the needs of society—grade equivalents to be reached in the basic skills of reading and mathematics; society's needs for the patriotic and citizenship teachings incorporated into social studies; and, in recent times, science's needs for meeting the Sputnik challenge. "Transmitting the cultural heritage" has been assumed to be of prime importance—an assumption apparently based on the premise that there is one ideal culture.

Taba recognized the difficulty of adding the complex dimension of psychological needs to curriculum development and, in essence, assigned this dimension elsewhere by stating (p. 287):

Many psychological needs lie outside the power of educational approach either within or outside the school. Yet, these psychological needs must be understood and taken into account in curriculum building, because they are a part of the constellation of conditions under which learning takes place. While schools may not be in a position to eliminate deep-seated psychological insecurities, curricula must be adjusted to the demands of security needs, and schools need to provide learning conditions which at least do not create additional insecurities. In this sense, then, all needs are of concern to the educator, but only some of these can be provided for explicitly through the curriculum. Others may be of greater concern to the psychologist and the mental hygienist.

Admittedly, curriculum developers face an awesome task in meeting the challenge of universal education. They bear the heavy burden of determining essential educational (subject-centered) needs and societal needs, without opening the "Pandora's box" of existential, psychological, ethical, and other inner needs. Nevertheless, these responsibilities exist, and in recent years psychological need has gained ground in attracting the attention of curriculum-planners.

## PSYCHOLOGICAL NEED

The inclusion of psychological need in curriculum development is advocated by those who fear that overemphasis on behavioral objectives, academic achievement, and grading may develop negativism among students toward school learning. Academic objectives retain their importance, but these planners also stress the importance of psychological processes, human relations, positive mental health, and student involvement in setting goals, selecting options, learning how to work toward goals, and developing persistence in spite of occasional failures.

George Willis (1971), who traced the treatment of psychological need in an analytical survey of the literature on curriculum development, notes an acceleration of attention to this aspect of need (pp. 46-47):

Happily, a growing body of curriculum literature is beginning to move, however tentatively, toward the problem of accounting for quality in experience. Articles [see the references at the end of this chapter] by Herbert Kliebard, Robert M. W. Travers, and Elliot Eisner have raised serious questions about the desirability of Tyleresque instructional objectives, not on the grounds that such objectives ignore the problem of experience, but rather on the basis that they do not meet instructional needs nearly so well as has commonly been supposed. Nonetheless, these attacks have implicitly raised doubts as to how well these objectives can be consistent with psychological needs. In addition, a persistent stream of publications from the Association for Supervision and Curriculum Development during the 1960's has continued to raise curriculum issues about the inward experience of students, dealing with these issues in terms of mental health, psychological processes, existential situations, perceptions, and the formulation of meanings. Further, most instrumental in outlining the topography of the problem have been several papers by Dwayne Huebner, who has identified the technological bias inherent in most curriculum formulations, emphasizing that curriculum is an "environment-producing" discipline and pointing out the ethical and aesthetic dimensions of educational environments. Finally, in the same vein are papers by John S. Mann, further contributing to the idea of curriculum as environment and to its aesthetic dimensions.

Attention to psychological needs began to be expressed in the late 1960s in courses and programs of a loosely organized field known as psychological education. Possibly inspired by the shock of assassinations, riots, crime in the streets, and other crises in that decade, a number of research and development projects were funded to introduce affective education into schools. Much of this work is based on interpretations of Maslow (1970) and others, who postulate a need for self-esteem and self-actualization as a major source of human motivation.

Psychological education courses are variously alleged to increase achievement motivation, awareness and excitement, creative thinking, interpersonal sensitivity, joy, self-reliance, self-esteem, self-understanding, self-actualization, moral development, identity, nonverbal communication, value clarification, and other aspects of ideal psychological functioning. Although these terms are vague, varied, overlapping, and universally desirable, the psychological education movement does not discount the importance of stated goals and objectives. Courses offered in psychological education are based on particular objectives. For example, Outward Bound courses are designed to promote self-reliance. Other programs are designed specifically to increase channels of communication. The affective domain is the focus of numerous courses and programs, and specific procedures are being developed to reach the objective of self-actualization (see chapter two of this book; Alschuler 1972; and Mosher et al. 1972).

Worthy as the psychological education movement is in providing more comprehensive dimensions to curriculum development, there is some danger that adults are continuing to determine the needs of students in this effort. In some instances "packaged" psychological curricula are prepared, inferring that a decision about need has preceded development of the plan and the instructional materials.

An important contribution of the psychological education movement, however, has been its attention to the necessity for broadening the concept of need in education, by involving the student, the teacher, the parent, and others close to the consumer level of curriculum development in providing new views of needs. The tempo of a rapidly changing world has also stimulated attention to procedures for having those most closely affected by curriculum plans assess their own needs.

## NEEDS ASSESSMENT

Needs assessment, whether formal or informal, implies a technique or planned procedure for identifying the most important objectives to be accomplished in a given learning situation and that therefore must be recognized in developing a curriculum.

Student needs may be assessed through interviews, observation analyses, informal communications, normative tests, criterion-referenced tests, and other opportunities for learning an individual's perception of the relevance and importance of a situation or curriculum plan. Normative measures are designed to compare students with each other in terms of standardized tests, thus establishing relative needs. Criterion-referenced measures are designed to measure a student's performance in mastering a given set of objectives, without reference to the performance of any other student, thus identifying personal instructional needs. Despite the availability of other needs assessment procedures, comparison of student scores on standardized achievement tests with national norms has, in the past, been the common—and frequently the sole—needs assessment procedure. Its limitations as a single measure of needs are obvious.

Needs assessment procedures and instruments designed for wider audiences are varied and directed toward multiple sources of data. They include surveys, analyses of statements submitted in surveys, skillful interviews, panels of experts to analyze data, studies of trends, and adaptations of the Delphi technique.

Recent attention to needs assessment has elicited much ingenuity in endeavors to ascertain what parents, teachers, students, professors, researchers, and other citizens consider needs to be. Statewide and national needs assessments are not uncommon. Students or student representatives are more and more frequently included in communitywide or schoolwide surveys to learn their views of what needs should be fulfilled by the school's offerings. The new dimension in needs assessment is the attempt to assess the views of a wide range of consumers of curriculum rather than relying on determination of student needs by the producers of curricula: textbook writers, policymakers at state and district levels, university experts, curriculum committees, etc.

## DISCUSSION TECHNIQUES IN ASSESSING NEEDS

Consultations of students for their perceptions of their own needs are taking some imaginative forms that go beyond the traditional conference in the school counselor's office or pencil-and-paper survey. "Classroom meetings," so-called by William Glasser (1972), provide informal nonthreatening settings strategically arranged by teachers for seeking student opinions. Glasser reviews numerous studies in which he engaged directly in classroom work with children and demonstrated extended opportunities for adults to listen in open discussions to children's expressions of feelings about their needs. He found that this technique led to success in motivating children to take a greater interest in the elementary school curriculum. Glasser emphasized that, particularly in central-city schools where failure is a way of life, adults require far more persistence and patience in encouraging children to talk and in becoming better listeners. Not only have the students experienced constant failure in school but their parents have also "failed" in school and their teachers often believe that they are failures as teachers.

Opening a classroom discussion, Glasser found, requires attention to such details as convincing teachers that it is a good idea to move the children's chairs into a circle, despite arguments that "the custodian doesn't want the chairs moved," or "we'll lose control." But these same teachers found that if they arranged the children in a circle and talked to them in a way that showed they wanted to make friends with the children, conversation began. Teachers' attitudes concerning this process are frequently a deterrent at the outset, says Glasser, but positive benefits—improved attitudes of the children, improved behavior in the classroom, and improved motivation for school learning—influence teachers' attitudes positively.

In high schools, new concepts of adviser-advisee relationships are moving some areas of counseling out of the counselors' offices and into teacher-student discussions. At James Madison Memorial High School in Madison, Wisconsin, and McCluer North High School in Ferguson-Florissant, Missouri, new concepts of advising have been instituted that provide a means for teacher-student interaction to discover students' perceptions of their needs. This then leads to curriculum development that is more meaningful to individuals and groups. Each professional staff member of the high school, whether teacher, principal, band director, coach, or other member, serves as an ombudsman adviser to a number of student advisees, meeting with them regularly to listen to their problems and concerns and conferring with them about educational decisions. Counselors' roles in these programs are to assist other faculty members in developing skills for leading discussions, assessing needs as perceived by students, and collectively planning options for students to meet their needs. Reports available from the principals' offices indicate more successes than failures.

The concept of involving learners in identifying needs and formulating purposes is not new, although its implementation in an organized manner is recent. John Dewey (1938, pp. 67, 45), discussing the meaning of purpose, states:

There is no point in the philosophy of progressive education which is sounder than its emphasis upon the importance of the participation of the learner in the formation of the purposes which direct his activities in the learning process, just as there is no defect in traditional education greater than its failure to secure the active cooperation of the pupil in construction of the purposes of his studying. . . . The trouble with traditional education was not that educators took upon themselves the responsibility for providing an environment. The trouble was that they did not consider the other factor in creating an experience; namely, the powers and purposes of those taught.

Even earlier, Harold Rugg (1926 p. 82) wrote:

The purposes of education . . . are discovered by thought and feeling. . . . The setting up of goals, therefore, is a matter of judgments—of the best judgments we can find. . . . [I]t is of great importance for the curriculum-maker to see that the determination of goals for a given social order will be most soundly made only when he has at hand adequate knowledge and a deep and broad perspective.

## INVOLVING MULTIPLE GROUPS IN OPEN-ENDED NEEDS ASSESSMENTS

Needs assessment procedures that reach out to the various participants and referent groups of the curriculum development process range from open-ended surveys to structured, and sometimes complex, procedures. Needs assessments are being conducted at local, state, and national levels for policymaking purposes. Open-ended assessment, the theme of this section, is illustrated by local school district experiences. More structured assessment techniques are described later in this chapter.

### Rounds of Surveys

A Delphi-type needs assessment conducted in 1971 by the School District of University City, Missouri (*Survey of Critical Needs* 1971), surveyed curricular and instructional needs as viewed by four referent or participant groups. Successive rounds of questionnaires were used to seek opinions. A statistical sampling method selected respondents from the professional staff, students of grades five through twelve, parents, and representatives of civic, philanthropic, and religious organizations of the community.

On the first round, each person was provided with an almost blank sheet of paper headed by the single question: "In your opinion, what are the most important or critical needs of the school's program?" This resulted in a wealth of written detail on changes and improvements perceived as desirable by the four groups. From the material submitted on the first round, an item analysis was made. Persons in each group who had been surveyed the first time received a second questionnaire listing the needs suggested by that particular group and were asked to assign priorities to them according to a weighting method. A tally of the results provided a rank order of items by each group. About 60 percent of the persons surveyed responded to both rounds of questionnaires.

Students' perceptions included several needs relating to the immediate school environment. Adults' perceptions tended to emphasize basic skills, societal concerns, and various benefits and resources that make the teaching career more enjoyable. Despite the diversity of emphases, all groups concurred on several needs. Mentioned by all groups in the first round, although not necessarily assigned a high priority in the second round, were the following needs, some phrased in different terminology but with similar intent:

Teaching students to assume more responsibility for their own work and behavior.

Orderly behavior in the schools.

Improved communication among students, staff, parents, and community.

Individual attention to students.

More interesting courses.

Racial harmony among students.

More civic projects and use of community resources.

Improvement of the counseling program.

The top ten needs (including tie votes) identified by each group were:

*Students, grades five through twelve*

The school should have fair rules and apply them to all students, reduce favoritism to some students, and find ways to prevent fights.

The school building and grounds should be cleaner, with no trash lying around.

The school should teach more responsibility to children and give more attention to children who cause problems.

The school should take some action after receiving our replies to this questionnaire.

Black and white students should work together for common goals and harmony.

Courses should be developed to include more practical experiences, such as field trips, visits to corporations, and visits to community organizations.

Students should have more involvement with the community and with community projects.

Counselors should communicate more with students, give more information, listen to students as individuals, and devote more time and effort to student problems.

Air conditioners should be provided in warm weather.

More variety and more interesting work should be provided in the various school subjects, with more choice allowed in the kinds of classes and time spent in class.

Rules of discipline should be enforced firmly for all offenders by teachers and administrators.

School buildings and the facilities within them, including lockers, drinking fountains, and heating systems, should be kept in better repair, and more attractive paint and decorations should be used.

*Parents*

Adequate salaries should be offered to attract and keep good teachers.

There are too many pupils per teacher, which lessens individual instruction.

Technical and vocational training is needed for both male and female students who do not care to go on to higher education.

Reading specialists are needed for all grade levels to improve reading skills.

Curriculum should be designed to teach children how to live and cope in a pluralistic society and to improve the child's acceptance of his or her elders and of minority groups. Curriculum should also stress manners and courtesy.

More effective teachers and better qualified ones are needed.

Emphasis should be placed on the causes and consequences of good and bad health habits.

Questionnaires should be sent out periodically to parents so that they can express their ideas on a continuing basis.

Black experiences should be recognized throughout the curriculum, not in a separate program.

Children should have more time with teachers; there should be more one-to-one teacher-student dialogues.

*Civic, philanthropic, and religious organizations*

Each child should be taught to assume responsibility for his or her acts.

Efforts should be made by school and community to generate faith in the board of education.

Ineffective teachers should not be retained.

There should be greater emphasis on verbal and written skills.

Tutoring programs should be expanded to meet the needs of individual students.

There should be a critical analysis and evaluation of each teacher's ability to teach in an interracial environment.

Efforts should be made to achieve greater trust among all those concerned with schools.

Counseling at the junior and senior high schools should be improved.

Parents should be given a full explanation of any increased funds (taxes, etc.).

There should be objective evaluations of all programs.

*Teachers and administrators*

A more attractive salary schedule is needed.

Additional assistance in reading is needed for low achievers.

Assistance with learning disabilities is needed.

Ways to reduce vandalism should be designed.

Additional help is needed with behavior and discipline problems.

Knowledge from research should be used to teach "unreachable" children.

Control and orderliness in buildings is necessary; a laissez-faire atmosphere is undesirable.

Improved communication with staff is needed.

More materials are needed for individual prescriptions.

Basic courses are necessary for slow students.

Following the open-ended needs survey, the school district developed long-range plans for meeting priority needs expressed by the various groups. Not only has curriculum development subsequently been directed toward expressed needs but also renewed efforts have been made to improve communication within the school and between the school and the community, to improve the aesthetic appearance of the school buildings, as requested by students, and to involve parents, students, and teachers in curriculum planning on a continuing basis through various committee structures.

## Round-Table Discussions

Another style of open-ended needs assessment was used in the school district of the city of Charlotte and of Mecklenburg County, North Carolina, in 1974. The participants there engaged in round-table discussions rather than written surveys. Ellen Scarborough (1974) reported the process in which thirty neighborhood meetings attracted 2,500 citizens and produced tape recordings pinpointing key areas of discussion and potential controversy about the educational and community needs of the area.

Discussions centered around goals and objectives. The original input for each discussion was a common list of ninety-four goals that had been prepared by a committee of community volunteers before the rounds of neighborhood discussions began. From the opinions expressed in the discussion meetings, a revised list of goals was adopted, task forces were organized, and priorities were established for putting them into action.

## Professionally Designed Needs Assessment Instruments

A carefully prepared instrument that offers a procedure for assigning priorities to educational goals and, at the same time, assessing needs of the local district or school unit in relation to these goals and objectives is *Educational Goals and Objectives* (n.d.) produced by the Program Development Center of Northern California and distributed by the Commission on Educational Planning of Phi Delta Kappa. Numerous communities and schools have used this program. It provides directions, strategies, and techniques for drawing cross section representatives from citizens at large, adults directly involved in the educational process, and students. Both discussions and written responses are used. Several rounds of meetings are required, and specific procedures are followed. Once the district's needs have been assessed, the program provides instructions for translating them into objectives at a program level. The program also accommodates additional goals and objectives that may be contributed by the participants. The original list (Phi Delta Kappa EG Form 4) was:

## EDUCATIONAL GOALS
### These are not in any order of importance.

*Learn how to be a good citizen*
A. Develop an awareness of civic rights and responsibilities.
B. Develop attitudes for productive citizenship in a democracy.
C. Develop an attitude of respect for personal and public property.
D. Develop an understanding of the obligations and responsibilities of citizenship.

*Learn how to respect and get along with people who think, dress, and act differently*
A. Develop an appreciation for and an understanding of other people and other cultures.
B. Develop an understanding of political, economic, and social patterns of the rest of the world.
C. Develop awareness of the interdependence of races, creeds, nations, and cultures.
D. Develop an awareness of the processes of group relationships.

*Learn about and try to understand the changes that take place in the world*
A. Develop ability to adjust to the changing demands of society.
B. Develop an awareness and the ability to adjust to a changing world and its problems.
C. Develop understanding of the past, identity with the present, and the ability to meet the future.

*Develop skills in reading, writing, speaking, and listening*
A. Develop ability to communicate ideas and feelings effectively.
B. Develop skills in oral and written English.

*Understand and practice democratic ideas and ideals*
A. Develop loyalty to American democratic ideals.
B. Develop patriotism and loyalty to ideas of democracy.
C. Develop knowledge and appreciation of the rights and privileges in our democracy.
D. Develop an understanding of our American heritage.

*Learn how to examine and use information*
A. Develop ability to examine constructively and creatively.
B. Develop ability to use scientific methods.

C. Develop reasoning abilities.

D. Develop skills to think and proceed logically.

*Understand and practice the skills of family living*

A. Develop understanding and appreciation of the principles of living in the family group.

B. Develop attitudes leading to acceptance of responsibilities as family members.

C. Develop an awareness of future family responsibilities and achievement of skills in preparing to accept them.

*Learn to respect and get along with people with whom we work and live*

A. Develop appreciation and respect for the worth and dignity of individuals.

B. Develop respect for individual worth and understanding of minority opinions and acceptance of majority decisions.

C. Develop a cooperative attitude toward living and working with others.

*Develop skills to enter a specific field of work*

A. Develop abilities and skills needed for immediate employment.

B. Develop an awareness of opportunities and requirements related to a specific field of work.

C. Develop an appreciation of good workmanship.

*Learn how to be a good manager of money, property, and resources*

A. Develop an understanding of economic principles and responsibilities.

B. Develop ability and understanding in personal buying, selling, and investment.

C. Develop skills in management of natural and human resources and man's environment.

*Develop a desire for learning now and in the future*

A. Develop intellectual curiosity and eagerness for lifelong learning.

B. Develop a positive attitude toward learning.

C. Develop a positive attitude toward continuing independent education.

*Learn how to use leisure time*

A. Develop ability to use leisure time productively.

B. Develop a positive attitude toward participation in a range of leisure time activities—physical, intellectual, and creative.

C. Develop appreciation and interests which will lead to wise and enjoyable use of leisure time.

*Practice and understand the ideas of health and safety*

A. Establish an effective individual physical fitness program.

B. Develop an understanding of good physical health and well being.

C. Establish sound personal health habits and information.

D. Develop a concern for public health and safety.

*Appreciate culture and beauty in the world*
A. Develop abilities for effective expression of ideas and cultural appreciation (fine arts).
B. Cultivate appreciation for beauty in various forms.
C. Develop creative self-expression through various media (art, music, writing, etc.).
D. Develop special talents in music, art, literature, and foreign languages.

*Gain information needed to make job selections*
A. Promote self-understanding and self-direction in relation to student's occupational interests.
B. Develop the ability to use information and counseling services related to the selection of a job.
C. Develop a knowledge of specific information about a particular vocation.

*Develop pride in work and a feeling of self-worth*
A. Develop a feeling of student pride in his achievements and progress.
B. Develop self-understanding and self-awareness.
C. Develop the student's feeling of positive self-worth, security, and self-assurance.

*Develop good character and self-respect*
A. Develop moral responsibility and a sound ethical and moral behavior.
B. Develop the student's capacity to discipline himself to work, study, and play constructively.
C. Develop a moral and ethical sense of values, goals, and processes of free society.
D. Develop standards of personal character and ideas.

*Gain a general education*
A. Develop background and skills in the use of numbers, natural sciences, mathematics, and social sciences.
B. Develop a fund of information and concepts.
C. Develop special interests and abilities.

The St. Louis Public School System used an instrument designed by the Center of Research and Program Development of the Wisconsin Department of Public Instruction for conducting an educational needs assessment study on the basis of which educational programs for disadvantaged children were later developed. School board members, educators, citizens, and students participated through a statistical sampling technique. A prepared list of subject fields, levels of education (i.e., early childhood, adult education), types of programs, teacher personnel concerns, administrative services, pupil services, budget allocations, instructional approaches, educational programs, and types of in-service education was used in seeking opinions on needs. From the results, a matrix was produced that identified high priorities and interrelationships. Open-ended questions provided additional information, and the curriculum development process reached toward the needs assessed by this representative cross section of the school and the community.

The needs assessment yielded the following composite ranking of critical educational needs in all categories by the total sample:

| Rank | Educational Need |
|------|------------------|
| 1 | Early childhood (three- to four-year-olds) |
| 2 | Reading |
| 3 | Teaching personnel |
| 4 | Individually prescribed instruction |
| 5 | Analysis of community needs and strengths |
| 6 | Guidance services (high school and element; ry school) |
| 7 | Education in human relations |
| 8 | Methods of teacher selection |
| 9 | Ineffective teachers (weak, unsuccessful) |
| 10 | Education in motivating pupils |
| 11 | Education in diagnosing pupil needs |
| 12 | Business (stenography, accounting, clerical, etc.) |
| 13 | Specialized personnel (counselors, psychologists) |
| 13 | Quality of teacher candidates |
| 15 | Primary education (grades one to three) |
| 15 | Program for average pupils |
| 17 | Classroom facilities |
| 18 | Program for educationally disadvantaged pupils |
| 18 | Program for alienated youth |
| 20 | Supervision of instruction |

## STATE NEEDS ASSESSMENT PROGRAMS

Three events in the national scene of the middle 1960s inspired interest in and attention to educational needs assessment at the state level. One was the National Assessment of Education Program. A second was the enactment of the Elementary and Secondary

Education Act (ESEA) of 1965, which included a requirement that school systems assess by objective means the effects on student achievement produced by federally funded programs for the educationally deprived. Following the lead of the ESEA, practically all federal funds and most private grants now require an assessment of needs based on documented evidence. The third event of the 1960s was the publication of the Coleman Report, *Equality of Educational Opportunity* (1966), which attempted to assess the quality of services schools were supplying to various segments of the population in terms of measured pupil achievement.

These events and various writings on the crises of the 1960s stimulated demands from state legislators, other state officials, and various public interest groups for more specific and detailed information about the level and progress of education in their communities and states. Consequently, statewide assessment plans and programs began developing in every state of the union (see Dyer and Rosenthal, 1971). Although needs assessment, properly viewed, involves a great deal more than statewide testing programs, relatively few states in the early 1970s were going beyond the three Rs to get information on how education was affecting student values and attitudes. States seemed mainly concerned with how well their educational systems were succeeding in imparting basic skills. However, some states are now producing instruments to gauge educational needs in such aspects of human life as self-concept, understanding of others, responsible citizenship, health habits, creativity, acquisition of salable skills, understanding of human accomplishments, readiness for change, and attitudes toward school.

Wisconsin's needs assessment "perception" instrument provides a means for identifying imperative educational needs statewide as perceived by school board members, educators, students, and selected citizens. It then provides for assigning priorities to specific and composite educational needs and ascertaining need priorities by geographic region of the state. Similar procedures are being used in Nevada, Missouri, and other states.

Kentucky delineates perceived needs or educational inadequacies across the state by means of a survey questionnaire followed by assistance in developing diagnostic instructional approaches at the local level. Indiana's statewide assessment of educational needs includes testing in reading, mathematics, psychomotor abilities, personal values, and attitudes toward self. Needs assessment surveys done under emergency conditions to secure federal funds have themselves created other needs at the state level, including needs for greater attention to the goal-setting process, relating needs assessment data to financial resources, and greater efforts in communication and coordination of the curriculum development process.

## PROGRAM NEEDS

Assessments of needs in relation to specific programs, such as career education, "right to read," arts and humanities, bilingual education, and dropout prevention, are also being done in recognition of the necessity for participants in and consumers of curriculum development to contribute to the process of identifying needs.

An example of a needs assessment procedure in relation to a specific program is a survey conducted in Texas to identify needs for curriculum development in career education. Students, parents, educators, and business and industry representatives are being surveyed in a sample that is representative of the state's geographic distribution, ethnic makeup, and socioeconomic groups. The survey offers respondents an opportunity to identify needs in basic skills in reading, writing, and mathematics, communication skills, the humanities, task-completion skills, decision-making skills, use of resources, attitudes toward quality, performance, and personal satisfaction in achievement, among several others.

## SUMMARY

The preceding discussion gives numerous examples of needs assessment procedures that encompass far broader concepts of needs than the traditional expert-determined or producer-determined needs or the narrow definition of needs that arises from comparison of student achievement scores with national norms on standardized tests. The examples given here include psychological needs as well as educational needs and describe ongoing procedures in various parts of the country in which individuals and groups directly concerned with a curriculum development process are also involved in identifying the needs that curriculum and instruction should meet.

Both implicit and explicit in this discussion is the point of view that curriculum development must seek to match learning experiences not only to desired outcomes but also to the learners' own perceptions of their needs so that their attention and efforts may become a motivational force. The work of the curriculum developer includes planning for means that develop in the learner a constantly growing maturity in setting his or her own goals.

## REFERENCES

Alschuler, Alfred S. "Psychological Education." In *Curriculum and the Cultural Revolution*, edited by David E. Purpel and Maurice Belanger, pp. 256-71. Berkeley: McCutchan, 1972.

Coleman, James S.; Campbell, Ernest Q.; Hobson, Carol J.; McPartland, James; Mood, Alexander M.; Weinfeld, Frederic D.; and York, Robert L. *Equality of Educational Opportunity*. Washington, D.C.: U.S. Government Printing Office, 1966.

Combs, Arthur W., ed. *Perceiving, Behaving, Becoming*. Washington, D.C.: Association for Supervision and Curriculum Development, 1962.

Dewey, John. *Experience and Education*. New York: Collier Books, 1938.

Dyer, Henry S., and Rosenthal, Elsa. *State Educational Assessment Programs*. Princeton, N.J.: Educational Testing Service, 1971.

*Educational Goals and Objectives*. Bloomington, Ind.: Commission on Educational Planning, Phi Delta Kappa, n.d. (probably 1973).

Eisner, Elliot. "Educational Objectives: Help or Hindrance?" *School Review* 75 (autumn 1957): 250-60.

Erikson, Erik H. *Childhood and Society*. Rev. ed. Baltimore: Penguin Books, 1965.

Frazier, Alexander, ed. *New Insights and the Curriculum*. Washington, D.C.: Association for Supervision and Curriculum Development, 1963.

Glasser, William. "The Identity Society." Paper presented at the Futures Conference, "New Directions in Education, Educational Systems for the Seventies," Washington, D.C., May 1972.

——.*Schools without Failure*. New York: Harper and Row, 1969.

Havighurst, Robert J. *Human Development and Education*. New York: Longmans, Green, 1953.

Haysom, John T., and Sutton, Clive R. "Motivation: A Neglected Component in Models for Curriculum Improvement." *Curriculum Theory Network* 4, no. 1 (1974): 23-35.

Huebner, Dwayne. "Implications of Psychological Thought for the Curriculum." In *Influences in Curriculum Change*. Washington, D.C.: Association for Supervision and Curriculum Development, 1968.

Kliebard, Herbert M. "Curricular Objectives and Evaluation: A Reassessment." *High School Journal* 51 (March 1968): 241-47.

Leeper, Robert R., ed. *Humanizing Education: The Person in the Process.* Washington, D.C.: Association for Supervision and Curriculum Development, 1967.

Macdonald, James B.; Wolfson, Bernice J.; and Zaret, Esther. *Reschooling Society: A Conceptual Model.* Washington, D.C.: Association for Supervision and Curriculum Development, 1973.

McNeil, John D. "Forces Influencing Curriculum." *Review of Educational Research* 39 (June 1969): 293-318.

Mager, Robert F. *Preparing Objectives for Programmed Instruction.* Palo Alto, Calif.: Fearon, 1962.

Mann, John S. "Functions of Curriculum Research." *Educational Leadership* 24 (October 1966): 77-88.

Maslow, Abraham H. *Motivation and Personality.* 2d ed. New York: Harper and Row, 1970.

Mosher, Ralph L.; Sprinthall, Norman A.; Atkins, Victor S.; Dowell, R. Chris; Greenspan, Barbara Meyer; Griffin, Andrew H., Jr.; and Mager, George C. "Psychological Education: A Means to Promote Personal Development during Adolescence." In *Curriculum and the Cultural Revolution,* edited by David E. Purpel and Maurice Belanger, pp. 284-410. Berkeley: McCutchan, 1972.

*National Assessment of Educational Progress.* Denver: Education Commission of the States. (Continuing series of publications.)

Passow, A. Harry, ed. *Nurturing Individual Potential.* Washington, D.C.: Association for Supervision and Curriculum Development, 1964.

Popham, W. James. "Educational Needs Assessment." In *Curriculum Evaluation: Potentiality and Reality,* p. 23. Monograph supplement of *Curriculum Theory Network.* Toronto: Ontario Institute for Studies in Education, 1972.

Provus, Malcolm. "Evaluation as Public Policy." In *Curriculum Evaluation: Potentiality and Reality,* pp. 33-44. Monograph supplement of *Curriculum Theory Network.* Toronto: Ontario Institute for Studies in Education, 1972.

Rugg, Harold, ed. *Curriculum Making: Past and Present,* part I. Twenty-sixth Yearbook of the National Society for the Study of Education. Bloomington, Ill.: Public School Publishing, 1926.

St. Louis Public Schools. *Educational Needs Assessment Tabulation.* St. Louis: Project TREND, 1972.

Scarborough, Ellen. "Voices of Dimensions: What Did They Say?" *Charlotte Observer,* 11 July 1974, p. 1F.

*A Survey concerning Desirable Characteristics and Outcomes for Seventeen Year Old Students.* Austin: Texas Education Agency, n.d. (probably 1973).

*Survey of Critical Needs of the Educational Program.* University City, Mo.: School District of University City, 1971.

Sweigert, Ray L. "The Discovery of Need in Education: Developing a Need Inquiry System." *Journal of Secondary Education* 43 (December 1968): 345-48.

Taba, Hilda. *Curriculum Development: Theory and Practice.* New York: Harcourt, Brace and World, 1962.

Travers, Robert M. W. "Towards Taking the Fun Out of Building a Theory of Instruction." *Teachers College Record* 68 (October 1966): 49-60.

Tyler, Ralph W. *Basic Principles of Curriculum and Instruction.* Chicago: University of Chicago Press, 1950.

Waetjen, Walter B., and Leeper, Robert R., eds. *Mental Health in the School.* Washington, D.C.: Association for Supervision and Curriculum Development, 1966.

Willis, George. "Curriculum Theory and the Context of Curriculum." *Curriculum Theory Network* no. 6 (1971): 41-59.

## ADDITIONAL READINGS

Browder, Lesley H., Jr.; Atkins, William A., Jr.; and Kaya, Esin. *Developing an Educationally Accountable Program*, pp. 75-105. Berkeley: McCutchan, 1973.

Cawelti, Gordon, ed. *Vitalizing High Schools: A Summary of Six National Proposals for Reforming Secondary Schools, and a Curriculum Critique.* Washington, D.C.: Association for Supervision and Curriculum Development, 1974.

de Charms, Richard. *Personal Causation.* New York: Academic Press, 1968.

Hunt, David E., and Sullivan, Edmund V. *Between Psychology and Education.* Hinsdale, Ill.: Dryden Press, 1974.

Kerr, John F., ed. *Changing the Curriculum.* London: University of London Press, 1968.

Kohlberg, Lawrence. "Moral Education in the Schools: A Developmental View." In *Curriculum and the Cultural Revolution*, edited by David E. Purpel and Maurice Belanger, pp. 455-78. Berkeley: McCutchan, 1972.

Kopan, Andrew T. and Walberg, Herbert J., eds. *Rethinking Educational Equality.* Berkeley: McCutchan, 1974.

McClelland, David C., and Atkinson, J. W. *The Achievement Motive.* New York: Appleton-Century-Crofts, 1953.

Pfeiffer, John. *New Look at Education.* New York: Odyssey Press, 1968.

Piaget, Jean. *The Moral Judgment of the Child.* New York: Free Press, 1965.

Walberg, Herbert J., and Rasher, Sue Pinzer. "Public School Effectiveness and Equality: New Evidence and Its Implications." *Phi Delta Kappan* 56 (September 1974): 3-9.

# Strengthening Links among Participants

PROPOSITION: If the number and intensity of links among participants increase, the curriculum development process will become more responsive to their common needs.

Collaborative efforts, interaction, and communication among participants and referent groups can generate power for responsiveness in curriculum development. Arguments presented here support this view with some illustrations showing that lack of collaboration leads to lack of success in curriculum development.

*Participants* are those who have a direct share in curriculum development at some level: policy-making, producing, or using. *Referent groups* are those who should be consulted about curriculum development but have more indirect relationships, interests, and concerns. *Links* are cooperative actions or communication systems that interconnect the persons concerned with a given unit of curriculum development and the resultant curriculum and instruction. The roles and responsibilities of each category of participants and each referent group are described in chapter five.

Statements and evidence to support the proposition range far and wide in the literature. Well-known researchers, scholars, and observers provide analytical and philosophical views, investigative data, theoretical positions, and journalistic reports. Sources include human relations programs, organizational theory, the work of research and development centers in education, school-university efforts, school-community endeavors, and new involvements of students.

## DEMOCRATIC IDEALS

John Dewey, in *Democracy and Education* (1916), emphasized the need for social participation in planning and carrying out educational activities. Dewey argued (p. 115) that, since education is a social process and there are many kinds of societies, one criterion for educational criticism and construction implies that

a society which makes provision for participation in its good of all its members on equal terms and which secures flexible readjustment of all its institutions through interaction of the different forms of associated life is insofar democratic. Such a society must have a type of education which gives individuals a personal interest in social relationships and control, and the habits of mind which secure social changes without introducing disorder.

## NONPARTICIPANTS

Fifty years after Dewey's pronouncement, Harry Broudy (1966) noted the need for participation and pointed to the problems that arise in curriculum development when participation is lacking. Failure to include various groups and interests led to widespread rejection of the curriculum "reform" products of the 1960s, in which scholars directed their efforts toward refurbishing the separate disciplines, expecting schools and teacher education institutions to adopt the new approaches although they had been called on to give a bare minimum of consultation during the planning stages. (A description of the curriculum reform decade and its place in the history of curriculum development is provided in chapter one.)

Broudy detects in the scholars' approach to curriculum development a tinge of elitism, intellectual snobbery, and impatience with the limitations of the common man. Combined with ample funds for experimentation, these attitudes gave the scholars a heady feeling of power that seemed to be expressed in the voice of an elite dedicated to training an elite to think *for* the common man rather than educating the common man to think for himself. The curriculum plans produced were oriented to the "upper middle class products of the ivy colleges for models of excellence and huge corporations for patterns of decision making" (Broudy 1966, p. 15), while the heterogeneous assortment of schools, teachers, pupils, and school boards that were expected to adopt these reforms with dispatch represented less lofty layers of the social order and looked to the American town meeting model for patterns of policy-making.

Teacher education institutions seemed less than cooperative—probably, in Broudy's view, because they not only were bypassed by the "reformers" but also seemed to be relegated to some unimportant status. This attitude of snobbery was conveyed by use of the term "educationist" and by the suggestion that teacher preparation could better take place in institutes and in-service improvisations designed by leaders within the separate disciplines than it could in teacher education institutions.

On the other hand, Broudy emphasizes that curriculum development cannot be left to the hunches of the average person any more than it can be left to the scholars alone. Curriculum development must take into account the pressures of a highly complex, interdependent, bureaucratically organized society in which many educational matters are collectivized and institutionalized. Although it may be preferable to have curriculum alternatives freely and competently chosen by individuals, curriculum development is still highly dependent on the contributions of specialists. That the participation of all in curriculum development is necessary is a generalization derived by Broudy from observations of the curriculum development era of the 1960s.

Joseph Featherstone (1974) who has written widely about education, particularly open or informal education, also comments on the reformers of the 1960s. He notes (p. 214) that, although they brought forth excellent materials in some cases, they failed to engage teachers in continuous thought and creation, with the result that teachers taught the new materials in the old ways.

Being for the most part university people and specialists, the reformers were ignorant of classrooms and children; of pedagogy. They concentrated on content—organized in the form of the standard graduate school disciplines. . . . [T]he reformers lacked a coherent vision of the school environment as a whole.

Robert Schaefer (1967) also deplores the 1960s curriculum movement on the basis that it was relatively indifferent to teachers. The essential effort had been to produce materials that permitted scholars to speak directly to the child. The scholars seemed to view teachers as mere technicians who were not to be assigned an intellectual and professional role. Unless curriculum development can find a viable means of attracting teachers to the intellectual excitement it seeks to create in children, it cannot succeed, says Schaefer.

## INVOLVEMENT PROBLEMS

Featherstone (1974) comments that the "free school" movement, which reemerged in the 1960s from progressive education ancestry, has at times demonstrated again a failure to involve the many participants in education. Overenthusiastic free school advocates seem, to Featherstone, to associate freedom with nothingness. He discovered that many children in "free schools" are not happy, possibly because they realize they are not accomplishing very much and are bored with their lack of intellectual progress.

Jonathan Kozol (1972) makes this point even more strongly in describing a free school established in 1966 that closed after a short life because the children had not learned to read there. The founders of the school were committed to helping black children, but "rejected the terms on which the black parents wanted their children to be helped." Kozol emphasizes (p. 34) that

these elite ideologies and ideals do not meet the actual needs of the specific, real and non-theoretical children who are sitting here before us. . . . [I] t is too often the rich college graduate who speaks three languages with native fluency, at the price of sixteen years of high-cost, rigorous, and sequential education, who is most determined that poor kids should make clay vases, weave Indian headbands, play with Polaroid cameras, and climb over geodesic domes.

Humane schools are needed, states Featherstone, but we also need a steady concern for intellectual progress and workmanship. Enough people from different walks of life must interact and participate in sharing knowledge about the various aspects of the curriculum, if real progress is to be made toward meeting common needs.

## HUMAN RELATIONS STUDIES

Human relations studies further support the concept of need for broader links among participants. L. K. Frank (1961) emphasizes that no discipline or profession can cope alone and unaided with the immense taks of making living more orderly, significant, and fulfilling of human dignity. Also from studies of human relations, Kenneth Benne (1961) notes that ideally all parts of the system cooperate in identifying difficulties in operation, finding alternative responses to each difficulty, and evaluating the results of the response selected. He does not see this as denying leadership in order to achieve decisive collaboration. Rather, Benne asserts it is a necessity if decisions are to be relevant to the analyzed environment and to all parts of the system.

Arthur Combs, from his studies of the helping professions (1970), has generalized that humaneness is learned from the quality of an individual's interactions with significant others. From his observation of student-teachers, Combs makes comparisons to the needs of all students. He states that, if increasing humaneness is to be a major function of the schools they will have to find much better ways of involving students in the educational process—and involving them deeply.

To involve others deeply, the leader must exhibit supportive behavior and a human relations orientation. A formal study by Wayne Doyle and William Ahlbrand (1973) supports this statement. Subjects were principals and teachers in elementary schools of three large suburban school districts. Hypotheses were: (1) as the human relations orientation of the leader increases, his or her supportive behavior for the ideas of subordinates increases, and (2) as the leader's supportive behavior for the ideas of subordinates increases, generation of ideas by subordinates increases.

Using an instrument designed by Fred Fiedler in previous studies of task-oriented and human-relations-oriented leaders, Doyle and Ahlbrand designed a study to test links among the orientations of the leaders, the ways leaders reacted to ideas of subordinates, and the subsequent generation of additional ideas by subordinates. Both hypotheses were supported by the data. Principals with high human relations orientation sources were more supportive of teachers' ideas, while principals with low human relations scores (task orientation) were more critical of teachers' ideas. Teachers generated significantly more ideas in the groups where principals were more supportive of their ideas (had a human relations orientation).

The investigators noted the following implications for links among group members: the problem-solving performance of hierarchically differentiated groups is enhanced when the power figure (1) attempts to create a "freedom to fail" atmosphere in the group, (2) is more occupied with eliciting ideas from subordinates than in submitting ideas himself or herself, recognizing that the ideas of all group members are needed to progress toward a successful solution, (3) delays expressing a negative opinion on an idea submitted by a subordinate until the full resources of the group have been brought to bear on the issue, and (4) makes every effort to develop a receptive relationship with group members by questioning ideas of subordinates in a supportive, nonthreatening manner.

## ORGANIZATIONAL THEORY

Further support for the value of interaction and collaboration is available from organizational theory. Reviews of developments in organization and management since 1900 note three phases: efficiency, bureaucracy, and human relations (March and Simon 1959).

Chester Barnard (1938) is credited with ushering in a new era in the understanding of organizations. His work is said to have inspired students of organization to greater efforts to create a discipline of organization based on scientific inquiry. During the 1940s, behavioral scientists were attracted to this growing field and drew from organizational theory a specialized knowledge of human behavior, research methods for studying human behavior, and theoretical concepts, which led to greater insights into organizational behavior. Ideas from these insights can be borrowed and transformed for curriculum development.

Douglas McGregor (1960) contrasts two theories on the relationships among people in an organization, which he calls Theory X and Theory Y. He rejects Theory X, which assumes that (1) the average human being has an inherent dislike of work and will avoid it if he can, (2) because of this, most people must be coerced, controlled, directed, and threatened with punishment to get them to put forth adequate effort toward the achievement of organizational objectives, and (3) the average human being prefers to be directed, wishes to avoid responsibility, has relatively little ambition, and wants security.

Theory Y, which McGregor advocates, rests on the assumptions that (1) the expenditure of physical and mental effort in work is as natural to human beings as play or rest, and the average person does not inherently dislike work, (2) people will exercise self-direction and self-control in the service of objectives to which they are committed, (3) under proper conditions, the average human being learns not only to accept but also to seek responsibility, (4) the capacity to exercise a relatively high degree of imagination, ingenuity, and creativity in the solution of organizational problems is widely, not narrowly, distributed in the population, and (5) the intellectual potential of the average human being is only partially used. Active and responsible participation of the individual in decisions affecting his or her career is a principle derived from Theory Y.

Another contribution from organizational theory is operations research, developing from a systems concept, which has brought highly skilled techniques to organization and management with implications for processes of curriculum development. Most pertinent in the context of this proposition are interdisciplinary teams that pool their knowledge of approaches to a problem. Teamwork in approaching a problem is more important in operations research than specific techniques and tools.

## RESEARCH AND DEVELOPMENT IN EDUCATION

Some of the most prominent examples of applications of organizational and management theory in education are illustrated by the regional educational laboratories and research and development centers. These institutions have applied the theories both in the management aspect of organizing for the tasks of curriculum development and in developing instructional packages.

Both successes and failures are reported. Among the successes are numerous highly developed curriculum materials and methods based on the best knowledge from learning theory. These were created with the help of highly specialized experts, using carefully monitored feedback from both hothouse and field trials in the schools, and constantly revising materials to meet formative evaluative findings. The materials are marketed only after completion of the expensive development processes. However, prodigious efforts seem necessary to "install" the packages in the schools, and there are indications that wider participation of the potential users would be desirable.

Roger Pillet (1971) asserts that researchers have perpetuated a separation of theory and practice. He lists as shortcomings (1) the locus of the leadership function in curriculum development that is external to the teachers, administrators, parents, and students who are expected to become users; (2) the negation of reality that occurs when new programs are designed on paper without regard to the knowledge and experience of the learners and educators who are expected to become the users; and (3) the use of abstract language that reduces the possibility of communication among those involved in various aspects of curriculum development.

Howard Merriman (1971) notes heightened demands at the local level for participation with researchers and developers in decision-making. Merriman urges curriculum researchers and developers to seek participation by the educational community, and he defines an educational community as those persons in a community who have an interest in education—parents, teachers, students, administrators, and other interested citizens. Parents may decide to support the school or not. Teachers make decisions to follow an administrative directive to use a given program or package or covertly to ignore it. Students choose to learn or not to learn. Other groups have other means of expressing satisfaction and dissatisfaction with the schools. Failure to involve the education community in studying the day-to-day reality and failure to communicate clearly indicate the need for researchers and developers to initiate new links.

Amitai Etzioni (1971) views the laboratories as somewhat ineffectual because of the weak link between the knowledge-makers and the decision-makers. The disassociation of the laboratories from their clientele is an example of the inadequate links between different segments of the educational community. Interaction is required, states Etzioni, not only for the production of relevant knowledge, but also to assist in its introduction into the curriculum development process.

## SCHOOL-UNIVERSITY COLLABORATION

School and university collaboration in curriculum development has had a history of fits and starts with occasional periods of extensive effort. Arthur Foshay (1970), who was involved in cooperative university-school research in the 1940s, analyzes the causes of its failure to continue although it was intended to stimulate cooperative approaches to curriculum development. Based on his Teachers College experience, Foshay concludes that the cooperative university-school research movement was badly flawed by its ad hoc character. It was directed toward pupil-teacher problems as the teacher viewed them and did not take into account other broad goals of curriculum development. To avoid failure in cooperative efforts and narrowness of point of view, Foshay asserts (p. 151) that

curriculum development has to provide within itself a very large number of options for those who take part in it. It has to be tentative, it has to be interactive, it has to play to individual strength, to be cooperative, and within all of these conditions it still has to be rigorous in the sense that its consequences have to be examined constantly.

More recently, experiments in collaborative efforts within the District of Columbia school system have produced descriptions and inferential statements on cooperative action. The Cardozo Project in Urban Teaching, reported by Lindley Stiles et al. (1967) and quoted in Larry Cuban (1969), was based on a model involving the university, the school, and the community in curriculum development. Successes from these collaborative efforts, cautiously stated from subjective observations, include intellectual stimulation from active, continuing involvement with adults and children, creation of more humane relationships when teachers reached out beyond the class-room into the community, and greater opportunities for imaginative and resourceful teacher training, when the center for training was shifted from the university to the District of Columbia school system.

A less successful experiment in the District of Columbia, reported by Lauter (1968), was the Adams-Morgan Community School Project. In cooperation with the Antioch-Putney Graduate School of Education, the Morgan Elementary School was a testing ground for community-university-school cooperation. Conflict prevailed throughout the life of the experiment, and little progress in curriculum development was made. Lauter ascribed the failure to the lack of advance planning and inadequate participation by all parties to the project.

More harmonious participation is reported by Raphael Nystrand

and Luvern Cunningham (1970) in an experiment involving staff members from the University of Chicago, and teachers, principals, janitors, secretaries, and cafeteria workers of the Benjamin Wright Raymond School, an inner-city school serving a deprived neighborhood. A series of workshops was held for these purposes: (1) to identify common problem areas and responsibilities confronting the adults of the school; (2) to explore the processes by which these problems might be resolved through cooperative action; (3) to practice various proved methods of group participation and decision-making; and (4) to use role-playing techniques in the analysis of school-related problems.

Results from pre- and postworkshop measurements indicated that the group did establish goals and work toward their attainment; that communication among persons and groups in the school improved; that staff morale, rapport, and spirit improved to the extent that expressed desires to leave the school system were reduced; that openness and exchange of views among staff members increased; and that several individuals emerged with increased self-esteem and peer support by virtue of the leadership opportunities afforded them through increased participation in school affairs.

One of the most notable examples of school-university collaboration is the application of a proposal made by Robert Schaefer in the John Dewey lecture series. John Adams High School, which opened in Portland, Oregon, in September 1969, was created from ideas generated by and translated from Schaefer's model, as reported in a monograph by researchers Fletcher and Williamson (1969).

Schaefer had suggested that reform literature of the 1960s had concentrated on pre-service education as it takes place in the colleges and universities and had failed to examine the total educational experience of teachers on the job. He also observed that educational discourse had remained mainly within the universities and had not gone inside the schools. Therefore, his model proposed that the school be organized as a center of inquiry in which school and university persons (in education departments and other disciplines) would work together. The institution should be characterized by a vigorous pursuit of pedagogy and substantive scholarship through adult interaction between teachers and professors or between teachers and teachers as well as interaction with the students. Schaefer also proposed new modes of inquiry for students, in which they would break out of the school's rigid schedule and the Carnegie unit and seek learning in libraries, museums, and various unconventional places. In the model, administrators were to be facilitators of inquiry for themselves and their associates, and the assumption was that, if adults grew and learned and wrestled with intellectual problems, high school students would also be inspired to do so. One of the major purposes of a school as a center for inquiry would be to discover new knowledge about the instructional process and free teachers to inquire into the nature of what and how they are teaching. Schaefer maintained that pedagogical strategies could not be meaningfully separated from content, and thus teachers also must have continuing opportunities to inquire into the substance being taught.

Trudy Johnson (1974) describes the planning and preparation that went into the organization of John Adams High School and recounts its beginning experiences. In the summer before its opening, scholars, teachers, students, and citizens from the community worked together to prepare the curriculum and to plan instructional processes. A basic premise for the task was that "the university will keep the school intellectual and serious, and the community will keep it relevant and honest."

While John Adams probably developed somewhat differently from the original model that Schaefer described, it has in most ways followed his general concepts. The idea for the high school was born in the fall of 1967, when seven students in the Harvard Graduate School of Education discussed the direction of education and how they would like to develop a school as the central unit for educational change, thus putting into practice current educational theories that often seem to be so far from the realities of a live school setting (Johnson 1974, p. 145). The group proposed a "clinical high school." Portland accepted the idea and implemented it in a school that was currently being opened. Thirteen hundred students were drawn from other Portland high schools, and a staff of about one hundred was gathered primarily from the Portland area. Staff members were chiefly persons who were more interested in current educational theories than the usual faculty. The opening weeks were a testing period in many ways: the conglomeration of students, teachers, and administrators who were new to each other, the university influence, and the presence of student-teachers, paraprofessionals, and other adults who assisted in many different ways were all novel experiences to be assimilated. The school has continued to pursue forward-looking developments in education, to create a unique curriculum, and to explore the effectiveness of varying styles of instruction. All has not been smooth sailing, but persistence and devotion to the original concept have maintained its unique character, and it appears to be a model worth long-range study in school-university relationships.

Schaefer's model provides a reply and a solution to the problem set forth by the National Education Association (1971), which sharply criticized educators of universities and colleges for the continuing dispute and failure of communication between teacher education divisions and liberal arts divisions. The NEA observed that educators had been so divided on whether a teacher's professional preparation should stress the techniques of pedagogy or should focus on a discipline such as history or science that presents programs for teacher education were often doing neither well. The NEA report (p. 78) recognized the need for prospective teachers and their professors in the universities to be brought into realistic involvement:

Perhaps the major defect of teacher education is its isolation from the practical classroom work and the problems of the schools. Teacher education curriculums have been designed entirely by university faculty members—usually the senior faculty, such as department heads, whose school-level teaching experience, if any, is long behind them. Schooled in a quieter age, before the pace of educational change accelerated and before the problems of dropouts and cultural differences received national attention, and accustomed to teaching college students—quite a different breed from the children whom young teachers encounter in the public schools—university faculties have generally been slow to recognize the irrelevance of much of their instruction for new teachers.

While these expressions of dissatisfaction, proposals for solutions, and experiments were coming to light other new projects in school-university collaboration were being funded by foundations (e.g., the Ford Foundation experiments in teacher education), the federal government under the Education Professions Development Act (EPDA), and other innovative categories of funding.

The successful establishment of new links, which continue past the period of outside funding, is characteristic of these projects. A typical example is the joint endeavor of Washington University in St. Louis and the Nathaniel Hawthorne Elementary School in University City, Missouri. University professors and pre-service teachers are highly involved with the principal, teachers, aides, students, and a community advisory committee in developing the curriculum for a new organizational mode. Since 1970 the school has changed from a traditional graded school to an ungraded school with multiple-age arrangements. Although the building is of early 1930s architecture, the interior has been remodeled satisfactorily to adapt to newer, more open concepts of instruction. Professors and student-teachers participate with the school staff in all aspects of the school's program. Courses for the university students are conducted in the elementary school by the professors. School staff members participate both as consultants and as peer-learners. Professors and their students try out segments of curriculum by actually teaching in the school in a clinic situation.

From these collaborative professional efforts, assisted by lay citizens, a new and exciting model has developed that offers a constant program of responsiveness to new knowledge and new constituents. Since the beginning of the joint project in 1970, the school's population, which is migratory, has changed almost totally several times. The project has constantly welcomed newcomers from various ethnic and minority groups. This model of school-university cooperation serves well in a constantly renewing situation (Wirth 1973).

## STUDENT INVOLVEMENT

The literature reports only very recent recognition of the inclusion of young students in the process of curriculum development. Schools have tended to use democratic processes, if at all, at the teacher-teacher level, the teacher-administrator level, or the teacher-administrator-community level.

James House (1969) made a comparative study in Wayne County, Michigan, of how schools that valued student participation differed from schools that did not. In the former, teachers and administrators elicited student opinions and sought to strengthen communication links. A characteristic of these schools was an exciting and relevant curriculum that showed evidence of being responsive to current sociological problems by reshaping the teaching program and eliminating track systems that segregated pupils. The schools encouraged pupils to teach courses without credit, to volunteer for essential community services, to attend department meetings as advisers, to suggest course content for black studies, and to share the spotlight with teachers on curriculum advisory councils. In contrast, in schools where students had little voice in curriculum or administrative decisions, protest and unhappiness seem to prevail.

Other reports indicate that high school students are increasingly taking part in educational planning and curriculum development. In 1971, high school students were serving as nonvoting members of school boards in Richland, Washington; Santa Barbara, California; and Monticello, New York. They served as advisers to state boards of education in California, New Jersey, and South Carolina. In Buffalo, New York, San Diego, California, and Atlanta, Georgia, students were paid to work with teachers during the summer to help revise the curriculum. In Pittsburg, Pennsylvania, students assisted in selecting textbooks, and in Englewood, New Jersey, they had a part in screening administrative personnel for school jobs. In Wilmington, Delaware, students were aiding in the selection of paraprofessionals and in Beverly Hills, California, students helped screen prospective teachers (Education U.S.A. 1971).

In response to student unrest and student apathy, the National Education Association in 1970 appointed a task force on student involvement to investigate current widespread problems (McKenna 1971). The task force identified three problems: dull and irrelevant curricular content and nonmotivating teaching methods, lack of broad involvement of students in the decision-making process, and poor human relations between students and their instructors. The task force noted that the United States Supreme Court in *In re Gault* had stated that "neither the Fourteenth Amendment nor the Bill of Rights is for adults alone." This decision signified to the task force that all students, and particularly those in secondary schools, have the same rights afforded other citizens regardless of age. The task force identified more than one hundred potential techniques for responding to the main causes of unrest. From its study it derived the principle that "all parties to the educational process—students, teachers, administrators, parents—will need to seek better ways cooperatively, and then continually revise and replace them as the rapidly changing society requires" (McKenna 1971, p. 60).

Mark Shedd, Norman Newberg, and Richard Delone (1971), who were closely associated with the "schools without walls" programs in the Philadelphia schools, observe that relevance in the curriculum depends on having students, parents, teachers, and administrators share status, power, and decision-making. These authors cite Philadelphia's Parkway Program, John Adams High School in Portland, Oregon, the British primary schools, and, in an earlier time, Dewey's Laboratory School and the Quincy school system under Colonel Francis Parker as examples of how the collaborative process provides links that create relevance, even though participation sometimes leads to ambiguity. In fact, ambiguity is a precondition of relevance, they assert.

Mario Fantini (1973) describes numerous schools across the United States in which students, teachers, and parents are working together successfully to develop various choices so that each school user can have the type of education she or he wants and needs. A few of the many examples Fantini describes are Quincy Senior High II in Quincy, Illinois; the Berkeley, California, series of alternatives; Murray Road High School in Newton, Massachusetts; and St. Paul Open School, Minnesota.

Research studies have found that very young as well as older students formed important and serious work groups to discuss, plan, and carry out activities in cooperation with adults. In the cases reported, the schools provided constructive learning situations in which children were involved in forging their own roles, working out relationships, and assuming responsibility for self-evaluation. In these situations the teacher acted as guide and resource rather than a not-to-be-questioned authority, critic, and judge. Several studies provide evidence that highly authoritarian situations led to alienation, tension, and destructive activity (see Minuchin 1965; Lippitt and Gold 1959; Mallery 1962; Friedenberg 1963; Henry 1957).

That the curriculum will better serve youth if it extends into the community to bring young people and adults together in working relationships and mutual approaches to problem-solving is expressed by several investigators. William Kvaraceus, Professor of Education and Director of Youth Studies at the Lincoln Filene Center for Citizenship and Public Affairs at Tufts University, deplores the fact that "generally youths are kept powerless in adult society. They have no vote; they are locked out of significant jobs; they are kept dependent through prolonged education in a credential society; they are unorganized" (1969, p. 63). He points to youth problems of delinquency, drug abuse, and alienation, and states that these cannot be solved by professionals working on their own; only youths can solve youth problems, and, when youths begin to serve themselves and the community, solutions will be found.

Sherif and Sherif (1965), after summarizing many studies on the characteristic problems of adolescence, find that, unless the gulf between adolescents and parents or other adults can be bridged, a young person will gravitate toward age-mates who then become his or her reference set, with consequent crippling effects on motivation and attitudes. This concern is shared by Urie Bronfenbrenner (1970, pp. 116-17), who states:

As we read the evidence, both from our own research and that of others we cannot escape the conclusion that, if the current trend persists, if the institutions of our society continue to remove parents, other adults, and older youth from active participation in the lives of children, and if the resulting vacuum is filled by the age-segregated peer group, we can anticipate increased alienation, indifference, antagonism, and violence on the part of the younger generation in all segments of our society—middle-class children as well as the disadvantaged.

A survey conducted by Glenys Unruh and William Alexander (1974, p. 54) identified numerous locations where the curriculum is being extended into the community and students are becoming involved with a wide range of adults.

Juniors and seniors of Lincoln High School, Portland, Oregon, are participating in a unique social studies intern program which takes them into actual professional career situations in governmental and private agencies. Students have been assigned to one or more agencies, including a public interest research group, county offices, a community college, the American Civil Liberties Union, a university, a metropolitan youth commission, hospitals, the city planning commission, and an architectural firm. Specific activities have covered environment, police science, theater arts, freeway and airport studies, law enforcement, domestic relations, urban studies, corrections, parole, education, and medical research. The purpose of the course is to allow students to learn about career possibilities in the social sciences and develop greater insights into urban institutions.

In Los Angeles, high school students have been invited to attend classes sponsored by various industries on their sites to introduce students to industrial careers. Opportunities have been made available in the areas of computer programming, stenography, engineering, photography, and aircraft related industries among others.

Other innovative plans to help students gain more information about the adult world are being practiced. Rochester High School of Rochester, Vermont, sets aside a week in May of each year for students to engage in a community-oriented program. Choices include studies of farming and related occupations, housing construction, forestry studies, Indian reservations, governmental agencies, and others.

An environmental control program of Katahdin (Maine) High School is part of a broader plan for community involvement. Students enrolled in an environmental control course are released from two to four hours each day for learning activities at various sites in nearby forests and state parks. The course involves about 110 hours of instruction and grants one high school credit. A sequential curriculum includes an introduction to the need for environmental improvement, studies of woods fire control, woods safety, entomology, woodlot management, and the work of game biologists, park rangers, state wardens, and the forest service. Trips are made to fish stream projects and wilderness waterways. The course culminates in a five-day wilderness trip.

The Panel on Youth of the President's Science Advisory Committee (1973) recommends extension of this sort of youth-community involvement. These learning experiences, it finds, benefit both youths and adults, as common activities lead each to see the other's point of view. An additional benefit to society is that the contacts facilitate social order and lessen social conflict between age groups.

## COMMUNITY INVOLVEMENT

New experiments with community involvement in curriculum planning that involve parents with school groups are reported in the literature. Fantini (1970) reports an apparently successful experiment in an urban ghetto area in Syracuse, New York, where parents and students were given decision-making powers on curriculum-planning, teacher selection, and allocation of budget resources.

Although the demand for inclusion of parents with teachers and students in educational decision-making is relatively new, several examples of participation can be cited, some successful, others leading toward animosity. A report of the National Education Association (1971) concludes that the fate of education may hang on whether the participants engage in raucous power struggles that harm the schools or instead change the concept of power and realign themselves to engage in cooperative decision-making.

Successful examples of community involvement in curriculum planning include the Berkeley plan, in which a master plan committee of 138 citizens, working over two and one-half years, involved the

community in group meetings. Blacks and whites, liberals and conservatives learned to recognize common interests and to trust each
other sufficiently to demand that their children participate in a
genuine school community (Halpern 1968). An outgrowth of this
extensive involvement of diverse groups was the Experimental
Schools Program of the Berkeley school district, through which
extensive curriculum development is taking place. The program
offers many types of alternatives so that broad humanistic goals of
the schools can be reached (*Experimental Schools Program* 1971).

Frey and Sanchez (1971) describe a project in San Diego, California, in which, over a three-year period, conflict and dissatisfaction
with the school's program have been channeled into meaningful
progress through involvement of parents, administrators, teachers,
and students. Beginning with the objective of opening communication channels, a variety of ad hoc committees with no power
initiated dialogue among minority groups, activist students, interested educators, and some researchers. Proceeding in the second year
to a "groping-striving-identifying" phase, the program in the third
year emerged as a district program actively at work for meaningful
cross-group involvement in activities contributing to responsive curriculum development.

In another study of the San Diego city schools, Stone and Pegas
(1971) report the implementation of a multiple-link system in which
federal, state, and local resources and personnel joined together to
survey needs, establish priorities, and design a curriculum that
focused the most effective combination of resources on the educational goals of the schools. The project, centering on career education, is served by an advisory council that includes representatives
of the federal government, the state government, the city schools,
the teachers' association, parents, community members, and community organizations.

Further support for collaborative action comes from the third
annual report of the President's National Advisory Council on
Supplementary Centers and Services (1971). From a study of innovative Title III (ESEA) projects in the fifty states, the advisory council
made nine recommendations, of which five emphasized the need to
involve many different groups and individuals in educational planning. The council stressed involvement of low-income and minority
groups, non-public-school children and teachers, and representatives

of youth on educational advisory councils; student involvement in the development and improvement of the educational system; and citizen participation at state and local levels in strengthening the work of educational agencies.

A case study of program development in the Dallas, Texas, schools was presented by Nolan Estes (1973) and several associates at an annual conference of professional education associations. In Operation Involvement, the Dallas model for shared decision-making, approximately 600 participants play major roles each year in a complex process for determining program goals and objectives for the city's public school system. The participants take part in program and budget decisions beginning more than a year in advance of preparation of the annual budget. Operation Involvement brings together representatives of various groups, including teachers, students, parents, support staff, principals, and central office staff. The 600 members are divided into twenty-five small groups to focus on various areas of the school program. Employees are given released time for monthly sessions, which range from discussions on the latest school problem to field trips for background information. Several times a year, representatives from each small group meet with the superintendent to assist in setting program priorities. Each representative comes armed with input gained through intensive and extensive discussions at the unit level.

Parent groups represented in Operation Involvement include the Dallas PTA City Council (representing 40,000 PTA members); advisory committees on bilingual education, career education, textbooks, food services, and other areas of concern; and ad hoc groups with whom the superintendent periodically meets by taking his office to various parts of the city for discussions with citizens who cannot or will not come to the central office.

Students are represented through SUPER-SAC, an acronym for the Superintendent's Student Advisory Committee, composed of representatives from eighteen high schools. This group meets regularly with the superintendent to present the students' viewpoints. Each principal of the district's 185 schools has a Teacher Advisory Committee selected by the teachers to represent the views of the entire faculty. These committees meet regularly to discuss concerns and act as sounding boards for new ideas and solutions for school problems.

Secretarial, clerical, maintenance, and custodial personnel each have organizations and are active participants in another large group that feeds into Operation Involvement—the District Communications Committee. Every employee group in the school system is represented on the DCC. Employee groups meet independently on a regular schedule, alternating with meetings of the District Communications Committee, to which they send representatives to provide input and get feedback.

The interests of principals, supervisors, and other administrators are represented through the Dallas School Administrators Association. This group has a full-time president who serves on leave for a year as an ombudsman in the superintendent's office. The position rotates to a different administrative staff member each year.

Operation Involvement, made up of representatives from all these groups, follows a systems approach to shared decision-making. The Dallas group does not assert that it has all the answers, but satisfaction with the development process is evident, and the group is working on the problems of shared decisions.

## SUMMARY

In this chapter, observable findings and research data are provided to support the proposition that better links among participants make the curriculum development process more responsive. Arguments are drawn from studies of successful links among participants that have led to renewal in curriculum development and studies of unsuccessful endeavors in curriculum development in which one or more major sets of participants were omitted during the planning and preparation stages. Examples come from human relations studies, organizational theory, research and development efforts in education, school-university collaborations, new modes of student involvement, and programs of community participation in curriculum development.

## REFERENCES

Barnard, Chester I. *The Functions of the Executive.* Cambridge: Harvard University Press, 1938.

Benne, Kenneth D. "Deliberate Changing as the Facilitation of Growth." In *The Planning of Change,* edited by Warren G. Bennis, Kenneth D. Benne, and Robert Chin, pp. 230-34. New York: Holt, Rinehart and Winston, 1961.

Bronfenbrenner, Urie. *Two Worlds of Childhood: U.S. and U.S.S.R.* New York: Russell Sage, 1970.

Broudy, Harry S. "Needed: A Unifying Theory of Education." In *Curriculum Change: Direction and Process,* pp. 15-26. Washington, D.C.: Association for Supervision and Curriculum Development, 1966.

Combs, Arthur W. "An Educational Imperative: The Human Dimension." In *To Nurture Humaneness*, pp. 173-8. Yearbook of the Association for Supervision and Curriculum Development. Washington, D.C.: ASCD, 1970.

Cuban, Larry. "Teacher and Community." *Harvard Educational Review* 39 (1969): 253-72.

Dewey, John. *Democracy and Education.* New York: Macmillan, 1916.

Doyle, Wayne J., and Ahlbrand, William P. "Hierarchical Group Performance and Leader Orientation." *Administrator's Notebook* 22, no. 3 (1973): 1-4. Published by the Midwest Administration Center of the University of Chicago.

Education U.S.A. "Student Revolt Cooling Off?" In *The Shape of Education for 1971-72*, pp. 60-64. Washington, D.C.: National School Public Relations Association, 1971.

Estes, Nolan. "Case Study of Shared Decision Making in the Dallas Schools." Paper presented at the annual conference of the Alliance of Associations for the Advancement of Education, Dallas, 17 May 1973.

Etzioni, Amitai. "Schools as a 'Guidable' System." In *Freedom, Bureaucracy, and Schooling*, pp. 29-45. Yearbook of the Association for Supervision and Curriculum Development. Washington, D.C.: ASCD, 1971.

*The Experimental Schools Program of the Berkeley School District.* Berkeley: Berkeley School District, 1971.

Fantini, Mario D. *Public Schools of Choice.* New York: Simon and Schuster, 1973.

———. *The Reform of Urban Schools.* Washington, D.C.: National Education Association, 1970.

Featherstone, Joseph. "Tempering a Fad." In *Curriculum: Quest for Relevance*, edited by William Van Til, pp. 212-19. Boston: Houghton Mifflin, 1974.

Fletcher, J., and Williamson, J. "Research and Evaluation at John Adams High School." Mimeographed. Portland, Ore.: John Adams High School, October 1969.

Foshay, Arthur W. "Curriculum Development and the Humane Qualities." In *To Nurture Humaneness*, pp. 143-53. Yearbook of the Association for Supervision and Curriculum Development. Washington, D.C.: ASCD, 1970.

Frank, L. K. "Fragmentation in the Helping Professions." In *The Planning of Change*, edited by Warren G. Bennis, Kenneth D. Benne, and Robert Chin, pp. 43-48. New York: Holt, Rinehart and Winston, 1961.

Frey, G. T., and Sanchez, E. L. "Are You Ready for Community Involvement?" *Thrust* 1 (1971): 21-24.

Friedenberg, Edgar Z. "The Modern High School: A Profile." *Commentary* 36 (November 1963): 373-80.

Halpern, R. "The Berkeley Plan: Tactics for Integration." *Saturday Review*, 21 December 1968, pp. 47-49.

Henry, J. "Attitude Organization in Elementary School Classrooms." *American Journal of Orthopsychiatry* 27 (1957): 117-33.

House, James E. "A Study of Innovative Youth Involvement Activities in Selected Secondary Schools in Wayne County, Michigan." Ed.D. dissertation, Wayne State University, 1969.

Johnson, Trudy M. "Adams High: The First Hundred Days." In *Curriculum: Quest for Relevance*, edited by William Van Til, pp. 142-50. Boston: Houghton Mifflin, 1974.

Kozol, Jonathan. "Free Schools." In *Curriculum: Quest for Relevance*, edited by William Van Til, pp. 194-201. Boston: Houghton Mifflin, 1974.

Kvaraceus, William C. "Working with Youth: Some Operational Principles and Youth Values." *Bulletin of the National Association of Secondary School Principals* 53 (December 1969): 62-71.

Lauter, P. "The Short Happy Life of the Adams-Morgan Community School Project." *Harvard Educational Review* 38 (1968): 235-62.

Lippitt, Ronald, and Gold, M. "Classroom Social Structure as a Mental Health Problem." *Journal of Social Issues* 15 (1959): 40-49.

Litwak, Eugene; Shiroi, Earl; Zimmerman, Libby; and Bernstein, Jessie. "Community Participation in Bureaucratic Organizations: Principles and Strategies." *Interchange* 1, no. 4 (1970): 44-60. Published by the Ontario Institute for Studies in Education, Toronto.

McGregor, Douglas. *The Human Side of Enterprise*. New York: McGraw-Hill, 1960.

McKenna, Bernard. "Student Unrest: Some Causes and Cures." *Bulletin of the National Association of Secondary School Principals* 55 (February 1971): 54-60.

Mallery, David. *High School Students Speak Out*. New York: Harper and Row, 1962.

March, James G., and Simon, Herbert A. *Organizations*. New York: John Wiley, 1959.

Merriman, Howard O. "A Conception of Curriculum Evaluation involving Teachers, Parents, and Other Educational Decision-makers." In *Elements of Curriculum Development*, pp. 23-34. Monograph supplement of *Curriculum Theory Network*. Toronto: Ontario Institute for Studies in Education, 1971.

Minuchin, P. P. "Solving Problems Cooperatively: A Comparison of Three Classroom Groups." *Childhood Education* 41 (1965): 480-84.

National Education Association. *Schools for the 70's and Beyond: A Call to Action*. Washington, D.C.: NEA, 1971.

———. *Rational Planning in Curriculum and Instruction*. Washington, D.C.: NEA, 1967.

Nystrand, Raphael O., and Cunningham, Luvern L. "Organizing Schools to Develop Human Capabilities." In *To Nurture Humaneness*, pp. 120-42. Yearbook of the Association for Supervision and Curriculum Development. Washington, D.C.: ASCD, 1970.

Panel on Youth of the President's Science Advisory Committee. *Youth: Transition to Adulthood*. Washington, D.C.: U.S. Government Printing Office, 1973.

Pillet, Roger A. "Boundaries of a Curriculum Network." In *Elements of Curriculum Development*, pp. 7-11. Monograph supplement of *Curriculum Theory Network*. Toronto: Ontario Institute for Studies in Education, 1971.

President's National Advisory Council on Supplementary Centers and Services. *Educational Reform through Innovation*. Washington, D.C.: Educational Policy Group, George Washington University, 1971.

Rubin, Louis J., ed. *Improving In-Service Education*. Boston: Allyn and Bacon, 1971.

Schaefer, Robert J. *The School as a Center of Inquiry*. New York: Harper and Row, 1967.

Shedd, Mark R.; Newberg, Norman A.; and DeLone, Richard H. "Yesterday's Curriculum/Today's World: Time to Reinvent the Wheel." In *The Curriculum: Retrospect and Prospect*, part I, pp. 153-60. Seventieth Yearbook of the National Society for the Study of Education. Chicago: University of Chicago Press, 1971.

Sherif, M., and Sherif, C. M., eds. *Problems of Youth: Transition to Adulthood in a Changing World*. Chicago: Aldine Press, 1965.

Stiles, Lindley, et al. "Cardoza Project in Urban Teaching: Evaluation and Recommendations." Mimeographed. February 1967, pp. 13-15. Quoted in Cuban, Larry. "Teacher and Community." *Harvard Educational Review* 39 (spring 1969): 253-72.

Stone, W. J., and Pegas, B. "Linkages: Federal, State, and District Cooperation." *Thrust* 1 (1971): 16-20.

Unruh, Glenys G., and Alexander, William M. *Innovations in Secondary Education*. 2d ed. New York: Holt, Rinehart and Winston, 1974.

Wirth, Arthur G. *An Inquiry-Personal Commitment Model of Teacher Education: The Hawthorne Teacher Education Project, Washington University*. St. Louis: Washington University, 1973.

# Systems Concepts in Curriculum Development

**PROPOSITION: If concepts of open systems are used, the curriculum development process will become more responsive to the need for interrelating its factors and participants.**

This is the seventh of a set of interrelated propositions, presented in chapters six through twelve, that explicate the complex nature of curriculum development. In chapter thirteen, these propositions are brought together to form a theory that generates constructs and hypotheses. Single-principle or linear approaches, which have prevailed at times in curriculum history, lack the scope and breadth of vision for curriculum development that is responsive to humanistic and democratic ideals, moral values, changing knowledge, new skills, and the findings of futures research.

This seventh proposition focuses on systems concepts in curriculum development. Significant propositions (needs, planning, links) are discussed in three preceding chapters and interwoven here in the interacting relationships of systems concepts.

## DEFINITIONS AND CHARACTERISTICS
## OF SYSTEMS APPROACHES

A *system* is a complex unity of parts related to each other in a manner that serves a common purpose. As curriculum development is not a single system but is a combination of interacting systems and subsystems, the terms systems concept and systems approach are used in this discussion rather than system concept or approach.

Throughout this discussion, the term systems in relation to responsiveness in curriculum development refers to open systems concepts as distinguished from closed systems. These two terms were defined in chapter nine as follows: *Open systems* concepts imply a constant state of self-renewal. Such systems continuously reorganize to meet new problems, to examine new complexities, and to use new ideas and information as a part of the planning and renewal process. *Closed systems* approaches to problems analyze them in terms of some internal structure and ignore external environments (societal issues, for example).

Open systems concepts in curriculum development are directed toward making education responsive to the student and his or her world. By emphasizing the critical role of people in identifying needs and in planning, and by developing thoughtful procedures and processes for achieving results, systems concepts provide orderly, self-adjusting processes for curriculum development to identify needs and design effective ways to meet them.

Systems *concepts* imply a search for relationships and ways of optimizing the interaction of components. Systems *approaches* apply systems concepts to human endeavors. A systems approach offers a decision-making structure and a set of decision-making strategies. It makes available a self-correcting, logical process for the planning, development, and implementation of man-made entities. Systems approaches look at more than one system and determine ways of combining and integrating systems to solve problems. Open systems approaches emphasize a process that begins with the needs perceived by the participants in the curriculum development process rather than needs predetermined by external producers of curriculum plans and materials.

A systems approach is action-oriented. It responds to needs in a logical, orderly manner. It requires that something be done and, when done, that it be evaluated. A systems approach is an analytic rather than an erratic approach. It requires planning and action to be accomplished in a manner that allows participants to revise the plans, as action and experience proceed, and incorporate constructive improvements. A systems approach requires initiative and commitment. Curriculum-planners using a systems approach must be ready to document and make public exactly what they are doing, why they are doing it, and how the curriculum is being developed. The participants and consumers must evaluate the curriculum development effort so that it can be continually improved.

It is important to emphasize that any systems approach is a process, a means, a way of achieving something; it is not the product itself. In curriculum development, systems approaches recognize the interactions of the factors and participants engaged in the process and recognize that it is necessary to organize, integrate, and manage those components that contribute to achievement of learning outcomes. This means obligating each human and material resource to make its unique contribution to the learning-teaching situation. This also necessitates mutual planning for, agreement on, and assessment of the use of material resources and the roles of humans.

Donald Miller (1970) observes that systems concepts enhance human capabilities to make decisions and solve problems and that systems approaches accept as input many relatively intangible factors derived from human judgment. The education-related problems of our time are so complex and massive in scope, Miller contends, that they require an integrated approach, a systems concept.

John Pfeiffer (1968, pp. 2-3) emphasizes the role of systems in decision-making:

> The systems approach can be regarded as a disciplined way of using specialists in a variety of fields to analyze as precisely as possible sets of activities whose interrelationships are very complicated, and of formulating comprehensive and flexible plans on the basis of the analysis. The frame of reference is unequivocally the real world. . . . The systems approach concerns itself above all with the nature of decision making. Intangibles have always played a leading role in the process and there is no substitute for judgment, the unique contribution of the man shaping major policies. He is always on his own when the chips are down. No one can help him at the moment of decision when he selects one course of action over another. Before he reaches this stage, the systems approach comes in to provide guidelines and evaluations, on the theory that a combination of his judgment and an analysis drawing on the advanced technology of assessment may be more effective than either alone.

Systems concepts may be applied to complex or simple organizations, to broad or narrow societal contexts, and to various sizes of units of human interaction. A wide range of procedures is available. In no case, observes Pfeiffer, does the use of a systems approach imply a "one-shot" solution to curriculum problems. Pfeiffer also points out that the coming together of the systems approach and education is by no means an isolated phenomenon and that, broadly viewed, it is part of a significant shift in social values. Application of the systems approach to human problems he views as a trend toward giving humanism a higher place among our priorities, instead of subordinating it to military and industrial problems.

Raphael Nystrand and Luvern Cunningham (1970), and Robert Gilchrist and J. W. Gott (1971) are among those who view systems as having the potential for helping education to support and enhance human values through better curriculum decision-making. Systems approaches can relate goals, objectives, educational experiences, educational outcomes, costs, and resources in ways that are supportive of human values. In systems approaches to the development of curriculum, alternatives for achieving objectives must be examined. To quote Gilchrist and Gott (p. 28):

System logic need not be and, indeed, within education must not be mechanistic and aloof from life. . . . [A] system approach wisely applied will enable educators, citizens, and students to become partners in developing an educational program that is the best current knowledge, research, and resources can provide. Not only so, but a system approach will enable educators to see the interdependence of their individual roles in the total educational program.

Arthur Foshay (1970, pp. 152-53) relates curriculum development in a broad sense to systems concepts when he observes that it seems more productive to undertake curriculum development as

an inquiry in a highly interactive fashion which attempts to take advantage of the strengths of individuals as they are perceived by themselves in a cooperative setting, to pursue rigorously all of the human qualities, and to examine constantly the apparent consequences of one's efforts. . . . Curriculum development probably is best regarded as a set of actions intended to bring about improvement, constantly corrected so that improvement is brought more nearly within the grasp of those who would bring it about.

## HISTORICAL ROOTS

The beginnings of the systems concept, observes Roger Kaufman (1970), can be traced back to early philosophers who concerned themselves with human beings, environment, and knowledge. Anthony Oettinger (1968) also remarks that systems concepts have roots reaching back through Roger Bacon to Aristotle and not, as some believe, just to the RAND Corporation. Early philosophers identified several alternative ways of acquiring knowledge, including intuition, phenomenology, rationalism, and empiricism. Of particular interest to systems thinking is empiricism, or the acquisition of knowledge gained from experience. As the scientific method evolved, it was found to be fairly reliable for acquiring information and for making reasonable predictions about future events.

General system theory began to attract attention in physics and biology during the 1920s, but it was not until the late 1940s that a trend began to emerge in several disciplines. Norbert Wiener's book *Cybernetics* (1948) brought the concepts of feedback and information processing to the attention of both biological and social sciences and made a lasting impression throughout the realm of science, with "fallout" in other fields. During and after World War II, research and development in problem-solving and the development of complex man-machine systems produced new methods of planning and development. These made available new ways of thinking about complex problems and their changing relationships, with applications to education and, in this discussion, to curriculum development.

Numerous writings began to appear in educational literature in the early 1950s and have increased since. Added impetus to use systems concepts was given by federal funding guidelines that required cognizance of the elements of systems approaches. Needs assessment, now demanded by nearly all states of the union, represents an element of systems concepts.

The extensive use of systems concepts in military enterprises, explorations in space, and business and industry, however, has to some extent inhibited the use of systems approaches in educational and other humanistic endeavors. Oettinger critically observes that advocating systems analysis as a panacea ranks with advocating making the world safe for democracy; nevertheless, he adds, "not to believe in the usefulness of systems analysis is to deny the value of

reason, common sense, and, indeed, the scientific method" (p. 77).
James Macdonald (1967), while recognizing the importance of
systems concepts for educational planning, emphasizes that systems
methods must be "transformed" and "not merely transferred" from
industry, business, and government to educational uses. This proposition is directed toward transforming systems concepts and drawing
on related studies, to fashion an aspect of responsive curriculum
development.

## ELEMENTS OF SYSTEMS APPROACHES

Although terminology, interpretations, and sequences vary from
source to source, several basic elements, aspects, or steps are significant in applications of systems concepts to problems of education
and specifically of curriculum development. Broad goals, needs,
objectives, constraints, alternatives, selection, implementation, evaluation, and modification are generally accepted as the elements of
systems approaches in education. Each element is initiated by human
action, has a particular intent and function, and is related to the
other elements. Each element is a field of study in itself and is
represented by a body of literature and information composed of
factual descriptions, concepts, generalizations, and principles that
can be submitted to further analysis and interpretation.

### Broad Goals

The overarching goals of an enterprise are usually expressed in
philosophical statements that serve as guides for the school's program
and as standards against which needs are assessed. Statements of
goals may list such desirable outcomes as personal self-fulfillment,
moral responsibility, social consciousness and effectiveness, economic awareness, and acquisition of knowledge and skills.

National curriculum groups and commissions have frequently
formulated goals that are very broad in scope; for example, "worthy
use of leisure time," and "development of an appreciation of the
value and power of science in our technological society." Broad goals
are designed to give direction to policymakers at the national, state,
and local levels; though lofty, they provide value bases for curriculum development.

A goal is something broader, longer range, and more visionary than an objective. F. R. Kappel (1960, p. 38) describes it as

something presently out of reach; it is something to strive for, to move toward, or to become. It is an aim or purpose so stated that it excites the imagination and gives people something they want to work for, something they don't yet know how to do, something they can be proud of when they achieve it.

Curriculum developers need to have both broad goals and more immediate objectives of curriculum and instruction.

### Need

Need is defined as the discrepancy between the actual and the ideal or desirable. The first step in a systems approach is to assess the real needs of the participants. Identified needs must be actual human needs if the curriculum is to have relevance. Frequently a symptom or perception is thought to be an actual need; for example, "We need new math books," may be offered as a need. Determining need in a systems approach entails making a comprehensive analysis of subjective and objective baseline data for use in measuring progress. The determination recognizes dimensions of need related to society, the learner, and the nature of knowledge. The identification of need as a discrepancy leads to the derivation of a problem statement. In our hypothetical example, the need might be: "Children in school $X$ have an average mathematics score of 1 standard deviation or more below the mean of standardized test $Y$, which indicates low performance and interest." To ensure relevance in the curriculum development process, a valid needs assessment should be a first step in a systems approach. An extensive discussion of needs and needs assessments is provided in chapter ten.

### Objectives

From needs, problems are identified and are stated in terms of meaningful, desirable, and measurable or observable learning objectives. This is the most important step of the systems approach, because all subsequent steps are designed to generate learnings to meet the objectives. Expressing objectives entails asking the right questions, says John Pfeiffer (1968), an essential step in coming to grips with a problem. A systems approach depends on the art of expressing objectives in terms that can be used in the process of evaluation to provide feedback for modification.

Objectives may be formulated at several levels of specificity, ranging from general objectives for a comprehensive curriculum plan to objectives devised by a teacher for a lesson plan. Figure 4 presents an ordering of objectives for a science curriculum prepared by the Northwest Regional Educational Laboratory of Portland, Oregon, and is an example of levels of objectives ranging from general to specific. Figure 5 presents objectives related to the self-knowledge domain of a career development program. These two examples (science and self-knowledge) typify objectives in the factual and the abstract areas of curriculum.

FIGURE 4
Types of Goals and Objectives for Student Learning

| | | |
|---|---|---|
| System Goal | The student knows and is able to apply basic scientific and technological processes. | *Planning* |
| Program Goal | The student is able to use the conventional language, instruments, and operations of science. | |
| Course Goal | The student is able to classify organisms according to their conventional taxonomic categories. | |
| Instructional Goal | The student is able to classify correctly as needleleaf the cuttings of hemlocks, pines, spruces, firs, larches, cypresses, redwoods, and cedars. | |
| Behavioral Objective | Given cuttings of ten trees, several of which are needleleaf, the student is able to identify correctly which are needleleaf. | *Measurement* |
| Performance Objective | Given cuttings of ten trees, seven of which are needleleaf, the student is able to identify correctly at least six of the seven as belonging to the needleleaf class. | |

Example from "Science," provided by Northwest Regional Educational Laboratory, Portland, Oregon 97204. Used by permission.

## FIGURE 5
### Self-Knowledge Domain

---

*Goal:*
For individuals to have an understanding of self that will enable them
to make life career decisions.

*Developmental Objectives (K-12)*

K-3        For individuals to develop an awareness of their own
                characteristics
                For individuals to be aware that the personal characteristics
                of individuals differ

4-6        For individuals to develop the ability to assess their own
                characteristics
                For individuals to understand their current attitudes,
                beliefs, and values

7-9        For individuals to assume responsibility for continuous
                self-appraisal

                For individuals to understand that successes and failures
                contribute to self-understanding.

10-12     For individuals to formulate tentative career plans
                consistent with knowledge of self
                For individuals to begin to formulate plans for participation
                in adult social roles consistent with their self-understand-
                ing

Example of a developmental objective translated into more specific
objectives:

*Performance Objectives*

1. The individual will demonstrate in a written self-report, an
understanding of the nonstatic nature of personal characteristics by
identifying recent changes in his or her interests.

2. The individual will demonstrate an ability to gather self-information
from both internal and external sources by writing a self-appraisal
including a description of his or her information-seeking process.

3. The individual will assume the responsibility to make a positive
effort toward improving a personal weakness that he or she has
identified in a process of self-appraisal.

From Norman C. Gysbers and Earl J. Moore, *The Career Conscious Individual
Career Education Model* (Columbia: University of Missouri, 1973). Reprinted by
permission.

Problems may surround the preparation and use of educational objectives if curriculum developers select trivial objectives, objectives that are wrong for the particular situation, or objectives that overemphasize small, detailed facts and skills and omit more subtle abilities and attitudes. It is relatively easy to express such objectives as the ability to identify parts of a flower correctly or to list the names of all the presidents in sequential order; however, humanistic, creative, social, and problem-solving abilities and attitudes can also be stated in measurable terms, and this is an open challenge to the curriculum developer.

Objectives must be meaningful as well as measurable. Bruce Joyce (1971) calls attention to the power of purpose in curriculum-planning and says that systems procedures can be the curriculum field's most powerful program planning tool, if used to generate alternative goals and means rather than to identify the most economical or narrow path to given ends.

The typical approach to working out curriculum objectives for students, schools, or school systems is for a group of educators, academicians, or psychometricians, or some mixture of these to decide what they believe should happen to students as a consequence of curriculum-planning. In the past, representatives of the citizenry at large have occasionally been included in the group but usually in token numbers. If there is assent without understanding, objectives may seem meaningless and irrelevant at the point of implementation. The students themselves, as well as their teachers, their parents, their prospective employers, and educational policymakers must be cognizant of the goal-setting process and have some part in the development of meaningful goals and objectives. A systems approach, by involving the participants, will avoid a long-standing problem in curriculum development—basing a curriculum on the assumption that educational goals are "given" and that the only problem is to figure out how to attain them.

Henry Dyer (1972, p. 114) makes this point clearly:

Each individual and each generation has to create its own truth by which to know the world of its own time and place, and, by the same token, it has to create its own goals for ordering its efforts to cope with the world. Thus, the discovery and development of educational goals have to be part of the educational process itself, starting with the child and continuing with the adult as he works his way through to the personal, social, and economic decisions that determine the shape of the free world he is to live in.

This may be what John Dewey had in mind when he said (1938, p. 71) that "freedom resides in the operations of intelligent observation and judgment by which a purpose is developed."

## Constraints

It is imperative that constraints be identified, listed, and analyzed for authenticity to guide the selection of alternative activities. The school setting for which a curriculum plan is developed will undoubtedly lack certain resources that may be suggested as highly desirable. Physical facilities, equipment, material resources, teaching aids, fiscal limitations, and legal requirements must all be considered, as well as a variety of societal factors. The amount of in-service education needed to install a new curriculum plan may be prohibitive. On the other hand, a mathematics curriculum that might be easily installed and require no in-service training might be such a weak solution to instructional problems that it would have very little impact.

It is also necessary to examine purported constraints to determine whether they are imaginary or real. Mediocrity can be perpetuated by seeking to retain the status quo or to reflect years of tradition. Much of the technological progress that has occurred during the twentieth century has resulted from an attitude that "there must be a better way." This approach inspires a constant search for potential solutions to problems in many fields, including education.

## Alternatives

Seeking alternatives is an important concept in systems approaches. Unless alternative activities for meeting each objective are present, a systems approach is not being used. When a planning group offers a single course of action for reaching a given objective, the group tends to assume the role of salesman rather than that of planner in the sense used in systems approaches. Once objectives and criteria for evaluation have been determined, the next step is to identify different methods of meeting each objective. States Pfeiffer (1968, p. 5):

This is an active, not a passive step. There must be an organized effort to search out alternatives, perhaps the most important and creative phase of systems analysis. It demands open-mindedness and readiness to discard pre-conceived notions. Furthermore, the alternatives may be combined in different ways and each combination represents a possible plan, a set of activities which may bring about a desired set of changes.

l solutions can be generated through a "brainstorming"
r through opinion surveys, discussion sessions, interviews,
...nes of the literature, visits to other sites, discussions with
experts, and exchanges within and among peer groups. The development of alternatives should be done in an atmosphere of intellectual
freedom, with participation from as many different groups of people
as possible. No potential solution should be rejected or discarded
until all possible solutions are on the table. A general procedure for
seeking alternatives is: (1) gather data based on current and projected
solutions to the identified problem, (2) solicit ideas from a wide
range of sources, (3) keep a written list of all suggested ideas, even
though some may seem impractical at the time. If ideas submitted
are insufficient in quantity or scope, further search is necessary.

## Selection

Choice of the best alternative or alternatives is a critical point in
the systems approach. Selection criteria must be clearly stated. They
include such factors as the cost, the time required for implementation, the degree of risk involved, and the impact on other portions of
the system. Criteria may be translated into numerical weights as a
part of the process of selection, although alternatives carrying the
greatest numerical weight must still be subjected to rigorous analysis
and judged on the basis of experience and common sense in making
selections.

In the selection of alternative activities or strategies, consideration
must be given to:

1. *people to be affected*—their capabilities, their availability, the
number involved, their grade level, etc.
2. *time*—the length of time during which the change is to occur or
the work is to be done.
3. *resources*—the availability of specialized personnel, if needed,
material resources, services such as transportation for field trips, etc.
4. *cost*—careful consideration should be given to the reasonable-
ness of the probable cost of the activity.

## Implementation

Preparation of a timetable, design of a flow chart, task analysis,
assignment of job responsibilities, and other aspects of organizing

activities from week to week or day to day are essential. Monitoring provides constant information on progress toward objectives and goals. Curriculum plans and materials being developed for wide use usually are field-tested in part or whole, while in the process of development. The reactions of students and teachers during the trial stages are essential feedback for further modification. In a large-scale endeavor, a pilot stage may follow, in which the prototype is given a test run and still further feedback is provided. But even after the product is ready for wide distribution its responsiveness to changing times, places, and people will depend on its capacity for renewal.

The following figures illustrate applications of systems approaches graphically. Figure 6 presents a curriculum development model based on a systems approach. Figure 7 illustrates a task-breakdown technique. Both of these are examples of procedures that are part of systems approaches such as those used in regional laboratories and other research and development centers. Curriculum development products now available through these centers include the Wisconsin Design for Reading Skill Development, produced at the University of Wisconsin by the Wisconsin Research and Development Center for Cognitive Learning; the Language and Thinking Program and the Aesthetic Education Program developed by CEMREL in St. Louis; and Bilingual Continuous Progress Mathematics and Exploring Number Concepts produced by the Southwest Educational Development Laboratory in Austin, Texas. Pilot tryouts with controlled situations for collecting data have been a part of each of these curriculum development processes. Favorable results are reported in "Curriculum Development" (1974).

In figure 8 a systems approach is employed to provide for instructional management for the curriculum plan. In this model, both individual self-directed learning environments and group processes are planned. This figure represents the process developed at Valley High School, Las Vegas, Nevada, and is adapted from Philip Kapfer's model (1968).

## Evaluation

In systems approaches, evaluation provides constant feedback to appraise how well specified objectives are being met and to suggest revisions of the curriculum. Both formative and summative evaluations are essential in a systems approach. Michael Scriven (1967),

**FIGURE 6**

**Curriculum Development Steps Using Systems Approach**

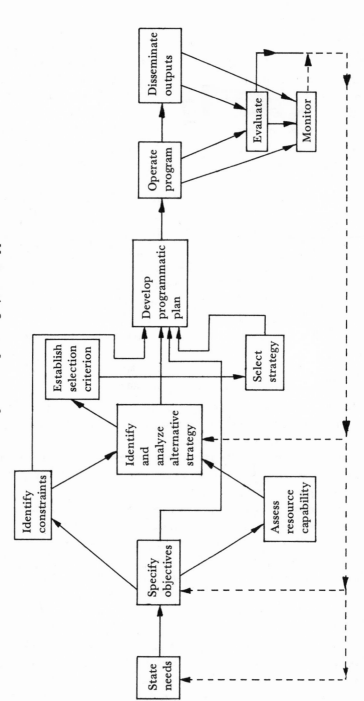

From James A. Hopson, *Managing Educational Development: A Systems Approach* (University City, Mo.: School District, 1973). Reprinted by permission.

who is credited with coining the terms *summative* and *formative* evaluation, defines formative evaluation in relation to curriculum development as the collection of appropriate evidence during the construction and trial of a new curriculum in such a way that revisions of the curriculum can be based on this evidence. Formative evaluation is almost exclusively aimed at improving the educational experience or product during its developmental phases. Benjamin Bloom et al. (1971, pp. 117-18) note that formative evaluation is the use of systematic evaluation in the process of curriculum

### FIGURE 7
**Tabular Work-Breakdown Structure Technique**

| Level 0 | Level 1 | Level 2 | Level 3 |
|---------|---------|---------|---------|
| Entire program | Design and develop | Collect knowledge | |
| | | Prototype development | |
| | | Redevelopment | |
| | Test | Formative testing | |
| | | Summative testing | Pilot test |
| | | | Field test |
| | Produce materials | | |
| | | | |
| | Disseminate | | |

The first step is to break the total activity into a few major segments, related to either the main products to be produced or the major functions to be performed in developing a single product. These sets are then progressively broken into subsets until the task level is reached.

From James A. Hopson, *Managing Educational Development: A Systems Approach* (University City, Mo.: School District, 1973). Reprinted by permission.

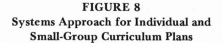

FIGURE 8
Systems Approach for Individual and
Small-Group Curriculum Plans

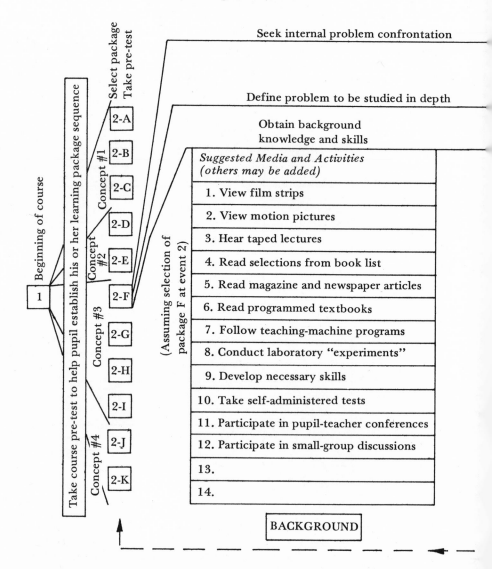

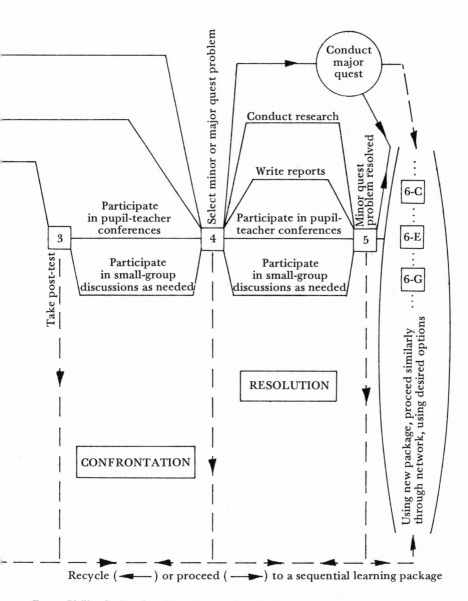

Recycle ( ◀── ) or proceed ( ──▶ ) to a sequential learning package

From Philip G. Kapfer, "An Instructional Management Strategy for Individualized Learning," *Phi Delta Kappan* 49 (January 1968): 262. Reprinted by
permission.

construction, teaching, and learning, for the purpose of improving any of these processes.

This means that in formative evaluation one must strive to develop the kind of evidence that will be most useful in the process, seek the most useful method of reporting the evidence, and search for ways of reducing the negative effect associated with evaluation—perhaps by reducing the judgmental aspects of evaluation, or, at the least, by having the users of the formative evaluation (teacher, students, curriculum makers) make the judgments. The hope is that the users of the formative evaluation will find ways of relating the results of the evaluation to the learning and instructional goals they regard as important and worthwhile.

Summative evaluation implies that a judgment is made about the effectiveness of learning or instruction under the curriculum after the learning or instruction has taken place. It is the type of evaluation used at the end of a term, course, or program for making an overall decision. Summative evaluation may employ either absolute or comparative standards and judgments; however, it frequently uses judgments. It sometimes produces anxiety and defensiveness in students, teachers, and curriculum-makers, but it is hardly possible to avoid responsibility for making a summative evaluation.

In a systems approach, both summative and formative evaluations are used diagnostically—for revising objectives, seeking better alternatives, and finding ways to assist the learner in achieving anticipated learning outcomes. Feedback is an important element in a systems approach. The system constantly gathers information about how it is doing and feeds the information back to planners to steer future operations. The power of evaluation rests on the nature of the feedback operation generated by the process. Feedback is a major concept in designing action to correct or increase the system's diagnostic sensitivity to the effects of given actions on learning outcomes.

Desirable characteristics of the evaluation process are listed by David Payne (1974, p. 6):

1. Evaluation is effective as it provides evidence of the extent of the changes in students.

2. Evaluation is most conducive to learning when it provides for and encourages self-evaluation.

3. Evaluation is conducive to good instruction when it reveals major types of inadequate behavior and the contributory causes.

4. Evaluation is most significant in learning when it permits and encourages the exercise of individual initiative.

5. Activities or exercises developed for the purposes of evaluating specified behavior are also useful for the teaching and learning of that behavior.

Robert Stake (1974) has identified the key emphases of the nine curriculum evaluation models shown in figure 9. All emphasize feedback and recycling phases, and all share the assumption that an assessment of needs has been made before program development. Models for the evaluation of a single curriculum differ from those that are comparative in nature. All models emphasize decision-making and reflect the biases and individual intents of their

**FIGURE 9**
**Key Emphases of Selected Curriculum Evaluation Models**

| Model Developer | Key Emphasis |
| --- | --- |
| Tyler (1942) | Curriculum objectives and evaluation of student progress |
| Provus (1969) | Assessment of discrepancy between program performance and standards |
| Taylor and Maguire (1966); Metfessel and Michael (1967) | Objectives and involvement of variety of personnel (laymen, professional educators, students, philosophers, psychologists) |
| NSSSE (1960) | Staff self-study with overview of content, facilities, and procedures |
| Stake (1967) | Gathering and processing description and judgment data |
| Crane and Abt (1969) | Estimation of cost-effectiveness of alternative curriculum materials |
| Welch and Walberg (1968) | Improvement of college physics curriculum using change data |
| Stufflebeam (1968); Klein et al. (1970) | Rational decision-making among alternatives by administrator |
| Light and Smith (1970) | Evaluation of national intervention programs through post hoc survey |

Based on an idea suggested by a chart developed by Dr. Robert E. Stake of the Center for Instructional Research and Curriculum Evaluation, University of Illinois, 1969. From David A. Payne, *Curriculum Evaluation* (Lexington, Mass.: D. C. Heath and Company 1974), p. 12. Reprinted by permission.

developers. The specification of instructional objectives plays a central role in nearly all models. Overlap among these models in terms of approach, content, and method is considerable, and they are presented to identify emphases in curriculum-related evaluation and to offer sources for further investigation.

## Modification

The evaluation process is by no means a stopping point in a systems approach. Any failure to fulfill the objectives must now be studied, changes must be made in the alternatives offered, selected alternatives must be implemented, and the results must again be evaluated. Since objectives also change in time, owing to changing conditions of society, knowledge, and the nature of learners, the process of modifying the system, based on successes and failures in meeting objectives, continues. Responsive curriculum development uses an open systems approach—it constantly receives new inputs, gathers new knowledge, and operates under changing conditions. The interactive nature of a systems model demands organization and integration of its elements.

Inputs affecting modification may be professional advice, new knowledge, the learners' reactions, etc., but connectives representing avenues for modification must be built into the systems model, so that not only interaction but also transaction takes place, in which each element gains from the other. Robert Chin (1969) emphasizes that a systems model offers a means for examining interaction both within and among units and is applicable to problems of leadership, power, communication, conflict in organizations, and intergroup relations as these affect curriculum development. If each input group is viewed as dependent on connectives to other groups and not solely on the relationships within its own group, the systems approach provides a tool for diagnosis and implementation of collaborative planning.

### OBJECTIONS TO SYSTEMS APPROACHES

Several objections and misconceptions are raised about systems approaches. Some persons consider a systems approach to be dehumanizing, noncreative, and unresponsive to human life and freedom. Some objections derive from a perception based on a behavioristic model. Others see the systems approach only as a closed system. It is sometimes thought to perpetuate the industrial model of education. Another major source of confusion about the systems approach is that it is mistaken for a total educational program for a given set of learners.

Kaufman (1970) argues that a systems approach is not dehumanizing, limiting, or narrowing. Because it takes into account distinct differences among people and among alternative objectives and procedures, it is uniquely human and humane. It is broad and inclusive by design. He maintains (p. 125), "Only people can dehumanize the educational process and its products, and they do not need a systems approach to do it."

Critics who perceive a systems approach as a behavioristic model allege that the pursuit of such a materialistic approach will dehumanize learners by putting them all into a single mold. The triviality of the measurable objectives that are used in some current educational activities are cited in support of this claim. To the extent that trivial objectives are central in a systems approach, the contention is true. To prevent this dehumanization, those using systems approaches should make sure that they respond fully to the needs of learners and of society, both present and future. Learners need to be provided with skills that enable them not only to survive in the current environment but also to reshape culture and society for the benefit of all mankind in the light of future trends. Responsiveness to human needs in a systems approach depends on the critical ingredients of (1) validity of input data, (2) integrity and objectivity, and (3) ability to state requirements in terms that can be included in a system.

Adherents of one model over the other (of the behavioristic model versus the humanistic or phenomenological model) are missing contributions from both positions, states Kaufman. He refers to W. D. Hitt's "Two Models of Man" (1969, pp. 651-52) for descriptions of these models:

The behavioristic model: Man can be described meaningfully in terms of his behavior; he is predictable; he is an information transmitter; he lives in an objective world; he is rational; he has traits in common with other men; he may be described in absolute terms; his characteristics can be studied independently of one another; he is a reality; he is knowable in scientific terms.

The phenomenological model: Man can be described meaningfully in terms of his consciousness; he is unpredictable; he is an information generator; he lives in a subjective world; he is arational; he is unique alongside millions of other unique personalities; he can be described in relative terms; he must be studied in a holistic manner; he is a potentiality; he is more than we can ever know about him.

The truth appears to lie in both directions; however, overreliance on narrow behavioral objectives may lead to a closed system of thinking. If teachers are preoccupied with narrow objectives that discourage innovation, stifle creativity, and make the classroom a dull, conforming place, then students will be taught in closed systems and are very likely to feel trapped, caught in a mesh over which they have no control, states Arthur Combs (1972). If they have no part in determining objectives and desirable outcomes, they are also likely to feel no commitment to them. Educational processes, in such a situation, become irrelevant, teachers are likely to be regarded as the enemy, and the system is seen as something to be sabotaged at every opportunity.

Combs also notes that, while behavioral objectives are useful in the achievement of specific skills, they do not lend themselves well to more general goals. If the systems approach is so narrowly conceived that it concentrates on specific skills to the exclusion of the general goals of the educational process, the major thrust of the system tends to be distorted.

The systems approach applied to curriculum development must be based on an open system, as described earlier in this chapter. Otherwise, the industrial model, with its batch processing and depersonalized attitude, will further alienate students. Systems approaches do not identify, define, and prescribe the total educational program; they are intended to identify only minimal requirements. When participants and consumers of the curriculum development process are included in identifying needs, designing objectives, selecting alternatives, and evaluating results, systems approaches can increase their motivation and self-actualization.

## CONTEXTUAL CONSIDERATIONS

Applications of systems approaches to curriculum development may take place in micro units (individuals, large or small groups of students) or in macro units (schools, districts, or states). At the macro level, curriculum development must meet the challenges of a rapidly changing society and fulfill demands that present a highly complex set of interrelated problems to education. Bela Banathy (1967, p. 283) lists these demands on contemporary curriculum development:

1. Increase education for all members of our society (particularly for those who are educationally disadvantaged).

2. Do this with a better productivity and economy of the instructional process.

3. Increase continuously the quality of learning experience.

4. Cope with the ever-accelerating information and knowledge explosion.

5. Provide for individual differences to permit the utilization of one's full potential.

Exploration of solutions to such complex interrelated problems requires a comprehensive framework. The systems approach, says Banathy, makes available to education a logical and psychological process for analyzing, coordinating, and controlling the array of interrelated factors. He notes that the systems approach is a way of looking at a process, a method that enables us to analyze a complex problem and then to synthesize a solution. Systems approaches, wisely used, help avoid panacea approaches.

Under pressure for solutions to meet urgent problems, curriculum-planners at any level may treat a symptom with a partial remedy when a deeper underlying cause is part of a complex problem requiring systematic diagnosis and solution. Marjorie Prentice (1973, p. 310) notes the holistic and synergistic qualities that are required for the management of curriculum development and observes:

Thus all parts of a system are seen as being interdependent, and the system itself is greater than the sum of its parts. When fully considering these qualities, one does not "band-aid" one part of the system without careful analysis of the consequences to other parts of the system; neither does one make decisions while in a crisis-mode without assessing potential alternatives.

The curriculum-planner, whether working with a micro unit or a macro unit, needs to be sensitive to the feelings, attitudes, and intuitions of those with whom he or she works and of those in the environmental context surrounding the planning unit. Prentice notes that, before a development task can get under way, the curriculum-planner must have realistic knowledge about a number of vital areas: the social-cultural milieu, the available resources, the possible organizational structures, the values held by the participants, the processes considered workable in that situation, the theoretical constructs underlying the plan, and a broad base of research and informational data.

Within this context, and with needs identified, it is the responsibility of the leaders to establish supportive working relationships and common understandings of terms, concepts, and modes of operation through techniques for reaching consensus on procedures and task responsibilities.

Contextual considerations inevitably include concepts generated by futures research (see chapter two). Michael Marien (1974) applies to curriculum development the central concept generated by Herman Kahn and Anthony Wiener in *The Year 2000* (1967), which they call the basic, long-term multifold trend (BLTMT). This trend provides a general sense of societal direction. According to Marien (p. 395), the following characteristics of the long-range shift must be considered in the context of systems approaches to curriculum development:

The growing quantity and complexity of knowledge and ignorance.

The growing demands for a skilled labor force and a sophisticated citizenry, increasingly raising the minimum level of functional literacy.

Social and technological change, increasingly requiring lifelong learning and unlearning.

Leisure, affluence, and increasing access to social position through educational attainment—all increasing the demand for educational services.

Mounting evidence that all people have a far greater capacity to learn than has been admitted.

Obsolescent institutions requiring personnel retraining.

Marien makes a further application of the BLTMT to education, and thus necessarily to curriculum development, by contrasting closed teaching systems with open learning systems. Responsiveness and openness are correlative, he finds. His comparisons are shown in figure 10.

Systems concepts that necessitate consideration of the needs of people, societal conditions, and changing knowledge can enhance the curriculum development process by including not only the realities of the academic disciplines but also human processes and by offering opportunities for participants to clarify their attitudes and values.

## SUMMARY

The discussion of open systems approaches emphasizes the complex nature of curriculum development, which necessitates a

## FIGURE 10
### From Yesterday to Tomorrow: The Basic Long-term
### Multifold Trend in Education

| Closed Teaching Systems | Open Learning Systems |
|---|---|
| *Alternate titles* | |
| Teacher- and/or institution-centered | Student- and/or child-centered |
| Tight system; rational mechanics; cause-effect paradigm | Loose system |
| Control-centered | Learning-centered; inquiry approach; developmental; discovery education |
| *Societal context* | |
| Agricultural; industrial | Postindustrial; knowledge-based; service society |
| Autocratic; plutocratic; gerontocratic | Democratic; meritocratic; self-renewing |
| Static and simple | Dynamic and complex |
| *Beliefs about learning* | |
| Teaching results in learning | Good teaching aids learning, bad teaching inhibits it |
| Learning requires discipline, work, drill, memorization, pain control | Learning is enjoyable, follows from pursuit of interests |
| Teacher as source of knowledge, student as passive absorber | Learning from many sources, including peers; student as active participant |
| Capability confined to a few—the geniuses, the gifted | Extensive latent potential in all |
| *Administration* | |
| Input-oriented | Input-service-benefit-oriented; PPBS |
| Hierarchical leadership | Pluralistic, participatory |
| *Curriculum* | |
| Narrow, fixed, retrospective | Broad, changing, present- and future-oriented |
| Classics, principles, truth, facts, deductions, maxims | Methods, principles, induction, creativity, intuition, randomness |
| Determined by teacher and/or extra-classroom authority | Determined by teacher and/or student |
| Programmatic, sequential; lesson plans strictly followed | Interchangeable programmettes, modular learning; lesson plan as guide to options |
| Group study prescribed for all students | Independent study designed to fit individual needs and interests |
| Western culture as superior to primitives, heathens, noble savages, the underdeveloped; us-them, emphasis on differences | Humanistic, pancultural; us, emphasis on similarities |

| *Closed Teaching Systems* | *Open Learning Systems* |
|---|---|
| *Student-teacher relations* | |
| Students are a collectivity | Compensatory education for exceptional children, the physically and linguistically handicapped, the underprivileged |
| Teacher as authority, student as follower; control as instrumental technique | Professional as learning facilitator or senior learner; student as junior colleague |
| Feeling withheld; I-it | Feelings exposed and respected, student evaluation of teachers; I-thou |
| Single teacher | Multiple adult exposure, team teaching, guests, differentiated staffing |
| *Student conduct* | |
| Compulsory attendance; no choice of institution | Optional participation; alternatives offered |
| Physical punishment for "misbehavior" | Counseling for personal difficulties |
| No student recourse for injustice | Ombudsman, legal measures |
| Dropping out is fault of student; shaming for ignorance | Many possible sources of failure—environmental, institutional, and individual |
| Established rules and routines | Democratic development of rules and routines as necessary |
| *Feedback* | |
| Formal, mechanistic, "right" answers | Multifaceted, formal and informal, open-ended |
| Strong reliance on quantitative measures | Use of quantitative measures as necessary |
| *Rewards* | |
| Grades, fixed proportion of failures, class rankings, honors, medals, degrees | Pass-fail, nongrading |
| Recognition through competition in a few areas of excellence | Deemphasis of competition, promotion of diversity, many areas of excellence; a taste of success for all |
| Learning has vocational and social utility | Rewards of learning are inherent |
| *Goals* | |
| Socialization, training, moral education, passing on civilization, knowing; education of intellect only | Development of whole individual, investigation of cultural heritage, questioning |
| Getting an education, being educated, terminal education | Learning how to learn, lifelong learning, education as a beginning |

| Closed Teaching Systems | Open Learning Systems |
|---|---|
| *Extraclassroom environment* | |
| Restrictive, "in loco parentis" | Permissive, largely peer-controlled |
| Physical and intellectual separation from world | Interlinkage of school and life, "school without walls" |
| *Space* | |
| "Grid" architecture, stationary furniture | Omnidirectional space, flexible furnishings, choice of environments |
| Arbitrarily assigned seats | Student freedom to choose seats |
| Teaching in classroom | Learning in classroom, learning resource center, home, dormitory, community, world |
| Specially designated learning institutions; outside learning ignored | Recognition and encouragement of formal and informal learning opportunities throughout society; equivalent credit for outside learning |
| *Time* | |
| Collective pace | Individual pace |
| Ordered structure of class hours and course credits | Flexible scheduling |
| Uninterrupted schooling, followed by uninterrupted work | Learning and work interspersed throughout lifetime; learning a living |

From *Futurist* 4 (December 1970): 222-23, published by the World Future Society, P.O. Box 30369 (Bethesda), Washington, D.C. 20014. Reprinted by permission.

system of interacting elements directed toward goals rather than an erratic linear or single-principle approach, examples of which have been inadequate in the past. A wide range of sources substantiates the appropriateness of open systems concepts for increasing responsiveness and humanism in curriculum development by interrelating the needs of people, societal conditions, and changing knowledge. Historical roots, definitions, and explanations of systems concepts are provided, and distinctions are made between open and closed systems. Objections to and misconceptions about systems approaches are explored.

The main elements of systems approaches are identified: broad goals, needs, objectives, constraints, alternatives, selection, implementation, evaluation, and modification. The functions and interrelationships of each are described. Various contexts of curriculum development for which systems concepts are useful are considered, and numerous examples are provided in table form to identify how responsiveness correlates with open systems.

## REFERENCES

Banathy, Bela H. "The Systems Approach." *Modern Language Journal* 51 (May 1967): 281-89.

Barnes, Ron. *Learning Systems for the Future*. Bloomington, Ind.: Phi Delta Kappa, 1972.

Bloom, Benjamin S.; Hastings, J. Thomas; and Madaus, George F. *Handbook on Formative and Summative Evaluation of Student Learning*. New York: McGraw-Hill, 1971.

Chin, Robert. "The Utility of System Models and Developmental Models for Practitioners." In *The Planning of Change*, edited by Warren G. Bennis, Kenneth D. Benne, and Robert Chin, pp. 297-312. 2d ed. New York: Holt, Rinehart and Winston, 1969.

Combs, Arthur W. *Educational Accountability: Beyond Behavioral Objectives*. Washington, D.C.: Association for Supervision and Curriculum Development, 1972.

Crane, P., and Abt, C. C. "A Model for Curriculum Evaluation." *Educational Technology* 9 (1969): 17-25.

"Curriculum Development." *D and R Report* 3 (February-March 1974): 1-20.

Dewey, John. *Experience and Education*. New York: Collier Books, 1938.

Dyer, Henry S. "Discovery and Development of Educational Goals." In *Accountability: Curricular Applications*, edited by Arthur V. Olson and Joe A. Richardson, pp. 109-20. Scranton: Intext Educational Publishers, 1972.

Foshay, Arthur W. *Curriculum for the 70s: An Agenda for Invention*. Washington, D.C.: National Education Association, 1970.

Gilchrist, Robert S., and Gott, J. W. "Strengthening Curriculum Decisions through a System Approach." *Thrust* 1 (1971): 27-29.

Hayden, Alice H., and Torkelson, Gerald M. *Systematic Thinking about Education*. Bloomington, Ind.: Phi Delta Kappa, 1973.

Hill, Joseph E. *How Schools Can Apply Systems Analysis*. Bloomington, Ind.: Phi Delta Kappa, 1972.

Hitt, William D. "Two Models of Man." *American Psychologist* 24 (July 1969): 651-58.

Hunt, David E., and Sullivan, Edmund V. *Between Psychology and Education*, chap. 3. Hillsdale, Ill.: Dryden Press, 1964.

Johnson, David W., and Johnson, Roger T. "Instructional Goal Structure: Cooperative, Competitive, or Individualistic." *Review of Educational Research* 44 (spring 1974): 213-40.

Joyce, Bruce R. "The Curriculum Worker of the Future." In *The Curriculum, Retrospect and Prospect*, part I, pp. 307-56. Seventieth Yearbook of the

National Society for the Study of Education. Chicago: University of Chicago Press, 1971.

Kahn, Herman, and Wiener, Anthony. *The Year 2000*. New York: Macmillan, 1967.

Kapfer, Philip G. "An Instructional Management Strategy for Individualized Learning." *Phi Delta Kappan* 49 (January 1968): 260-63.

Kappel, F. R. *Vitality in a Business Enterprise*. New York: McGraw-Hill, 1960.

Kaufman, Roger A. "System Approaches to Education." In *Social and Technological Change*, edited by Philip K. Piele, Terry L. Eidell, and Stuart C. Smith, pp. 121-90. Eugene: Center for the Advanced Study of Educational Administration, University of Oregon, 1970.

Klein, Stephen; Fenstermacher, Gary; and Alkin, Marvin C. "The Center's Changing Educational Model." *Evaluation Comment* 2 (January 1971): 9-12.

Lehmann, Henry. "The Systems Approach to Education." *Audiovisual Instruction* 13 (February 1968): 144-48.

Light, R. J., and Smith, P. V. "Choosing a Future: Strategies for Designing and Evaluating New Programs." *Harvard Educational Review* 40 (winter 1970): 1-28.

Macdonald, James B. "An Example of Disciplined Curriculum Thinking." *Theory into Practice* 6 (October 1967): 166-71.

Marien, Michael. "The Basic Long-term Multifold Trend in Education." In *Curriculum: Quest for Relevance*, edited by William Van Til, pp. 394-402. Boston: Houghton Mifflin, 1974.

Metfessel, N. S., and Michael, W. B. "A Paradigm involving Multiple Criterion Measures for the Evaluation of the Effectiveness of School Programs." *Educational and Psychological Measurement* 27 (1967): 931-43.

Miller, Donald R. *A System Approach to Planned Change in Education*. San Mateo, Calif.: San Mateo County Board of Education, 1970.

National Study of Secondary School Evaluation. *Evaluative Criteria*. Rev. ed. Washington, D.C.: NSSSE, 1960.

Nystrand, Raphael O., and Cunningham, Luvern L. "Organizing Schools to Develop Human Capabilities." In *To Nurture Humaneness*, pp. 120-42. Yearbook of the Association for Supervision and Curriculum Development. Washington, D.C.: ASCD, 1970.

Oettinger, Anthony G. "The Myths of Educational Technology." *Saturday Review*, 18 May 1968, pp. 76-77.

Payne, David A. "Toward a Characterization of Curriculum Evaluation." In *Curriculum Evaluation*, edited by David A. Payne, pp. 1-14. Lexington, Mass.: D. C. Heath, 1974.

Pfeiffer, John. *New Look at Education*. Poughkeepsie, N.Y.: Odyssey Press, 1968.

Prentice, Marjorie. "Management: Curse, Cure-all, or Workable Concept?" *Educational Leadership* 30 (January 1973): 310-12.

Provus, Malcolm. *Discrepancy Evaluation*. Berkeley: McCutchan, 1971.

———. "Evaluation of Ongoing Programs in the Public School System." In *Educational Evaluation: New Roles, New Means*, part II, pp. 242-83.

Sixty-eighth Yearbook of the National Society for the Study of Education. Chicago: University of Chicago Press, 1969.

Scriven, Michael. *The Methodology of Evaluation*. American Educational Research Association Monograph Series on Curriculum Evaluation. Chicago: Rand McNally, 1967.

Stake, Robert E. "Key Emphases of Selected Curriculum Evaluation Models." In *Curriculum Evaluation*, edited by David A. Payne, p. 12. Lexington, Mass.: D. C. Heath, 1974.

——. "The Countenance of Educational Evaluation." *Teachers College Record* 68 (1967): 523-40.

Stufflebeam, Daniel L. "Toward a Science of Educational Evaluation." *Educational Technology* 6 (1968): 5-12.

Taylor, P. A., and Maguire, T. O. "A Theoretical Evaluation Model." *Manitoba Journal of Educational Research* 1 (1966): 12-17.

Tyler, Ralph W. "General Statement on Evaluation." *Journal of Educational Research* 35 (March 1942): 492-501.

Welch, W. W., and Walberg, H. J. "A Design for Curriculum Evaluation." *Science Education* 52 (February 1968): 10-16.

Wiener, Norbert. *Cybernetics*. New York: John Wiley, 1948.

## ADDITIONAL READINGS

Bloom, Benjamin S.; Engelhart, Max D.; Furst, Edward J.; Hill, Walker H.; and Krathwohl, David R. *Taxonomy of Educational Objectives. Handbook I: Cognitive Domain*. New York: David McKay, 1956.

Harrow, Anita J. *A Taxonomy of the Psychomotor Domain: A Guide for Developing Behavioral Objectives*. New York: David McKay, 1972.

Krathwohl, David R.; Bloom, Benjamin S.; and Masia, Bertram B. *Taxonomy of Educational Objectives. Handbook II: Affective Domain*. New York: David McKay, 1956.

Prentice, Marjorie. "Systematic Instruction." *Educational Leadership* 30 (May 1973): 706-9.

# CHAPTER THIRTEEN

# Toward a Theory of Responsive Development

The seven propositions put forward in chapters six through twelve are brought together in this chapter and directed toward construction of a theory of responsive and responsible curriculum development.

## FRAME OF REFERENCE

Chapters one through five describe problems in curriculum development, the need for theory, what theory is and is not, how theory can be built, and the value base on which this theory is developed. A discussion of futures research in relation to curriculum development and the many factors bearing on curriculum development are also discussed. Responsive curriculum development is distinguished from unresponsive.

A long view of curriculum development over two centuries in the United States reveals that numerous piecemeal approaches have been tried and that a comprehensive theory of curriculum development has been lacking. Also lacking is a philosophical value base that can

incorporate the views of the nation's diverse peoples about the democratic and humanistic goals of education. Problems in curriculum
development have surged to the attention of the public time and
again over the decades, with increasing frequency in current times,
accompanied by calls for reform and warnings of crisis in the schools.
Lawrence Cremin observed recently (1974, p. 3) that "where various
educational programs have failed is at the point of theory: they have
not asked the right questions insistently enough, and as a result they
have tended to come up with superficial and shopworn answers."

Curriculum development in the past has often catered to the needs
of selected groups and individuals. It has frequently neglected
changes in knowledge, attended insufficiently to the actual needs of
children and other participants in the development process, and
ignored societal issues and concerns. Insufficient planning has been
undertaken to strengthen humanistic and democratic goals, and curriculum-planners have often wavered at the point of philosophical and
value decisions. The curriculum has historically been geared toward a
study of the past, with some attention to the present in recent times.
It has been devoid of studies of the future and has failed to stress
development of the learners' decision-making skills and abilities to
make reasoned choices when faced with alternative futures.

Theoretical frameworks for curriculum development are needed
that will (1) aid in continual analysis, revision, and growth; (2) relate
complex decisions to one another and to forces acting on the
schools; and (3) be applicable in diverse situations and at all levels of
curriculum development in the elementary and secondary schools. A
theoretical framework directs curriculum developers toward thinking
of curriculum-related factors; it directs them toward considering the
people, processes, and products of curriculum as a whole, rather than
following single-principle or linear approaches. A theoretical framework can help the curriculum-planner seek multiple approaches to
the broad goals of education.

Cultural changes are now commanding our attention to problems
of values and moral education, particularly in regard to student inquiry and decision-making. Curriculum development is also pressed
to meet new problems in a highly predictable future of dwindling
resources, increasing population, and interdependence of the people
and nations of the world. Thus, building a theory of curriculum
development to meet the needs of schools in a complex and changing

society requires a forward vision. It requires examination of value systems presently operating in our society, consideration of alternative futures, and development of a philosophical and value base.

The intent of this approach to a theory of curriculum development is to build responsiveness and responsibility into the development process, so that individuals and groups affected by curricular decisions are involved and a self-renewing system is established for setting goals and objectives, determining needs, assessing situational factors, developing plans, seeking alternatives, implementing actions, evaluating actions, and making modifications for improvement. To be adequate, curriculum development must reflect a moral commitment to human worth and freedom, to honesty and justice.

George Beauchamp (1968, p. 34), from his synthesis of various works in curriculum theory, points out that "the operational vistas opened up and explained by theories increase the possible choices of behaving for the practitioner" and that "a theory may clarify relationships among any given set of events." While theories do not tell teachers specifically what to do, nevertheless, "it is the job of educational theory to guide educational practices. In turn, theory is modified by practice and research that emanate from it."

The power of theories to generate new knowledge is a characteristic that is generally accepted. A theory is a set of interrelated constructs, definitions, and propositions that present a systematic way of identifying relations among variables for the purpose of explaining and predicting what may happen. Theories not only summarize ideas but also inspire the creation of new ideas and suggest hypotheses for further testing. Hans Zetterberg (1965, p. vii), from his studies of theory and verification, concludes that

theories may coordinate many methodologically imperfect findings in a rather trustworthy whole in the form of a small number of information-packed sentences or equations. Moreover, some of the bits and pieces coordinated into this trustworthy whole can be the challenging insights of the classics . . . and the celebrated writers of literature.

Daniel Griffiths (1959) reminds us that theories are developed to help identify problems here and now and in the immediate future. They are constructed so that better theories may be built in the future. The process of theory building itself is a necessary competence in the field of curriculum development.

Curriculum development is far from being a simple rational

process. The perceptive scope of curriculum developers must encompass the demands and needs of society, the growth and development of persons, the principles of learning, fundamental ideas and knowledge in the various areas of substantive content, and the modes of thought used in the disciplines and in multidisciplinary and interdisciplinary approaches. Curriculum development must yield an environment in which learners can experience and develop ideas, forms of thought, feelings, habits, and skills.

Responsive curriculum development implies the ability of the curriculum to meet diverse human needs, to receive new ideas, and to adapt to new situations, new knowledge, and new uses of knowledge. Responsive development is a process of continuing renewal of the curriculum that creates new forms to fit new conditions of the environment.

Unresponsive curriculum development implies that the ends are fixed and unyielding; that there is rigidity in principle and practice; and that opinion and judgment are inflexible. An unresponsive process of curriculum development reflects undeviating conformity to content, standards, and requirements that may be obsolete.

Involvement by the consumers, participants, and referent groups of the curriculum development process is a precondition of responsiveness and implies responsibility and sharing in the process. A fixed curriculum, the output of unresponsive curriculum development, does not require involvement by diverse groups and democratic decision-making processes; it operates chiefly by directive, coercion, or manipulation, rather than by group participation and inquiry. An unresponsive curriculum development process is revealed by a lack of sensitivity or adaptability to pluralistic values and cultures, to local needs and differences, to the changing national or international scene, to humanistic values, to students' needs and concerns, to teachers' needs and concerns, to the potential contributions of various referent groups, and to fields of knowledge or disciplines that were ignored in the original planning process.

Under conditions of rapid change, says Solon Kimball (1967, p. 8), we can no longer assume that the knowledge or the practices that served us adequately in the past are sufficient for either the present or the future; "we must consciously reconstruct an educational system to serve a society that is in a state of continuous emergence."

Involving diverse individuals and publics in cooperative decision-making in the process of curriculum development is not easy.

Communication problems, unequal access to resources, confrontations, and disagreements that may emerge are described in chapter five. In many cases, various participants have not previously been involved in curriculum-related decisions and need practical experience. Desirable roles, skills, and responsibilities of each of the participant and referent groups are described in chapter five, along with the bounds beyond which their behavior becomes irresponsible.

The process of building a theory of curriculum development and the uses of theory by practitioners are described in chapter three. Elements of theory, considerations to be observed, concepts, definitions, functions of a theory, and steps in constructing a theory are presented, as well as criteria to use in assessing the adequacy of a theory. Chapter three notes that propositions are the central elements of a theory; that they relate variates to one another; and that two variates are needed at a minimum to have one proposition. Theoretical propositions contain higher informative value than ordinary propositions and can account for a greater variety of events. Zetterberg (1965) asserts that theorists should be more courageous about using ordinary propositions to develop theoretical ones without first maximizing the evidence to support them. A matrix form is suggested by Zetterberg and by George Homans (1950) as useful in presenting propositions and searching out interrelationships among them.

## A MATRIX OF CONSTRUCTS

The seven propositions presented in part II each yield a key concept that contributes to responsiveness in curriculum development. These are shown in figure 11. From the propositions, a matrix of constructs is presented in figure 12. In the matrix the propositions are arranged as determinants (causes) on the horizontal axis and as results (effects, consequences) on the vertical axis. The matrix provides an inventory of propositions, both as determinants and as results, and a schema for studying their interrelationships at each point of intersection and at combinations of intersections. Each proposition interacting with another proposition strengthens both, and one leads to effects in the other, thus contributing to responsiveness in curriculum development. These interrelationships form broad constructs, derived from the points of intersection, that reach beyond the data and yield general hypotheses for testing. (See chapter three for definitions of construct, hypothesis, and other terms.)

In the cells of the matrix, C is used as a symbol for construct; thus, constructs are identified as $C_{1,2}$, $C_{1,3}$, and so forth. As an illustration, $C_{1,2}$ indicates that, if there is humanistic planning for freedom of the individual (determinant), then there is a more expanded view of culture (result).

## Types of Relationships

Global constructs from which hypotheses stem are studied in several types of relationships between two propositions. In the examples that follow, each construct is analyzed in terms of its type or

**FIGURE 11**
**Propositions**

| Concept | Statement |
|---|---|
| 1. Freedom for the individual | If planning for the freedom of individuals is included, the curriculum development process will become more responsive to social, ethical, and moral valuing. |
| 2. Expanded view of culture | If planners draw upon more of the total culture, the curriculum development process will respond to the needs and concerns of the persons served by the school. |
| 3. Democratic goals and means | If means are used that not only exemplify but also strengthen the nation's founding goals, curriculum development will respond to and embody the purposes of American democracy. |
| 4. Commitment to planned change | If there is a commitment to planned change, the curriculum development process will become responsive to dynamic and futuristic technological and social developments. |
| 5. Comprehensive assessment of needs | If there is a more comprehensive assessment of needs, the curriculum development process will be more responsive to both individual and group concerns. |
| 6. Links among participants | If the number and intensity of links among participants increase, the curriculum development process will become more responsive to their common needs. |
| 7. Open systems concepts | If concepts of open systems are used, the curriculum development process will become more responsive to the need for interrelating its factors and participants. |

## FIGURE 12
## Matrix of Constructs (C)

|  | | Results | | | | | | |
|---|---|---|---|---|---|---|---|
| *Propositions* | 1. Freedom for the individual | 2. Expanded view of culture | 3. Democratic goals and means | 4. Commitment to planned change | 5. Comprehensive assessment of needs | 6. Links among participants | 7. Open systems concepts |
| 1. Freedom for the individual | — | $C_{1,2}$ | $C_{1,3}$ | $C_{1,4}$ | $C_{1,5}$ | $C_{1,6}$ | $C_{1,7}$ |
| 2. Expanded view of culture | $C_{2,1}$ | — | $C_{2,3}$ | $C_{2,4}$ | $C_{2,5}$ | $C_{2,6}$ | $C_{2,7}$ |
| 3. Democratic goals and means | $C_{3,1}$ | $C_{3,2}$ | — | $C_{3,4}$ | $C_{3,5}$ | $C_{3,6}$ | $C_{3,7}$ |
| 4. Commitment to planned change | $C_{4,1}$ | $C_{4,2}$ | $C_{4,3}$ | — | $C_{4,5}$ | $C_{4,6}$ | $C_{4,7}$ |
| 5. Comprehensive assessment of needs | $C_{5,1}$ | $C_{5,2}$ | $C_{5,3}$ | $C_{5,4}$ | — | $C_{5,6}$ | $C_{5,7}$ |
| 6. Links among participants | $C_{6,1}$ | $C_{6,2}$ | $C_{6,3}$ | $C_{6,4}$ | $C_{6,5}$ | — | $C_{6,7}$ |
| 7. Open systems concepts | $C_{7,1}$ | $C_{7,2}$ | $C_{7,3}$ | $C_{7,4}$ | $C_{7,5}$ | $C_{7,6}$ | — |

*Determinants*

types of interrelationships as a means of looking for causal links. Relationships may have one or more of the following attributes (Zetterberg 1965, pp. 69-72):

1. *reversible* (if $x$, then $y$, and if $y$, then $x$) or *irreversible* (if $x$, then $y$, but if $y$, then no conclusion about $x$)

2. *deterministic* (if $x$, then always $y$) or *stochastic* (if $x$, then probably $y$)

3. *sequential* (if $x$, then later $y$) or *coextensive* (if $x$, then also $y$)

4. *sufficient* (if $x$, then $y$ regardless of anything else) or *contingent* (if $x$, then $y$ but only if $z$)

5. *necessary* (only if $x$, then $y$) or *substitutable* (if $x$, then $y$, but if $z$, then also $y$)

6. *interdependent* (a large change brought about through a series of interacting small changes)

## Construct $C_{2,1}$

*As a responsive curriculum development process includes an expanded view of the culture, a greater degree of planning for the freedom of the individual will result.* A coextensive relationship is illustrated by this construct: as culture is included more widely, curriculum development becomes more responsive to the values of planning for freedom.

### Hypotheses for Testing

If white and black curriculum developers investigate together the particular concerns of each race about the culture of the other, then their attitudes toward the opposite race, as measured by appropriate instruments, will increase positively.

If philosophical anthropology—study of the nature of man and society and of the human predicament and human development for the purpose of improving the human condition (Edel 1966)—is used by more curriculum developers as the organizing component of the social studies curriculum in the public schools (instead of history and geography), the behavior in schools of teachers, students, curriculum specialists, and administrators will change positively toward valuing planning for the freedom of the individual.

## Construct $C_{2,3}$

*As the responsive curriculum development process draws increasingly from an expanded view of culture, more influence is exerted toward designing educational means for strengthening American democratic goals.* A stochastic relationship exists: that is, if $x$, then probably $y$. If curriculum developers draw from an expanded concept of culture, it is probable that more resources will be brought to bear on designing educational means for reaching democratic goals.

### Hypothesis for Testing

If community and school interpenetrate (thus expanding each view of culture) by designing work experiences in the community for students and learning experiences in the schools for lay persons, then the degree of consensus will increase on those educational means that strengthen American democratic goals.

## Constructs $C_{1,3}$, $C_{1,4}$, and $C_{1,6}$

*In the responsive curriculum development process, when planning for the freedom of the individual is given a value priority, increased attention will be given to educational means that strengthen democratic goals, provisions for planned change, and links among referent groups.* An interdependent relationship is evident. Consideration of planning for the freedom of individuals leads to more knowledge about issues, which leads to greater consideration of principles involved, which leads to greater collaboration, and so forth. As each factor gains strength, the related factors also gain strength.

### Hypothesis for Testing

If dialogue on values is increased at the state and local boards of education, increased curriculum development priority will be given to systematic instruction in decision-making skills in the public schools.

## Constructs $C_{2,6}$ and $C_{6,2}$

*As curriculum developers draw knowledge, attitudes, and skills from an expanded view of the available culture, links among referent groups in curriculum development will increase, generating greater responsiveness in curriculum development.* This construct is the reversible type (broader inclusion of the culture leads to broader links, and vice versa), and is coextensive (an increase in either the inclusion of culture or group links leads to an increase in the other). It is also a contingent construct, because responsive curriculum development depends on links and an expanded view of culture.

*Hypothesis for Testing*

If interaction and collaboration in curriculum development increase among black and white students, teachers, parents, and administrators representing several socioeconomic strata, then polarizations and conflicts of values will decrease and the degree of consensus on curriculum development goals will increase.

## Construct $C_{4,1}$

*A commitment to planned change, which is necessary in response to dynamic futuristic developments, can exert influence toward planning for the freedom of individuals.* A stochastic relationship, as contrasted to a deterministic one, is expressed. Probability is high that applications of the concepts of planned change, if fully understood, can influence the present shifting situation in societal values and beliefs toward planning for freedom—human worth and dignity, respect for the individual, and a person-centered society.

*Hypotheses for Testing*

If dissatisfied students who have dropped out of a traditional high school participate with adults in planning an alternative high school (including problem-formulation, goal-setting, finding alternative means for reaching objectives, and self-evaluation), then the students will attend regularly and exhibit observable interest in achieving the goals that were set.

If opportunities are planned for secondary school students to experience interdisciplinary and action learnings related to a major social concern for the future (e.g., dwindling resources and increasing consumption of goods), then the students will be able to identify legislative decisions that either harm or benefit the goals of a person-centered society.

If young students are confronted with value dilemmas in case studies or role-playing situations, then they will be able to identify illustrations of honesty and justice.

## Construct $C_{4,3}$

*In the responsive curriculum development process, a commitment to planned change will expedite educational means that exemplify American democratic goals, and the degree of attainment of the goals of planned freedom for the individual will increase.* This construct shows an interdependent relationship. An increase in one variable leads to an increase in a second variable, which in turn improves the first variable, and so on. As more attention is given to planned change, which includes clarification and specification of goals and means, democratic goals become more effective in practice, and, as their effectiveness increases, planning becomes more effective.

### Hypothesis for Testing

If the school administrators of a local district systematically and collaboratively increase their skills in planning change, increased attention will be given to designing specific means for reaching the goals of American democracy in education.

## Construct $C_{4,5}$

*When the concepts of planned change expand in scope, assessment of the needs and purposes of the various participants becomes more comprehensive; the curriculum development process is then less subject to conflicting and competing pressures and more responsive.* A stochastic relationship exists: as planning skills increase, sensitivity to needs and purposes will probably increase.

### Hypothesis for Testing

If a regional laboratory or research and development center increases its staff skills in planning for change, its scope of inputs about the needs and purposes of referent groups will expand and its contacts with schools will increase.

## Constructs $C_{5,1}$, $C_{5,2}$, $C_{5,3}$, $C_{5,4}$, $C_{5,6}$, and $C_{5,7}$

*In the responsive curriculum development process, as needs assessment becomes comprehensive, strength will be gained in moral commitment to planning for the freedom of individuals, views of culture will expand, use of educational means to reach American democratic goals will increase, attention will be directed to the concept of planned change, links among referent groups will increase, and systems concepts will be more widely used.* Interdependent relationships are exemplified in this major construct; i.e., the more that is known about needs, the more importance is given to other factors in the curriculum development process.

*Hypotheses for Testing*

If an open-ended Delphi-type survey of local district needs solicits and uses the expressed curricular concerns of random samples of students, teachers, parents, curriculum specialists, administrators, and university professors of education, then curriculum development will give higher priority to humanistic and aesthetic development.

If a needs assessment by the state department of education for curriculum development purposes provides for feedback from students, teachers, administrators, parents, and representatives of research and development centers on their concerns about societal issues, personal development, and academic knowledge (rather than excluding one or more of these areas), statewide curriculum development processes will produce curricular and instructional plans providing for emphasis in all three areas—social relations, personal development, and academic knowledge.

## Constructs $C_{6,3}$ and $C_{3,6}$

*When links among the referent groups increase, educational means will be implemented that exemplify and strengthen American democratic goals for education.* This construct is the reversible type (links lead to means for reaching democratic goals and democratic means lead to links). It is also coextensive (as either increases, it affects the other positively).

*Hypotheses for Testing*

If children in elementary schools have practice in developing their curriculum plans in collaboration with teachers and curriculum specialists, all parties will increase their understanding and application of the democratic goals of education.

If secondary school teachers and students collaborate more in planning for curriculum and instruction, the dropout rate (physical and psychological) will decrease.

## Construct $C_{6,5}$

*If interaction and collaboration among referent groups increase, each group will become more knowledgeable of and empathetic to the needs and purposes of other groups, thus generating more responsiveness in curriculum development.* Here we have a reversible relationship, in that higher frequency of interaction and collaboration leads to greater empathy for the needs and purposes of others and greater empathy leads to higher frequency of interaction and collaboration.

## Hypothesis for Testing

In resolving value-laden curriculum problems and conflicts between students and local adult referent groups, if the needs and purposes of each group can be presented in orderly discussion settings to all others involved, then a mutually acceptable curriculum plan will be developed.

## Construct $C_{6,7}$

*In the responsive curriculum development process, links among referent groups are an essential factor in the use of systems concepts.* The relationship is the type Zetterberg describes as necessary. The inclusion of collaborative, interactive, and linking efforts among referent groups is a necessary factor in the success of systems concepts in increasing responsiveness in curriculum development.

## Hypothesis for Testing

If curriculum development includes adequate links among its referent groups, then it may start from various loci (e.g., psychology of learners, subject matter interests, research and development centers, local user-based developers, societal demands, or student protest movements) and become responsive in a comprehensive manner, avoiding either/or approaches to the needs of learners, to societal conditions, or to bodies of knowledge.

## Construct $C_{7,3}$

*The greater the use of systems concepts, the greater will be the focus on educational means that exemplify and strengthen the spirit of American democratic goals.* A stochastic relationship is expressed; that is, if systems approaches are used reliably, with adequate procedures for setting goals, assessing needs, specifying objectives and priorities, devising alternative procedures, and using evaluation as feedback for modification, then probably means for attainment of the broad democratic goals of American education will be practiced.

## Hypothesis for Testing

If curriculum development provides for instruction in decision-making, children will be able to differentiate practical applications of democratic values from undemocratic values.

## Constructs $C_{2,7}$, $C_{3,7}$, $C_{4,7}$, $C_{5,7}$, and $C_{6,7}$

*When curriculum development draws on the total culture, gives concerted attention to designing educational means to reach democratic goals, uses concepts of planned change, assesses the needs and purposes of the various participants, and establishes operational links among the referent groups, then there is greater use of systems concepts leading to responsiveness to the needs of people, societal conditions, and changing knowledge.* Here is a multivariate and interdependent relationship. The large change—a responsive curriculum development process—is brought about through a series of interacting interdependent factors and changes.

## Hypotheses for Testing

If three high schools in three diverse settings (ghetto, suburban, rural) that are presently using grading procedures that intentionally assign students to tracks according to rank order, or otherwise judge students as failures or successes, each initiate links among students, teachers, and administrators to accomplish comprehensive assessment of needs, planned change, mutual goal-setting, design of alternative means to reach goals, and wider use of the resources of culture, then systems concepts will be used and a responsive curriculum development process will produce these effects:

a. Formative evaluation will receive more emphasis than summative evaluation.

b. Teachers will use a wider variety of instructional methods.

c. In-service plans will center around the use of formative evaluation as a diagnostic tool to assist students in finding alternative ways to achieve learning outcomes.

d. Observation analyses will reveal a decrease in negative talk by teachers and an increase in positive student participation in classroom discourse.

e. Attitudes toward school will be more positive and less negative as measured by written instruments.

f. Time spent in class discussions of humanistic and American democratic values will increase.

g. The student dropout rate will decrease.

## Construct $C_{7,1}$

*The greater the use of open systems concepts in processes of curriculum development that are responsive to the needs of people, societal conditions, and changing knowledge, the more moral commitment will be generated toward planning for the freedom of individuals.* An interdependent relationship and an extension of the construct immediately preceding this one express the relationships of these factors. Here we have a chain pattern within the $C_{7,1}$ cell that expresses how an expanded view of the total culture, a focus on educational means to exemplify and strengthen democratic goals, a commitment to planned change, comprehensive needs assessment, and links among referent groups use systems concepts leading to values of planned freedom, which in turn lead to further chain patterns among the propositions and generate power by building on each other.

### Hypothesis for Testing

If a local school district organizes to use open systems concepts in curriculum development (as defined in this theory), then school practices and attitudes as measured on appropriate observational instruments will increase in the democratic values of planned freedom for individuals.

### SUMMARY

The hypotheses suggested here are examples that may inspire further hypotheses as well as applications of more specific aspects of these hypotheses, thus contributing to further knowledge for developing a theory of responsive curriculum development.

The matrix provides a means for bringing together the propositions that were developed in the earlier chapters and shows their interrelationships in the form of constructs or new concepts of the cause-and-effect relationships between propositions. From the constructs are formed several types of relationships: reversible or irreversible, deterministic or stochastic, sequential or coextensive, sufficient or contingent, necessary or substitutable, and interdependent.

Numerous examples are given of relationships at points of intersection and at combinations of intersections. The examples given not only bring together propositions in new ideas but also provide a means for generating further new knowledge.

## REFERENCES

Beauchamp, George A. "Basic Components of a Curriculum Theory." *Curriculum Theory Network*, no. 10 (fall 1972): 16-22.

———. *Curriculum Theory*. Wilmette, Ill.: Kagg, 1968.

Cremin, Lawrence A. "The Free School Movement: A Perspective." *Notes on Education*, October 1973. Newsletter published by Teachers College, Columbia University.

Edel, A. "The Contribution of Philosophical Anthropology to Educational Development." In *Philosophy and Educational Development*, edited by G. Barnett, pp. 69-91. Boston: Houghton Mifflin, 1966.

Griffiths, Daniel D. *Administrative Theory*. New York: Appleton-Century-Crofts, 1959.

Homans, George C. *The Human Group*. New York: Harcourt, Brace and World, 1950.

Kimball, Solon T. "Culture, Class, and Educational Congruency." In *Educational Requirements for the 1970s*, edited by Stanley Elam and William P. McLure, pp. 6-26. New York: Praeger, 1967.

Posner, George J. "The Use of Construct Validation Procedures in Curriculum Research." *Curriculum Theory Network*, no. 11 (spring 1973): 34-46.

Zetterberg, Hans L. *On Theory and Verification in Sociology*. Totowa, N.J.: Bedminster Press, 1965.